THE AMERICAN PEOPLE

A STUDY IN NATIONAL PSYCHOLOGY

THE AMERICAN PEOPLE

A STUDY IN NATIONAL PSYCHOLOGY

BY

A. MAURICE LOW

CHEVALIER DE L'ORDRE DE LÉOPOLD
IMPERIAL ORDER OF THE RISING SUN
AUTHOR OF "PROTECTION IN THE UNITED STATES"
"AMERICA AT HOME," ETC.

BOSTON AND NEW YORK
HOUGHTON MIFFLIN COMPANY
The Riverside Press Cambridge
1909

Published October 1909

My dear Lawrence,

This book will recall to you how we thrashed out and argued many a puzzling question and endeavored without prejudice to find the truth, which was not always easy, for an American and an Englishman do not see eye to eye in all things; but our purpose was ever the same: to ascertain the causes that have produced results. To me this book voices your always sympathetic but judicious criticism and your generous help — a companionship as precious as it is rare.

A. Maurice Low.

Washington, May, 1909.

CONTENTS

CONTENTS

THE PLANTING OF A NATION

THE AMERICAN PEOPLE

CHAPTER I

INTRODUCTORY

NEARLY nine years ago, after living for more than twenty years in the United States and studying its political and social institutions, I asked myself whether the American people were a new race with distinct racial characteristics and a developed psychology of their own or were simply the modification of a parent stock retaining the characteristics of their begetting. It was a question that has been widely discussed, but without an attempt, so far as I am aware, to reach a conclusion based on scientific deductions.

I began the inquiry for my own satisfaction and without any preconceived idea of putting my conclusions in permanent form, and it is, I think, due both to writer and to reader that I should say the investigation was made without prejudice or bias; I had no theory to sustain by alleged facts; it was immaterial where the adventure ended, whether it led to the discovery of a new race or the rediscovery of an old race amidst new surroundings unmodified by its new conditions, or only so slightly modified that the species had remained uninfluenced by environment and other circumstances. With an open mind, in the spirit of the investigator and not of the advocate, I began the study.

It seemed to offer no great difficulties, at least none that might not yield to reasonable intelligence and fair industry, but I was little to realize then how far I should wander, and how often I must retrace my steps and begin anew, before my quest was satisfied. There was a literature rich and voluminous and varied; a literature that showed much painstaking research and high ability, combined, in many instances, with a graceful and attractive style. In the writing of history treating of their country the Americans rank with any other modern nation; during the last quarter of a century America has been exploited by the literary *entrepreneur*, native as well as foreign, and the output has been thrown on the market in prodigious quantities; for the American loves to read about himself and is eager to see himself from the point of view of the foreigner, although he does not always agree with him; and the foreigner has found in America the romance of life that has long departed from Europe. America and the Americans were an undiscovered country and an unknown people, and each literary Columbus returned to feed the imagination with a newer and more untrustworthy tale.

Now all this, while interesting, was unsatisfactory, and brought me no nearer to my objective. History written by men with a claim to be regarded as serious historians subordinated everything to the historical narrative. To understand a people, to have a sympathetic comprehension of the spirit that is in them, to know what has made them what they are and what the future may have in store for them, to be able to grasp not alone their material development but the much more vital and elusive working of their mind, it is necessary as a foundation that one shall have a thorough knowledge of the history of that people; but history, using the word in its strictly technical sense, is too narrow and too concentrated. It remains for the historical psychologist to treat in his own way and as a special branch the subject in its widest relations. And the work of the literary *entrepreneur* was too superficial, too untrustworthy, too hasty, to be of value, although it served one useful purpose. It was an impressionist and brilliantly colored picture of the exaggerations of national character and usually a caricature; and caricature is not always malicious, for the supreme art of caricature is the perfect likeness with the accentuation of a salient feature.

If the impressions and observations and reflections of Englishmen and Frenchmen and Germans, of women as well as men, after a few weeks, and sometimes only a few days, spent in a country the size of all Europe, with a population more than twice that of their own country and with political and social institutions foreign to them and needing long and careful study to be understood, had any value, it was this: the foreigner found nothing the same as that to which he was accustomed, and he criticised or approved according to temperament or preconceived prejudice. The mind receives its most sensitive impression from things new, not from a reproduction of the old. The fact that every foreigner found in America something new — a new view of life, new social institutions, new methods of government — confirms perhaps more than anything else the conclusion reached by the writer through other sources of investigation, that America has given birth to a new race; that the term America to-day is something more than a mere geographical expression; that there has come into being an American Nation, for a nation is the product of not one but many things, and there must be certain well-defined elements to constitute nationality.

What those are shall be explained in their proper place. It is sufficient now to set down as an assertion capable of scientific demonstration a fact of the first importance.

My sole purpose being the ascertainment of this truth, it is only necessary briefly to explain the method pursued. In writing biography, in seeking for the causes that made this man great and another notorious, one does not begin when the character of his subject has been formed. If the true man is to be revealed, if we are to know him as he was, and especially if we are to know the influences that moulded him and so profoundly affected him for good or evil, we must begin at the beginning and follow his life through his struggles, his temptations, his triumphs. In a word, I have attempted to write the biography of a people; and the more I considered how that best could be done the stronger became the conviction that I must begin with the incunabula of the race. In the history of early struggles is found the cradle.

Every other civilization of which we have any knowledge is so much older than that of America that we can take much for granted; manners, morals, customs have become stereotyped and we do not have to ask the reasons for them or how they came into existence; we accept them as matter of course, precisely as we take the other phenomena of life; so much are we accustomed to them that they no longer excite wonder. But with America it is different. The why and the wherefore is the constant question; the meaning of it all can only be understood by an intimate knowledge of the fundamental. Thus it becomes possible for an Englishman to write a book on France and a Frenchman on England,[1] and neither finds it necessary to go back to history in his search for the foundation on which national character is laid.

It is impossible to write a history, using that word not merely to describe the deeds of a nation,

[1] Bodley: *France;* Boutmy: *The English People.*

but also its development and the formation of character, its physical and mental growth, and to bring into true relation all the various causes that make life, unless it is written as a consecutive whole. The proper function of the historian, the psychologist of history especially, as I conceive it, is from the summit of the present to look back with clear vision on the past, and with the advantage of unobscured view, free from the distraction of being an actor in the scene of life, behold the causes that produced results, observe the play of dædalian forces which once released gain from within themselves new impulses and form fresh centres of energy, and with the past and the present as a guide develop the future. The undulating wave of human action sets in motion agencies the consequences of which man can no more foresee at the time than he can follow each drop as it is hurled up from the depths and is dissipated in ether, not to be lost but to exert new power. Every human action forecasts futurity as inevitably as life forecasts death. History is acted in the present, but it is written in the past and read in the future.

I make no pretensions to original historical research. I have gone to the best and most accepted authorities for my information, carefully balancing conflicting statements and endeavoring to reconcile them by the preponderance of evidence. In the historical section everything has been purposely omitted that was not essential to a complete and, I hope, lucid explanation of the origin and development of the American people. Such things as encumber the pages of historians, which it is the duty of the historian to relate,—quarrels between parties, petty conflicts, even conflicts on a grander scale, — have been either omitted or dismissed with merely a reference; but those things that determine character, that distinguish the offspring of a race, that develop the mind, that prepare the ground for the acceptance of ideas which are to be so fruitful in results, have been treated at proper length. To students of American history it may seem as if I had simply repeated what is already well known; but to this criticism, if it shall be made, my answer is that it appeared to me to be essential to present certain historical facts in their just relation to psychological progress so as to show that the American people have not sprung from the air but are, similar to all other highly developed races, the product of evolution; in their case political and sociological.

It may perhaps be thought that disproportionate space has been given to the Puritan, but the more I have come to study the causes that produced this new race, the more I have been impressed with the imperfect knowledge possessed by Americans — and if it is so among Americans in how much greater degree must it be among Europeans? — of the great and lasting influence exercised on American civilization and the formation of character by the Puritans, who affected not only America but have influenced all the rest of the world.

Tradition has invested the Puritan with certain qualities. There lingers in the mind of every American, the dim recollection of school-days, the picture of the Puritan, grim, forbidding, sombre; and so difficult is it to efface the impressions of youth that Puritanism has become synonymous with all that is harsh and gloomy and opposed to innocent pleasure; and to be Puritanical implies rigidity of conscience and is construed as reproach. To the average American, almost to every American who is not a historical student, Puritan and Pilgrim are interchangeable terms; and so little is the distinction regarded that in a carefully prepared address made by a distinguished public man, himself a writer of American history, delivered at the dedication of a monument to the Pilgrims, he referred to the Puritans as if they and the Pilgrims were one; as if they shared the same views of religion and life; as if to the Pilgrims belonged the honor of having made New England.

"Acting at the sources of life, instruments otherwise weak became mighty for good or evil, and men, lost elsewhere in the crowd, stand forth as agents of Destiny."[1] In all history there is nothing so extraordinary as the effect of that religious persecution which led to the establishment of Massachusetts and laid the foundation of the great

[1] Parkman: *Pioneers of France in the New World*, Introduction, p. xv.

American Republic. Puritanism left its impress upon the life and thought of England, and having done its work as the agent of Destiny became merged in other forces. Puritanism in America, when it ceased to be merely a religious symbol, was still a social force, and it is to-day. "Vitalized by the principles of its foundation, the Puritan commonwealth grew apace." She sowed the seeds of intolerance and brought forth liberty. She preached blind obedience to authority and was the first to resist when it became galling. She taught thrift and elevated the material to the dignity of a virtue. She made acquisition a duty. She was free, and she was shackled to a narrow and harsh theology that dwarfed expansion. And yet she expanded, sending forth her sons into the barren places, who, full of energy and the love of gain that was as much a part of the Puritan character as his faith in the immutable workings of a higher power, gave new lustre to his name and made the world marvel. Where France failed, England succeeded. What Spain attempted, England accomplished. Holland planted and England reaped. Sweden dreamed and England worked.

In those long years of struggle and adversity, in those years when England was master of a continent and compelled the recognition of her power and Englishmen were competing with each other in the rivalry of trade and in widening their own possessions, those men of the North, inspired by a great purpose, were building a civilization different from Englishmen in the South, and as the agents of Destiny were unconsciously preparing for the part they were fated to play. Would the American Colonies have severed the tie that bound them to England if Massachusetts had been settled by the men who made Virginia and Maryland? There is, of course, no answer, but we can well believe that if there had been no Puritan element in America, if all that we understand by Puritanism had not vitalized the American, the breach might have come — possibly it was Destiny, and was inevitable — but it would have been closed in another way. But this, however, we do know, that while the men of the South were no less quick to respond to the clarion call that sounded the note of freedom, it was the spirit of the Puritan that pervaded the land; it was Puritanism that made resistance a duty; it was the influence of Puritanism, then as now, that has given the American character its stability, and has ever been an element to counterpoise the sometimes menacing mutability of the infusion of foreign blood; it was the Puritan love of gain and expansion that could be appeased only by new colonies planted in the wilderness; it was the Puritan sense of thrift and order and commerce that made the American people a nation devoted to business and more by the right of birth a nation of shopkeepers — using that historical expression in no sense derogatory but as characterizing the strongest quality of the American mind, its commercial instinct — than any other people in the world. There would, I am confident, have been an America if the Puritans had never been driven out of England and found shelter when and how they did, but it would not have been the America we now know.

Such comments as I make from time to time in sketching historical progress are to impress on the reader that almost against their will Englishmen were driven on the road that led to Americanism; that they became Americans without conscious effort, and ceased to be Englishmen, which was foreign to their inclination; and certainly with no conception of the tremendous results that were to follow. Actions in themselves trifling, but which produced momentous psychological consequences, have too often escaped notice. The historian feels that he has more important matters to record, but they are essential in tracing the growth of the mind of a people and observing how they were influenced by causes remote from the climax.

What follows is original in that the results of observation and study develop their own conclusions. It is an effort to search the spring to its source. It is the subjection of phenomena to minute analysis, and although at times there is seemingly no connection between the consequence and its primal cause, in the continuity of thought there is no break; the present foreshadows the future by the reflection of the past.

Avowing myself to be a uniformitarian, repudiating the doctrine of the catastrophic process of human development, believing that mental growth and social expansion are wrought by slow and gradual change, which is always working to a higher plane, the psychology of the American people presents no miracle and is reducible to exact terms. We have here no unfathomable mystery. There are no wide gaps to be filled by speculative soaring. It is a complex but at the same time compelling study of widening spiritual and mental powers, logical in all its processes; inevitable in its results.

Can the history of a people best be written by one of themselves or by a foreigner? It is a question which every one will answer for himself. My own opinion is that a foreigner who approaches his task with sympathy, who comes not as a critic but as a judicious investigator, who is neither a partisan nor a eulogist, who erects no false standard of comparison, and who is not afflicted with that distressing form of intellectual cecity which measures everything by the narrow vision of its own national perfection, is better qualified for the work. For it is axiomatic that we do not see ourselves as others see us, and what is true of the individual is even in a larger sense true of a people. They see themselves as a man looks at his mirror, who having seen his reflection every day for forty years is still a stranger to his own face; while the foreigner, if he is not blinded by patriotic conceit, has the definite advantage of comparison, which is the starting-point of investigation, which leads the inquiring mind to ask whether that which is new and strange may not be better than that which is old and familiar, and makes it necessary to try to ascertain what has brought about the change and the result it has produced. The foreigner has the advantage of detachment and is uninfluenced by prejudices which are accounted national virtues; he is frequently more discriminating but not less just than the native. And yet so profoundly am I impressed with the truism that almost no one understands any one else, and very seldom even himself, and so difficult is it to appreciate the motives and actions of our fellow beings, that one's feeling of confidence is shaken when he attempts the almost stupendous task of interpreting national psychology. Realizing this, I am very well aware that the point of view of the alien can never be that of the native, and that some of the conclusions reached in the following pages will be challenged. If so, they may be attributed to the impossibility of that mysterious barrier that nationality raises ever being quite leveled.[1] It may be over-

[1] This may appear to conflict with the views expressed in later pages on the absorption of the foreigner, the immigrant, into the American, but it does not. There is a difference between the immigrant who comes to America with the definite purpose to become an American and who divests himself of his nationality as he does his strange clothes the more quickly to adjust himself to his new life, and the foreigner, who while he may make his home in America, and perhaps contributes a little to its development and progress,

thrown by long years of residence, by constant and intimate association, by marriage and new family ties; but here and there a little of that barrier will be left, like an old walled city whose defenses have long crumbled, but where a tower still stands to remind the visitor that there were walls to be beaten down before the stranger could enter the gates.

Unless a writer is content merely to wander aimlessly in the beaten track and is satisfied so successfully to conceal his convictions that by pleasing everybody he satisfies nobody, he is forced at times to disagree with the conclusions reached by other authors and to view actions from his own experience. The rule imposed upon himself by Bodley[1] has been observed by me — never to make a harsh criticism unless my own impression was corroborated by the published opinion of a respected and impartial American authority. A regard for the feelings of others should make a foreigner sparing in his judgment. I do not concede that all disapprobation must necessarily be avoided, or that a useful purpose is served by profuse and indiscriminate praise, which is a sure and ready means of gaining an ephemeral popularity; neither is captious fault-finding to be indulged in simply to magnify one people or civilization at the expense of another; but

still retains his nationality and is always conscious that he is, say an Englishman instead of an English-American; and who while making no claim to being an American has not been influenced by Americanism. It is the foreigner, sharply to distinguish him from the American of foreign stock, to whom my remarks on the foreign point of view apply.

[1] Bodley: *France*, vol. i, p. 50.

a judicious discussion of national characteristics is not only valuable but essential if the evidence is sufficient to lead to a positive conclusion. No foreigner has more harshly criticised the Americans than the Americans have so often criticised themselves; much of which, I believe, is unwarranted. It is the idealism of the Americans that makes them such searching self-critics. Buried deep in the nature of every child of this race is an intense spiritual aspiration, overlaid, it is true, by the material, but against which the spiritual ever struggles. It is this idealism, this longing to triumph over the material, that is perpetually voiced in self-reproach, that breaks out in revolt against the sordidness of politics and the commercialism of life; it is this which makes the American criticise himself at times so fiercely, that makes him so quick to resent the criticism that comes from without; and that the American is extremely sensitive to foreign criticism cannot be denied. But this is not the place to elaborate the theme; later it will be discussed in its wider relation to the American character.

If I repeat that this work is the result of nine years' conscientious study and preparation, it is not to ask the indulgence of the reader for any deficiencies which the text may reveal,— and that it falls short of what such a book ought to be no one more keenly appreciates than myself,— but it is my protest against what I may, I hope with moderation, call the impertinence of the literary journalist, who approaches a serious task lightly, and without regard for his responsibilities turns out the stock book on America; who, after a week in New York or Boston and a couple of days in Washington and a day in Chicago, poses as an authority and considers himself qualified to instruct his own people on a subject of which he is totally ignorant, and frequently unsuited by temperament and training. Would it be making undignified a serious subject to suggest that in this day of frequent international conference and congresses it should be regarded as a violation of international comity for a person to write a book on a foreign country, its people or its customs, who has not given proof of the proper qualifications for the task?

CHAPTER II

THE AMERICAN PEOPLE A NEW RACE

I PURPOSE to write of the origin, growth, and development of the American people and to trace the causes that have produced a new race. From the feeble seed thrown by destiny on a rock-bound shore there has sprung a mighty race and a civilization the marvel of the world; a new system of political philosophy that made man conscious of the dignity of his birthright. The causes that have produced the American race and American civilization lie buried in no obscurity. No lava of a culture long dead must be cleared away before the truth stands revealed. On the palimpsest of a virgin continent, on verdure-clad mountains, in primeval forests, on the trackless waste of inland oceans, and rivers so vast that they gave to man a new conception of the might of nature, the American people have written in enduring language the record of a race.

Just as the story of the struggle and intellectual progress and spiritual development of a man is of vastly more interest than the record of his possessions and material success, so the history of the mental growth of a people is tenfold more vital and enthralling than the chronicle of their wars and conquests. With wars, with battles, with the rise and fall of political parties this history will not concern itself except as the aspirations and passions of men, now facing death in defense of an ideal, then engaged in a peaceful but equally determined struggle to preserve that ideal, so moulded character that they produced a new type and gave to the world a new race.

For although the American people spring from an old stock and have been influenced by many races and the civilization of all races, climate, environment, social conditions, and a system of political philosophy far-reaching in its moral influence have produced not a mongrel race but mentally and physically a new race. "In a society living, growing, changing, every new factor becomes a permanent force; modifying more or less the direction of movement determined by the aggregate of forces."[1] In both the animal and the vegetable kingdoms species, by the irresistible law of evolution and their adjustment to new conditions, retain many of the characteristics of the parent stock, but by conforming to their environment in the struggle for existence create a new type. This has been accomplished in the American people after little more than a century of national existence. They are not English, although they speak and think in English. They are not German, or Irish, or French, although the Germans, the Irish, the French, and many other races have influenced them. Saxon, Teuton, Celt, Latin

[1] Spencer: *The Study of Sociology*, p. 95.

have been the elements fused in the alembic of a social, political, and moral code which have produced a new metal with many of the attributes of its constituent elements but with properties of its own.

In history there are no haphazard events, although at times there is no juxtaposition of cause and effect, and the real meaning can be interpreted only when it is projected on the background of age. Superficial thinking and inaccurate investigation ascribe a divine or miraculous interposition to events that are the result of purely human action, which is as convenient for the historian and saves him as much trouble in his search for first causes as it was for the persecutors of witches to obtain a conviction on "spectral evidence."

In the study of race growth, which is the study of the ever advancing tide of civilization, although there are times when the tide appears to ebb, two facts obtrude themselves so insistently that their significance cannot be mistaken. One is that history — using that term in its broadest sense as embracing all human activity and its progress and development — is written on a palimpsest; the other is that mankind does not learn from the teachings of the past, but knowledge comes only from experience. In this the race differs not at all from the individual, who is taught the great lesson of life not from the wisdom of the ancients, which is common to all, but by that knowledge which is peculiar to himself.

If it were otherwise, if the discipline of the long line of the past counted for anything, the wheel of life would revolve more slowly but on a truer centre. With monotonous, exasperating regularity the follies, the errors, the crimes of former generations are repeated by the present. If the guide of the past were effectual the world after a thousand years would not allow its emotions to run riot; it would know that every emotion exacts its price, "for life goes on from generation to generation without heeding the wisdom of the wise or the goodness of the good. Her force breaks out afresh in every child that is born."

Fundamentally human nature does not change. It advances with the ever advancing perfection of mechanical progress (it is an interesting speculation whether civilization is the result of mechanical improvement or mechanical improvement produces civilization), its morals and manners adjust themselves to a conventional standard, and however inadequate they may appear viewed from the present were all sufficient for their age, and, it is important to remember, were a stage in the higher development of civilization. All the great developments of the internal man, Guizot says, have turned to the profit of society; all the great developments of the social stage to the profit of the individual man.[1] But while society has changed extrinsically, in all that is organic it is the same. Truth, honesty, jus-

[1] Guizot: *History of Civilization*, vol. i, p. 14.

tice are the cardinal virtues of an age that prides itself on having attained the summit of civilization, but they are the virtues that have been handed down from the past and are not the creation of the present. Wherein does the moral training of our children differ from that of the Persians, or how have we improved upon their theory or practice? "The moral nature of the child was trained with assiduous attention. As far as possible, it was preserved from contact with vice, while the virtues of self-control, truthfulness, and justice were constantly enjoined and practiced. Ingratitude and lying were considered the most shameful vices, while truthfulness was looked on as the highest virtue."[1] The wheel of civilization forever revolves, but its mass is so immense and it turns with such deliberation that man the pigmy, with narrowed vision, in the conceit of pride in what he believes to be discoveries, sees only what is before his eyes and thinks he has beheld a new truth, and all that he has seen is the civilization of the past in its periodic return coming to the surface to confound the present.

Nor is it only in morals that the present repeats the past. The diversions of the idle rich in all ages show a singular similitude. The unrestrained license of undergraduates celebrating their triumphs on the river or the football field is merely the survival of the days of the Restoration, when it was

[1] Painter: *A History of Education*, p. 22.

the fashion for dissolute young men to band together to molest respectable people in the streets. Yet the worthy burgesses of London who were the victims of the curious sense of humor entertained by the Mohocks simply experienced the fate of the citizens of Rome at the height of her glory, when elegant aristocrats found their sport in rudely assaulting quiet citizens returning from dinner, or plundering some poor huckster's stall in the Suburra, or insulting a lady in her chair.[1] In little things "often regarded as peculiar to America," an American writer satirically remarks, "we are only preserving old English forms and customs. For example, when a vigilance committee in the South or West decorate an obnoxious stranger with a coat of tar and feathers, they are only exercising a form of English hospitality practiced in the seventeenth century."[2] The wheel forever revolves.

If I emphasize that in the progress of society nothing is new and at every stage its virtues and vices are simply a reproduction of society at a former period, it is because the lesson is peculiarly applicable to the United States. Many Europeans who have written of the United States with the spirit of the philosopher or the historian, without deliberate intent, but in good faith, adopt this mental attitude: We have given you literature, science, art, the refinements of life; you have given us,

[1] Dill: *Roman Society from Nero to Marcus Aurelius*, p. 76.

[2] Campbell: *The Puritan in Holland, England, and America*, vol. i, p. 72.

what? Nothing except the materialism of life and the corruption of politics. Now the reason for this is not, as Americans have so frequently believed, "a certain condescension in foreigners," that condescension that makes the foreigner regard himself and his culture, his morals and his habits, as superior to the American. It is purely psychological. In viewing his own development the European cannot stand outside himself; the genesis of his civilization is too remote for him to be able to comprehend that it has experienced the same "cyclical evolution" as a much younger civilization.

No living European has seen the society with which he is most familiar and of which he is a part, that is, of his own country, come into existence with the resistless and at times destructive force of a volcano that levels mountains and fills valleys. In the memory of living man in Europe human advancement has been the slow, steady, almost unperceived progress of a river that scours its own bed and with calm but irresistible force, so placid despite its power that at times the drift of the current is unnoticed, bears its detritus to the ocean. But in America the movement has been cataclysmic. It has cut a new channel, violently, with a sudden wrench, at times with great disorder, when a new channel was necessary. Like its own Mississippi it has made mock of tradition and scoffed sociological geographers, with their precise charts and their mathematical lines of boundaries.

In America man stands face to face with a civilization in the making, and the making of civilization has always been the play of primordial forces. He sees all that is noble and all that is base revealed in all its nobility and all its baseness. He sees the mind stripped of its covering. Civilization that is old, that has become fashioned into a mould and is a stereotyped convention, conceals its workings. Much that is shameful and sordid exists, but as civilized men cover their bodies, so civilized society has a horror of frankly revealing its mental processes. In America that stage has not yet been reached. What is bad is candidly pronounced bad, so that a remedy may be found. What is good all the world shall be told; it shall be to the world an inspiration, and to Americans an encouragement for redoubled effort. In England, says Masterman, reticence still forbids an eager sincerity about ultimate questions, but in America "a new child race will discuss its own spiritual anatomy with all the candor of interested children." [1]

It is because the Americans came from England, it is because the mother tongue of America is English, and it is from England that America has derived her ideals, her law, and her literature, that England has been made the yardstick of comparison. The two countries have so much in common mentally and spiritually that Europe, which knows England so much better than it knows the United

[1] Masterman: *In Peril of Change*, p. 60.

States, has fallen into the fashion of using England as the common denominator in which to express the terms of American civilization. But this is a mistake and leads to an error so grave that it makes all calculation worthless. America is no longer England or even a reflex of England. America is American, and if the character of the American people is to be understood and their civilization is to be correctly interpreted they must be measured by their own standards and not weighed in the scales of foreign make. And bearing this in mind, we shall see again with what exact fidelity the present reproduces the past. The corruption of politics,—perhaps the most fruitful theme of European writers, and not entirely neglected by American commentators, — the sordidness of place-hunters, the dishonesty of demagogues, the lust for wealth, the vulgarity of display, — these things are neither new nor peculiar to America. For everything that has happened or is now happening in the United States we shall find its parallel and its precedent in English civilization in its various evolutionary stages; nor shall we find them at a time so remote from the present that they were merely the survival of the manners and customs of a people then but slowly emerging from barbarism and whose civilization was still rudimentary. Long after England had given to the world some of the world's greatest and most enduring literature; long after Newton had discovered his great principle, and Flamsteed had created the science of modern astronomy, and Hooke and Boyle and Wilkins (the list might be prolonged almost indefinitely) had made their great contributions to science; long after the courage and valor and patriotism of England had become the glorious heritage of Englishmen, the morals of England were so unspeakably vile that the titles of some of the poems of Lord Rochester, a fashionable poet, "are such as no pen of our day could copy";[1] and politics were so openly a matter of barter and sale that seats in Parliament were sold to the highest bidder. "I came into Parliament for Newton in the Isle of Wight, a borough of Sir Leonard Holmes," wrote Lord Palmerston in his diary, May, 1807. "One condition required was that I would never, even for the election, set foot in the place, so jealous was the patron lest any attempt be made to get a new interest in the borough." Samuel Wilberforce, the great philanthropist, paid £9000 for Hull, which he represented when he first entered Parliament; the Earl of Shaftesbury, the friend of the working classes and the champion of protective labor legislation, as Lord Ashley, contested the County of Dorset at a time so near the present as 1831, and spent £15,600 only to meet defeat.

Parliamentary seats are no longer put up at auction, but the lock to Saint Stephens turns with a

[1] Green: *A Short History of the English People*, p. 589.

golden key. The cost of getting a seat in England is often heavy. A considerable proportion of the English members of Parliament, a modern English writer says, would be satisfied if their annual outlay upon their divisions came to no more than £500. Many spend less, some a great deal more. There are large county divisions, and certain small and greedy urban communities, debauched by a succession of over-affluent members, in which the annual expenditure could be reckoned in thousands of pounds rather than hundreds. And this is exclusive of the actual cost of the election, which may be anything from £600 to £2000, and may have to be defrayed at any moment determined by the Fates and the Prime Minister. A man in straitened circumstances cannot meet all these demands with the open-handed liberality the electors appreciate. Against the average member of Parliament, especially if he be a Conservative, there can hardly be a more injurious imputation than that he "does nothing" for the place — that he spends no money there. And unless he is a politician of real distinction, or of exceptional personal popularity, he is in some danger of finding that his local association is angling industriously for a more munificent patron.[1]

"In these days of so-called debased politics," an American writer says, the Duke of Newcastle of George the Third's time, "would be denounced as

[1] Low: *The Governance of England*, p. 181.

a 'machine boss' of the most pronounced type; for it was he who controlled the patronage barrel; who received church dignitaries in quest of preferment; influenced Whigs in search of profitable contracts; and any individual that had rendered partisan service of any character and believed he should obtain a valuable concession of any kind. It was the Duke who patted this follower on the back, who gave money now and a promise then, who shook hands with the public generally and who tried to send away happy every person who called upon him for a favor. His methods were no better or no worse than political methods that have been practiced in our own day. To gain a point he never hesitated at bribery."[1]

Or we may go back to the century before George III reigned and see where the lesson of corruption was learned. When Randolph was sent to London in 1682 he wrote to the Bishop of London of "their great friend the L. P. S. [Lord Privy Seal] who cannot withstand their weighty arguments"; and it was the weight of gold. Anglesey was the Lord Privy Seal, and he is described by Burnet as one who "stuck at nothing and was ashamed of nothing; neither loved nor trusted by any man or any side; seemed to have no regard to common decencies, but sold everything that was in his power, and sold himself so often that at last the price fell so low that he grew useless."[2]

[1] Hastings: *Introduction to Public Papers of George Clinton,* vol. i, p. 24.
[2] Doyle: *English Colonies in America,* vol. iii, p. 208.

If England in the eighteenth century could have been compared say with Germany, Germany with two hundred years more of civilization behind her, with the same liberal political institutions and the same language as England, what would Germany have thought of English political corruption, of English manners, of the brutality of justice? England to-day is no longer the England of the eighteenth and the beginning of the nineteenth centuries, because she has experienced and learned. So will the United States. The political corruption in England, as I have already shown, was greater, more shameless, more destructive of popular liberties than it has ever been in the United States. In England men and women were hanged where the money value of the article stolen was trifling because the hanging of a thief was supposed to be for the protection of society. In the United States men — women seldom, if ever — are lynched because society, rude, violent, primitive, with stern ideas of justice, demands death for self-protection. Can any one doubt that the time will come when lynching in the United States will be as unknown as is to-day the spectacle of an English judge sentencing a woman to death for having stolen a few yards of cloth to save herself and her children from starvation?

Society is always striving for higher ethical standards and before attaining them it passes through the same stages of development that the body does physically. It must grow slowly, it must experience the pains of growth; life comes to it as a practical experience and not as the theoretical teachings of the past. The child learns only by experience. Society at every stage has been like the child dimly groping for something better, ignoring precept and counsel, often hurt before it reaches a higher development; but society like the child, if it survives, if in it is implanted the vital essence, rises to a higher standard as a result of its experiences, its stumblings, its pains, and its sorrows.

In their analysis of the American mind and their explanation of the psychology of the American people most writers have based their conclusion on a false premise. It has come to be the fashion to believe that the chain of English civilization was unbroken in its transmission to the American colonies; that in the century and a quarter of national existence the United States should have developed along the same lines, and at the same pace, and subject to the same influences as the mother land. The intellectual phases of American history, therefore, are to be judged as exalted, arrested, or retrograded according as they measure up with contemporaneous conditions in England.

It cannot be too strongly asserted that nothing is more misleading than this belief in the transmission intact and the continuance of the established civilization of England among pioneer colonizers in a new country and with severed political allegiance. Its constant iteration has invested it with the sanctity that age gives to a "natural law," and having been accepted by the world at large it has become a conviction. But even "natural laws" buttressed by the ignorance of centuries have been proved to be a perversion of the principles of truth when the test of knowledge has been scientifically applied. Copernicus destroyed the "natural law" of the universe and gave to man the truth of astronomy.

The English who came as the first settlers to America were in all things Englishmen in a foreign environment, at heart alien, just as the Englishman of to-day who serves his country in India or South America or Germany remains an Englishman, although he adopts the language of the country in which he lives and adjusts himself to its customs. But with the permanency of settlement, the revolutionizing influences of the struggle with natural conditions, and above all with a declared political independence of the British Crown, the bond with the old civilization snapped. Thus a new and distinct racial psychology began in America. After a race has been formed and bred to certain qualities within a limited field, Shaler says, after it has come to possess a certain body of characteristics which give it its peculiar stamp, the importance of the original cradle passes away.[1]

The civilization of England flowed on. Society was established, its traditions were fixed, there was no interruption in its orderly and progressive devel-

[1] Shaler: *Nature and Man in America*, p. 165.

opment. Civilization in America, when America was no longer English but was American in fact as well as in name, paused long enough to give birth to a new civilization, the like of which the world before had never dreamed of. A new system of political philosophy, which was a moral code no less than a political, that gave man "kingship in right of his mere manhood," produced its own needs of civilization, which was largely influenced by natural conditions, as society always has been at every stage in its development. And there began a new civilization, a civilization that, whether good or bad, whether superior to or inferior to the civilization of the English, obeyed the inexorable law of evolution and in its own way has served its own purpose.

Democracy is not alone a polity. It is something much more than that. A people born in a democracy unconsciously acquire ideas and a mental process that make them unlike the subjects of a monarchy or the citizens of a country in which established class distinctions exist. We shall see, as the theme unfolds, the moral and psychological effects of a democratic form of government.

American civilization is the youngest of which the world knows. It is still formative. This makes a serious study fantastic almost, for judgment is but another name for comparison; we can reach a conclusion only by comparing it with something else, and when we compare American civilization with that of any other modern people it is almost as if we had to resort to a miracle to explain causes. It is as if the boy overnight had been touched by the magician's wand and awakes a man, a giant in force and intellect, and yet with all the vital enthusiasm of youth, who is conscious of his strength and who has the stripling's contempt for age. Men sneer at his juvenescence and think it surprising that he is still so crude, and wonder when, if ever, he will emerge from adolescence and arrive at the dignity of man's estate, and yet they stand amazed at his power and his mind. He defies every tradition, the wisdom of his elders he laughs at and becomes a law unto himself, the fallacy of theory he joyously mocks, and with it all he grows stronger, better, spiritually more exalted.

The same difficulty that confronted Bagehot meets me, but in a much greater degree. There is great difficulty, he says, in the way of a writer who attempts to sketch a living Constitution — a Constitution that is an actual work and power. The difficulty is that the subject is in constant change. If this is so in the case of a Constitution, how much more so must it be when a study is made of a civilization that is still in a state of flux, that is constantly being moulded to receive new impressions? A contemporary writer, Bagehot says, who tries to paint what is before him is puzzled and perplexed; what he sees is changing daily.[1] In America this change

[1] Bagehot: *The English Constitution*, pp. 1–2.

is perpetual. I have watched it in the few years that have elapsed since I began this study; it has caused me more than once to revise my judgment. America, says Bryce, changes so fast that every few years a new crop of books is needed to describe the new face which things have put on, the new problems that have appeared, the new idea germinating among her people, the new and unexpected developments for evil as well as for good of which her established institutions have been found capable.[1]

With equal force Reich has pointed out the perplexities one encounters at every turn. But suppose we wish, he says, to investigate a question of national psychology, we have no laboratory to appeal to; we must seek sense impressions in the world abroad. In order to comprehend the characteristics of one's own nation, we must subject it to a scrutinizing comparison with other nations. How difficult is this comparison to make. How few have even the opportunity of making it. It implies a long sojourn in foreign countries of a person endowed with keen and critical faculties of observation, and a mastery of the literature and language of those countries. These are the essentials, and how rarely are they fulfilled. But without comparison after this manner there can be no real advance.[2]

When Europeans, and not alone Europeans but

[1] Bryce: *The American Commonwealth*, vol. i, p. 2.

[2] Reich: *Success Among Nations*, p. 91.

many Americans also, deplore the crudeness of American civilization and become despondent because America has not yet produced a Leonardo da Vinci, a Wren, a Shakespeare, a Mozart, and pronounce their *obiter dicta* that America is deaf to the higher voices, they forget that Europe has a heritage of a thousand years and America but a hundred; that men are the product of their soil and their environment, and art is born not in the stress of commercialism, but comes later. History has served us to no purpose if we do not recognize this. Art is the expression of luxury and fashion and idleness, of a certain form of voluptuousness; it flourishes best where there is a Mæcenas and his order to give to it the approval of their patronage; or it is the expression of religion; or it is the soul cry of a people despairing of the present and hopeless of the future. In the beginning art was the symbolism of religion or superstition; later it lost its original meaning and became conventionalized, and then commercialized. In America there is great luxury, fashion peculiar to American conditions, but little idleness; voluptuousness as a national quality does not exist; of religion there is much, but it does not take the form that inspired the Greeks and the cathedral builders of mediæval Europe; the American people instead of despairing face the problems of the present and the unknown questions of the future with supreme self-reliance. In a word, their national vitality is too high for them yet to have reached that stage when imagination makes a greater appeal than action. The artistic temperament and the strenuous, masterful, almost brutal qualities of the man of action do not reside in the same body. Almost universally the men who have sung their songs of incomparable beauty, "too wise to be wholly poets and yet too surely poets to be implacably wise," in whom *Weltschmerz* has colored their whole vision of life, have shrunk from the rough contact of the world and hated the very thought of strife.

If we have read history aright, if we do not confuse causes with effects or underestimate the forces that produced such momentous results, one conclusion is ineluctable. No race has ever given proof of a high order of mental attainments until after it has enjoyed a long period of great material prosperity. Art and literature are not born in the dregs of national poverty; no people struggling for a bare existence and content with food or raiment enough merely to keep themselves alive have given birth to the deathless voice of the bard. After the struggle for existence has been won there comes the desire for comfort, and then follows luxury; and what is luxury but the appeal to the senses, the gratification of the body or the delight of the mind, the enjoyment of the sensual or the quickening of the emotions aroused by music or art or poetry?

But it will be said that the poets whose songs

are in the hearts of the people have been of the people; that it was suffering and poverty and great compassion that made them articulate; that it was their protest against wrongs too great to be silently endured; that it was only because they knew the hopeless misery of the downtrodden that they were able to voice it; that prosperity would have made them content and dumb; which is much like saying that the world has been deprived of its great poets because there are so many successful greengrocers. The greater the wealth of a people, whether a community or a nation, the greater its poverty, so far apart are the two ends of the social scale, so far apart must they be when wealth is the reward of individual endeavor or is dependent upon audacity, courage, industry, or an intuitive sense of possibilities. Among a people where the dead level of conditions exists there is, it is true, no sense of social injustice because all are practically equal, but there is also no stimulus; there is no Promethean voice to flame, no heart to be touched. If it is true that the poets of the people have been of the people — and it is a generalization to be accepted only with the respect due to all generalizations — we now see why; we now see why there can be no great poets when life flows placidly like a stream in which there is not even a rock to add the variety of a ripple to its dull monotony or momentarily to reflect the sun's glint.

Out of the depths of his soul man voices his faith

or his despair; from his innermost self comes the hymn of victory or the cry of desolation. And the poets sing and the people hearken when there are great deeds to be done or great wrongs to be redressed, when men are to be inspired to resist or to defend themselves. War and poverty, the material — there is the inspiration of the poets.

It is something more than a theory that has here been advanced. It rests on the facts of history. The great art and literature of Greece and Rome were given to the world at a time when their splendor was unrivaled, when their riches were beyond compare, when with great wealth there was poverty equally as great. Ferrero calls our attention to the same phenomenon in Egypt. At the time when her agriculture was prosperous, her manufactures flourishing, her commerce widely spread, her schools famous, then also "her artistic life was vigorous." The artisans of Alexandria manufactured the most delicate fabrics, perfumes, glassware, papyrus, and numerous other articles of art and luxury which were ever sold in the markets of the world. Egypt was the home of luxury and elegance, and her painters and her decorators went everywhere, even to Italy; while to Egypt, then a centre of learning, from all parts of the world, even from Greece, students came to study in the schools of medicine and astronomy and literature at Alexandria.[1]

The great intellectual movement in England came

[1] Ferrero: *The Greatness and Decline of Rome*, vol. iii, pp. 240–241.

at a time when she was rich as she had never been before. The Elizabethan age was an age of intense material prosperity, when wealth was being rapidly accumulated, when commerce possessed the whole people, when the spirit of adventure had seized them, and yet it presented the same contrast that has always been witnessed at this stage of national development. On the one hand there was great luxury and great wealth, on the other there was great suffering and great poverty, and the condition of the poor was deplorable. The imagination is fired by the deeds of Raleigh and his captains; by that brave battle in the Channel; we stand with uncovered head before the tomb of Shakespeare; the great statesmen and philosophers have left their imperishable record; but let not our emotions nor our admiration blind us to the direful fact that it was in the reign of Elizabeth that the first poor-law was placed on the statute-books. In a subsequent chapter I shall more at length discuss the causes that have produced as well as arrested American art.

I have laid down the proposition that the civilization of America is not that of England; that the American people are no longer English, but a new race. I shall now endeavor to show how it came about that the civilization of England was checked in America and ran in new channels, the causes that have produced a new race, and the conclusions to be drawn from the facts established.

CHAPTER III

THE INFLUENCE OF ENVIRONMENT ON RACE

In tracing the development of American civilization, the growth of the American race, and the formation of national characteristics, we are impressed with the fact that the history of the American people properly divides itself into four grand divisions, each epochal in character-building. It is unnecessary to resort to empirical or arbitrary methods to ascertain where the dividing lines fall. They are the strata of human formation. These four epochs are:—

1. Colonial Days — the period from the arrival of the first settlers at Jamestown and the establishment of thc Plymouth Colony until the American nation was born in the throes of the revolt against oppression.

2. Independence — the period that saw the birth of a new political and moral creed.

3. The Civil War — the period that was the formative stage in the American character; that began in war in defense of justice and closed in war in defense of human liberty and political solidarity.

4. The Spanish War — the period from the close of the Civil War to the present; that hardened the mould of the American character and opened the vista to the future.

Observe, as throwing a vivid light on the causes that have produced the mental and moral characteristics of the American people, that each of these epochs was born in the passion of war, at each successive stage of American progress the heavens were riven with the storm of conflict, and the daughters of Jupiter came forth.

> "Can tyrants but by tyrants conquered be,
> And freedom find no champion and no child,
> Such as Columbia saw arise, when she
> Sprang forth a Pallas, armed and undefiled?"

The beginning of America was a resistance against religious oppression and a revolt against the suppression of personal liberty; and rebellion unless quickly checked leads to war, and it led, in this case, as was inevitable, to war to preserve liberty and to perpetuate an ideal. Each period was unconsciously but inexorably the preparation and precursor of that which followed, and each in passing wrought with iron hand in American development. Perhaps in all the history of all the world we shall find nothing so remarkable as this — race development that can be directly traced to the effects of war. But observe again, because it is one of those antinomies with which the history of the American people abounds, that while war has more profoundly affected their character than that of any other modern race, for the first one hundred and fifty years succeeding their birth they fought no war in defense of religious freedom or in the name of religion, they were not passed over like chattels from one sovereign to another, they knew no flag but their own, they engaged in no war of conquest solely to bring an alien people under their domination. While all Europe was involved in that great Thirty Years' struggle; while the history of Europe for a century and a half following the English settlement of America is a continuous record of war; while wars of the Spanish Succession, of the Polish Succession, of the Austrian Succession, even of Jenkins's Ear, burden the pages of history and make one weary to discover what it was all about and why it was worth fighting for; while Europe was one vast armed camp drenched in blood and the breeding-ground for the sordid ambitions of kings and statesmen, America, far removed from the scene of conflict, went forward in her spiritual and material development. We shall see later how profoundly American political institutions and American psychology were influenced by the conflict with the French and Indians, but the consequences were entirely different from those resulting from the wars of Europe, which made every man a soldier, who when he was not fighting under his sovereign's banner as his liegeman or as his mercenary became a rebel against the kingly power. The border warfare kept the colonist alert to defend his foothold in the New World, but his aim was security, his ambition the unmolested homestead right.

As the American mind gradually reveals itself, the effect of this political isolation at the formative stage of the race will be clearly seen.

A nation is the sum of many influences, but none have more weight in the formation of character and the mental type of a people than the natural phenomena of the country in which they live. Extreme heat and cold are reflected not only in the physical appearance of the race, but also in its mental characteristics. Nature, to help man adapt himself to his environment, has made the races that dwell nearest the sun more lithe, more sinewy, less burdened with superfluous flesh than those who live in colder climates, who need greater protection from the extreme rigors of their long winters; and as they are physically so they are mentally. The men and women of the south, in whose veins run the fire and heat of the sun, who bask in a riot of color, who are influenced by the witchery of radiant, caressing moonlight, have always been gifted with temperaments more vivid, more poetic, and more imaginative than the men and women of the north, slower, more precise, more practical. The plainsman is a different type from the mountaineer, and both show a variation from the inhabitant of the seacoast. An arid, sterile country produces a race unlike that in which the land is fruitful and rivers abound. Trees and mountains, valleys and prairies are the indelible pictures of memory that unconsciously color life, as the pictures of childhood leave an ineffaceable recollection.[1]

These things are not new, they are as old as creation itself. Man has always been influenced by his surroundings, always keenly sensitive to exterior impressions. To a certain extent their force is blunted when countless generations have looked upon the same mountains or the same valleys, for each succeeding generation has in it a part at least of the stored emotions and sensations of its predecessors, the inherent faculty of comprehension without ratiocination, exactly as the animal instinctively takes to the water or avoids it. To the child who opens his eyes on the unfathomable mystery of the sea, the sea is as natural as the mountain, which he beholds for the first time, is abnormal and terrifying. The civilization of most peoples runs too far back for us to appreciate the influences of climate and natural phenomena in moulding the characteristics of race, but in America we are so close to its genesis that we not only know but we can actually see what the effects have been.

To have a correct understanding of the American character it is necessary at the outset to establish certain facts which nearly all writers on American race development have treated, if they touched on them at all, as only incidental instead of being a primary cause. I maintain that when a highly

[1] *Cf.* May: *Democracy in Europe*, introduction, p. xxxix *et seq.*

civilized race is transplanted to a new environment, that environment entirely different from the old, different in climate and other physical characteristics, and to support life it is necessary for these people from the very first to engage in an unrelenting struggle against nature, the effect of that struggle will be seen in the mental characteristics of the people new to the soil. It is a remarkable fact that the great evolutionary authorities — Darwin, Spencer, Wallace, Haeckel, Le Conte, to mention only a few of the most eminent — are either silent on this important branch of psychological investigation, or else dismiss it with merely a passing reference, and yet its truth cannot be doubted. It is sustained by the teachings of biogeny, morphology, and sociology, and is further fortified by the historical study of race development. No one, I think, can study the psychology of history and not be profoundly impressed by the dominant influence that nature has exercised in the progress of organized society. In the ascertainment of the causes that have resulted in the shoot of the race varying so materially from the parent stem the importance of the physical cannot be overestimated.

Spencer says: "We see that . . . the changes or processes displayed by a living body are especially related to the changes or processes in its environment. And here we have the needful supplement to our conception of life. Adding this all important characteristic, our conception of life becomes —

the definite combination of heterogeneous changes, both simultaneous and successive, in *correspondence with external coexistences and sequences.*"[1]

At much greater length in his *Principles of Sociology*, under the title of "Original External Factors," Spencer treats of the influence of climate and physical conditions on race development, but stops just short of the question involved, frankly admitting that it is outside of his province and is the property of the specialist. After showing that temperature, heat, light, moisture, the configuration of the surface, the fertility of the soil, and the nature of the flora and fauna all "have their effects on human activities, and therefore on social phenomena," he says: "But a detailed account of the original external factors, whether of the more important kinds outlined in the preceding pages or of the less important kind exemplified, pertains to Special Sociology. Any one who, carrying with him the general principles of the science, undertook to interpret the evolution of each society, would have to describe completely these many local causes in their various kinds and degrees. Such an undertaking must be left for the sociologists of the future.

"Here my purpose has been," he says, "to give a general idea of the original external factors, in their different classes and orders; so as to impress on the reader the truth, barely enunciated in the preceding chapter, that the characters of the environment

[1] Spencer: *The Principles of Biology*, vol. i, p. 74.

coöperate with the characters of human beings in determining social phenomena."[1]

I give one more quotation from Spencer. "Divesting this conception of all superfluities, reducing it to its most abstract shape, we see that Life is definable as the continuous adjustment of internal relations to external relations. And when we so define it, we discover that the physical and the psychical life are equally comprehended by the definition."[2]

Huxley says: "It is a general belief that men of different stocks differ as much physically as they do morphologically; but it is very hard to prove, in any particular case, how much of a supposed national characteristic is due to inherent physiological peculiarities, and how much to the influence of circumstances."[3]

Darwin gives the weight of his authority to the influence of conditions upon physical development. "We have seen in the second chapter," he says, "that the conditions of life affect the development of the bodily frame in a direct manner, and that the effects are transmitted. Thus, as is generally admitted, the European settlers in the United States undergo a slight but extraordinarily rapid change of appearance. Their bodies and limbs become elongated; and I hear from Colonel Bernys that during the late war in the United States, good evidence was

[1] Spencer: *The Principles of Sociology*, vol. i, part 1, p. 16 *et seq.*

[2] Spencer: *First Principles*, p. 86.

[3] Huxley: *Methods and Results of Ethnology*, p. 240.

afforded of this fact by the ridiculous appearance presented by the German regiments, when dressed in ready-made clothes manufactured for the American market, and which were much too long for the men in every way. There is, also, a considerable body of evidence showing that in the Southern States the house slaves of the third generation presented a markedly different appearance from the field slaves."[1]

And Darwin again says: "Adaptation to any special climate may be looked at as a quality readily grafted on an innate wide flexibility of constitution, common to most animals. On this view, the capacity of enduring the most different climates by man himself . . . ought not to be looked at as anomalies, but as examples of a very common flexibility of constitution, brought, under peculiar circumstances, into action."[2]

"Races would advance and become improved," Wallace says, "merely by the harsh discipline of a sterile soil and inclement seasons. Under their influence a hardier, a more provident, a more social race would be developed than in those regions where the earth produces a perennial supply of vegetable food, and where neither foresight nor ingenuity is required to prepare for the rigors of winter. And is it not a fact that in all ages, and in every quarter of the globe, the inhabitants of temperate have been

[1] Darwin: *The Descent of Man*, p. 196.

[2] Darwin: *The Origin of Species*, vol. i, pp. 175–176.

superior to those of hotter countries? All the great invasions and displacements of races have been from north to south, rather than the reverse; and we have no record of there ever having existed, any more than there exists to-day, a solitary instance of an indigenous inter-tropical civilization."[1]

Buckle ascribes to climate, food, soil, and "the general aspect of nature" those physical agents "by which the human race is most powerfully influenced," and by "the general aspect of nature," he says, "I mean those appearances which, though presented chiefly to the sight, have, through the medium of that or other senses, directed the association of ideas, and hence in different countries have given rise to different habits of national thought."[2] That Buckle was a profound believer in the physical agents already mentioned is known to every student of his monumental work, and he elaborates his thesis at length. "It now remains for me," he says, "to examine the effects of those other physical agents to which I have given the collective name of Aspects of Nature, and which will be found suggestive of some very wide and comprehensive inquiries into the influence exercised by the external world in predisposing men to certain habits of thought, and thus giving a particular tone to religion, arts, literature, and, in a word, to all the principal manifestations of the human mind."[3]

[1] Wallace: *Natural Selection and Tropical Nature*, p. 177.

[2] Buckle: *History of Civilization*, vol. i, p. 29. [3] Buckle, *op. cit.*, p. 85.

I think the conclusion can be properly reached, based not on *a priori* reasoning but sustained by evidence, that environment has an enormous influence on the mind of man, and this influence is as powerful mentally as the physical characteristics of a country are upon his structure; just as the struggle for existence has developed certain organs, both in animals and men, and no physiologist will challenge the correctness of this assertion. But physical and structural variations are easily recognized; mental processes are not only slower but more subtle; the mind is concealed, and the changes that affect the mind of a race are so gradual that they can be ascertained only by long and laborious research. I may go further and assume an even more positive tone. With the sole exception of the American people it has been impossible scientifically to study the influence of environment on mentality, because of four obstacles.

In the first place, the early records of all other races are lost in obscurity, and although we have in many instances literature and traditions, we have no such precise literature, no such accurate record of any people from their beginning as we have of the Americans. Secondly, other races have been influenced in greater or lesser degree by the native civilization of which they became a part. This was absent in America. There was no native civilization. We shall have occasion later to refer to this. Again, every other race, whether as conqueror or emigrant, that have spread beyond the confines of their own country or territory, whether merely as a nomadic tribe or a people with a defined civilization, grafted themselves on the native stock or absorbed it into themselves, their own civilization becoming tempered and modified in the process. And lastly, all other races have engaged in wars and conquests, and the effect of war in the formative period of national character has lasting results. The American people, as we have remarked in a previous chapter, engaged in war in their formative period, but it was a war neither for conquest nor aggression; it was a war inspired by a cause unlike that of any other in history, and it produced certain well-defined psychological tendencies.

We shall now consider the climatal conditions found in the United States and see how far-reaching they have been in the formation of American character.

CHAPTER IV

CLIMATIC AMALGAMATION OF RACE

THE United States is in the temperate zone, but it enjoys all variations of temperature; in some parts its summers are almost tropical in their intensity and the winters are arctic in their severity. These wide variations in temperature in a people of common stock, under one political system, inspired by the same ambitions, have resulted in remarkable race characteristics. The people of the North — of all those states lying north of the fortieth degree of latitude, whose winters are long and severe, but whose summers compensate, the temperature rising west of the eightieth meridian — have the vigor, energy, and physical alertness of the people of northern Europe. South of the fortieth parallel of latitude winter is milder and summer long and hot, at times and in places rivaling the heat of the East, but still not so hot that the white man cannot labor and live without injury to his health. In some parts of some of the states of the South snow is practically unknown and frost is rarely experienced. The long hot summers and mild winters have made the Southern man different from the Northern; he is less energetic, more inclined to take life easy, in a measure less enterprising, and his resource and his initiative have not been so highly developed; and environment has also had its effect. The South was formerly purely an agricultural region, and the nature of its crops — cotton, tobacco, rice — and the conditions under which they were grown were conducive to *laissez-faire* and invited to a leisurely life. The struggle for existence pressed with less severity in the South and held latent those qualities that are brought out by the stress of competition or the conflict with nature. Since the South has ceased to be purely an agricultural region and has turned its energies to manufactures, its iron furnaces and cotton mills now fast competing with the North, it has lost some of its former characteristics and there is in progress another of those psychological transitions that have at successive periods produced American racial development. The change, however, is slow, and its full effect will not be seen in this generation.

Speaking broadly, it may be said that all the gradations of temperature to be found in Europe are experienced in the United States, which is one of the physical factors that have entered into the composition of a new race. The constant effort of breeders of stock and of floriculturists is to improve the breed or the flower by crossing it with a strain the product of a different environment, or to graft on it a growth that has its own peculiarities of soil and climate. Here we see the recognition of the fundamental law that in the animal and vegetable kingdoms what corresponds to character in man — in animals and fruits and flowers structure, size, color — is the result of environment. Man has less scientifically endeavored to improve the human race and has trusted to the happy-go-lucky chance of natural selection. There is to-day no unmixed race. The theory of the unvitiated strain, both in man and animals, is now known to be a fallacy. The great races are races of mixed blood and cross-breeding. King Cophetua needs the blood of the beggar maid to revive the royal line. Nations like trees die from the top and are strengthened at the roots; they must be fed from the ground up. A nation whose people marry and intermarry in their own class has pronounced its doom, for strength is to be found only in a judicious admixture of blood to overcome the degeneration of luxury and the absence of effort.

The effect on a homogeneous people living in a country whose climatic variations are extreme is eventually to amalgamate in the race the composite climatic influence. The daughter of a Russian father and a Spanish mother will, under normal conditions, inherit some of the temperamental or climatic qualities of one or both; and that child marrying an Englishman will transmit to her child, in a more or less marked degree, her own qualities as well as those of its father. But between the Russian and the Spaniard, between two people of alien races, there is always the insurmountable barrier of race and language, of customs and traditions, of history and political institutions, frequently of religion. In the United States climatic influence encounters no obstacles. The man from Maine, where winter is Siberian in its severity, marries a girl from Louisiana, whose summer is as voluptuously enticing as that of Spain, and they move to California, where in some parts roses bloom in the open air in winter and in other parts the fog is as cold and penetrating as it is off the English coast; their child marries a man from Dakota, where the summer is dry and hot and in winter the land lies buried deep under its covering of snow. But the man from Maine and the woman from Louisiana, the Californian or the Dakotan, are as one in language, in thought, in purpose, and the same ambitions animate both; both owe allegiance to the same political institutions; neither knows any other country which means more to the one than it does to the other. A woman, an alien, may merge herself in the life and country of her husband, and yet there is that indefinable something, the result of heredity and environment, that makes her a little apart from her husband and his people, no matter how completely she adjusts herself to her new surroundings. Nothing of this kind exists in the United States, where the people are one people; sectional rivalries and physical conditions and the influence of descent produce a variation in the type, but not a departure from it.[1]

The United States, as a whole, enjoys about the same average temperature as western Europe as a whole, but the winters are much colder and the summers are much warmer in America than in Europe.[2] Climatically the United States is a northern and a southern country, but with distinctive phenomena not elsewhere found. The isothermal lines ascend as they approach New York; the temperature at fifty-two degrees of latitude in the United Kingdom is similar to that at thirty-two degrees of latitude in the United States, a difference of nine hundred and fifty-six miles.[3] The inhabitants of the British Isles, Boutmy says, can travel from one end of the country to the other without experiencing any change of temperature, but in the United States the passage from ocean to ocean is marked by frequent changes of temperature, as it is also by frequent variations of soil. The soil is rich and fertile in places, arid and sterile in others, but the fertile area vastly overbalances the sterile regions, and the spirit of enterprise is encouraged because energy intelligently directed is sure to be

[1] "How rapidly nationalities merge in this country is seen in a case that is not imaginary, of a young man whose father was a Frenchman and whose mother was an American of English descent. His wife's mother is an Irish woman, and her father a German. Thus that marriage rolled four nationalities into one within two generations."—Horace Graves: "The Huguenot in New England," *The New England Magazine*, vol. xi, p. 503.

[2] Channing: *A Student's History of the United States*, p. 2 *et seq.*

[3] Boutmy: *The English People*, p. 4.

profitably rewarded. Nature says to the American that if he works hard and brings to his labor that intelligence which is demanded, he can feel sure of ample returns, but he must not relax his efforts.

It is one of the paradoxes of Nature, which has had its effect on the character of the people, that in those regions which produce the great staples to support life, the wheat- and corn-growing belts, the variations of temperature are extreme, intense heat as well as intense cold being necessary properly to germinate and ripen the crops. Hence it follows that the farmer and the agricultural laborer must be men of strong constitutions, able to withstand the great drain on their vital forces that comes from arduous labor under burning suns and the isolation of long, hard winters. Boutmy quotes Leroy-Beaulieu to the effect that the extreme severity of the climate in the Muscovite plains, and the great variations between the maximum and minimum temperatures, enervate and depress man instead of stimulating him. The effect of winter in causing mental depression has been well established in the United States. It is a fact resting on competent authority that when the West was even less sparsely settled than it is to-day insanity among the women living in farmhouses was not infrequent; the silence, the monotony, the absence of all society, the never-ending vista of the snow-covered plains, deathlike in their silence, with no moving creature or thing to afford even a momentary diversion, unbalanced these women, their physical vitality lowered by the enervating climate and unremitting toil. Men suffered less, because, while their lives were almost equally monotonous, they were much in the open, they went to the settlements and near-by towns; but the women saw nothing but the four walls of their houses and the interminable plains gripped in the iron hand of winter.

The latest evidence we have of the correspondence between climatic severity and isolation and insanity is found in the passage by the United States Senate, on February 28, 1908, of a bill to increase the appropriation for the care of the insane in Alaska. In 1905 Congress passed a law providing that "five per cent of the license moneys collected from outside of the incorporated towns in the district of Alaska" should be devoted to the care of the insane. This sum proving insufficient by reason of the increase of insanity, the law of 1905 was repealed and the Secretary of the Interior was given authority to draw on the Treasury for whatever funds might be necessary properly to care for the insane in Alaska. And in an American newspaper[1] I find stated that the Chief Signal Officer of the Army "has decided to withdraw from Alaska all men of the Signal Corps who have been there for two years or more." The immediate reason for this decision, it is explained, is the mental breakdown of Master Signal Electrician George Treffinger, who

[1] The Washington *Post*, March 8, 1908.

had been on duty in Alaska for four years. "The trouble with Mr. Treffinger," the account says, "is supposed to be due to the rigorous climate and the hardships of service in Alaska. . . . The Treffinger case is not the first in which mental trouble has resulted from long service in Alaska. Several years ago an officer of the Signal Corps returned home broken down in health and mentally impaired. While he improved for a time, he was finally placed on the retired list. Other officers, coming home from long service in Alaska, are reported to have exhibited abnormal mental tendencies, which, however, disappeared after remaining in a temperate climate for a short while."

It has often been erroneously asserted that the fierce stress of modern competition and the excitement of city life are the inciting causes of insanity, but careful investigation will show that isolation and long and severe winters, to persons born and reared under other circumstances, are largely responsible for the increase of mental disturbance.

The physical characteristics of the United States have had their effect on the American people through the influence of things so much a matter of course as clothing, food, and the structure of houses. The great mass of Americans must be warmly clad for more than half of every year; they must live in houses artificially heated, and they must eat meat and other foods rich in proteids to repair bodily waste. In this they are unlike the vine-growers of Italy or the planters of the West Indies, where a small amount of clothing suffices and natural heat supplies all the warmth necessary to keep their houses at a comfortable temperature, and the soil needs only lightly to be scratched to yield its harvest.

Nor must we overlook the effect of heat on the minds and bodies of men. For nearly six months in the year the average mean temperature of the United States, with a few isolated exceptions, is higher than that of Europe, and it drains the physical energies of Americans, who suffer intensely, especially in the large cities. It is true that men and women go about their allotted tasks in even the most torrid days, but they are made listless, nervous, irritable, and quick-tempered, and the effect is not merely transitory, but produces lasting structural and mental changes. Habits that have been long continued are not merely second nature, but become the very nature of man himself. From the beginning, Englishmen in America have been forced to adapt themselves to extremes of temperature which were unknown to them. The overheating of all American houses in winter, which is the perpetual and just complaint of every foreigner, who marvels how Americans live in such a superheated atmosphere, is easily explained. From the intense heat of summer there is the sudden transition to the fierce cold of winter, and the shock is too violent. The man working in the open, the farmer, the logger, the woodsman, can stand the cold, although not without discomfort; but the city dweller must make artificial conditions simulate the natural heat of summer. These thermometric variations are not conducive to poise or equability, they invite rather to nervousness and excitability; probably they are not without physiological effects. They dry up the secretions, and to keep the salivary glands moistened is perhaps the reason the American indulges in such copious libations of iced water; catarrh, I have been told, is more prevalent in the United States than elsewhere, which may be the result of excessive heat in summer and the dry artificial heat of winter; the unpleasant habit of expectoration so freely indulged in, and the fondness of Americans for tobacco-chewing, which is not confined as it is in England to the lowest classes, are the mechanical efforts of Nature to afford relief. But once again we see the effect of heredity. The seed of this new race was planted in the soil of New England and from there sent forth its shoots to make a continent blossom; the pioneers were the children of men who hardened under the touch of long winters and withstood the test of summer heat; who inured themselves to their surroundings, and who were able to carry ever westward their civilization because they had been tried and survived.

Two things the settler quickly learned were indispensable for his salvation — heat for his body and his home, and food containing the largest amount of strength-giving properties. Hence he became at an early day a trapper and a hunter, for the skins of the fur-bearing animals were necessary to clothe him and the carcasses of some of them to feed him; he felled the trees for fuel, until with greater knowledge he uncovered the stored-up riches of the earth and found in coal a better and more economical source for the creation of heat and energy.

As powerful as human institutions, political teachings, or the inspiration of religion, has been the influence of Nature on American race development. "The history of the United States, more than that of any Old World country, is the record of its physical achievements. The exploitation of virgin territory by a race of extraordinary intelligence, resource, and energy is the essential theme of our national history. Political events and social changes are conditioned on industrial evolution, and the story of America can be comprehended only in the light of her material aspirations and attainments."[1]

In America, perhaps to a greater degree than in any other country of which we have intimate knowledge, the basic characteristics of the race can be traced to natural causes. This necessity to be warmly clothed and warmly housed and well fed made men from the first devote much time and thought to purely material conditions, and at the same time it developed to an extraordinary degree the virtue of individual initiative. To suffer from

[1] Coman: *The Industrial History of the United States*, preface, p. vii.

the cold or to defy its rigor depended not upon the general effort of the community as it does at the present day when every activity of life is specialized, but upon the skill, the resource, the industry of the individual, who must match his cunning against the cunning of his quarry, learn its habits, display the same patience. And in this the huntsman differed in no wise from the farmer, the woodsman, the early trader. The sense of community was strong, each man felt himself a part of the body politic and social, and yet each knew that he must rely on his good right arm for success. In countries where life can be sustained on a handful of rice or a small quantity of fruit that requires little or no cultivation and clothing is a burden, Nature does not call upon her children to display their resource or their initiative, but in climates where these things are vital for the preservation and development of life the inexorable demand must either be met with the proper intelligence and skill or the race must perish. The law of survival, especially in those early days, has been strikingly demonstrated. Those unsuited for their new environment and conditions, who were too weak, or too lazy, or too ignorant to adapt themselves to their physical and other surroundings, died; the strong, the industrious, and the intelligent survived and transmitted to their descendants their own qualities of mind and body.

The English people have been vastly influenced by the physiography of their country, and it is peculiarly appropriate that the shoot from their race that spread across the sea and from which sprung a new race should have had its character moulded by the same influences. It was the custom of the early historians to attribute to certain influences, political, military, dynastic, the rise and fall of nations, and to find in them the causes that made or wrecked nations; and later historians, while not ignoring what may be termed primary historical causes, have included commerce as one of the elements that go to the making of national character. The methods of the historian and the political psychologist differ. The latter must examine more minutely remote causes, for he finds in them not only the motives of action, but discovers that those actions were the inexorable result of causes no more to be defied or prevented than the movements of the planets in their preordained orbits. No study of race development can be complete unless proper consideration is given to the geographic conditions under which the race was nurtured.

"The effect of the size of their country can be traced in the ideas of the American people, which are marked by a certain largeness and daring. The small territorial standards of the early European settlers have become profoundly modified by American continental conditions. The mere area of the individual states increases from the east towards the west. The commonwealths of New England seem pigmies in size compared with the trans-Mississippi states. There are twenty-six states in the smaller half of the country east of the Mississippi, and only twenty-three states and territories west of it."[1]

The larger area of the Western States show how "profoundly modified" the American temperament has become by American conditions. Beginning as an Englishman, accustomed to think in small areas, the geographical unit being the compact English county, it was natural for the pioneer to carry his conception of size with him and to begin his planting on a diminutive scale. The scattered and independent settlements and colonies, finally merged into states, were still to be held within restricted areas, because the imagination of man at that time was not vivid enough to grasp the truth, so foreign to all past experience and tradition, that danger did not necessarily reside in mere size, and that a political system was not dependent upon its geographic limits. It was only when the Englishman ceased to be an Englishman and became an American under the influence of American conditions that he cast off his insularity and became continental; it was then he quickly adapted himself to the wide range and vision that the size of the continent inspired, and size no longer had terrors for him. The men who went from New England to settle the West took on the largeness of the domain over which they ruled. To this day the less confined, broader view of the Westerner

[1] Semple: *American History and its Geographic Conditions*, p. 242.

is contrasted with the more rigid conception of life of the descendants of the Pilgrims and the Puritans. Between the men of the East and those of the West there is a difference, the difference that always distinguishes an older and a newer civilization; that is marked when the older civilization develops under the stimulus of man touching elbows with his fellow man and the majesty of Nature is less fearful; and the newer, when men are isolated and "range after range of mountains, and mile after mile of rugged plateau separate them from the seats of civilization and government."

To sum up and to bear in mind the physiographic conditions of the United States as affecting a people native to the soil or quickly brought in harmony with it by the force of circumstances, these are the principal things to be noticed: The climate is generally drier, the alternating seasons both cooler and hotter than those of northern Europe; because of the relatively unclouded sky there is more sunlight.[1] There is a greater quantity of ozone in the northern latitudes, and therefore it is more stimulating and produces a kinetic energy and vitality that finds its expression in constant activity and restlessness, both mental and physical.

This was quickly recognized by the first settlers. "Experience doth manifest," one of their chroniclers writes, "that there is hardly a more healthful place to be found in the world that agreeth better

[1] Shaler: *Nature and Man in America*, p. 264.

with our English bodies. Many that have been weak and sickly in Old England, by coming hither have been thoroughly healed, and grown healthful and strong. For here is an extraordinary clear and dry air, that is of most healing nature to all such as are of a cold, melancholy, phlegmatic, rheumatic temper of body." And he ends his glowing tribute to the life-giving properties of New England air with this happy epigram: "I think it is a wise course for all cold complexions to come to take physic in New England; for a sup of New England's air is better than a whole draught of Old England's ale."[1]

The "keen, alert mind" and the "incessant, unremitting energy" of the present-day American are ascribed by an American writer to climatic influences, and he finds in the so-called "cold wave," or sudden drop of temperature accompanying a downrush of cool air, something that clearly differentiates American from European weather. This is the theory of Gilbert H. Grosvenor,[2] and it is this cold wave, he believes, that stirs up the sluggish immigrant and fires his ambition. "We Americans," he says, "are always talking about our mountains of gold and coal and iron, of our fat fields of corn and wheat, but few of us ever realize that we have in our climate a great advantage over all other nations. In the cold wave, which

[1] Young's *Chronicles of Massachusetts*, pp. 251–252.

[2] *The Century Magazine*, June, 1905.

in summer and winter so often sweeps across the land and sends the thermometer tumbling thirty degrees in almost as many minutes, we have a constant, a never diminishing asset of priceless value. The wave acts as a tonic, but, unlike any tonic made by man, it carries no reaction. No other land has cold waves like ours. To the cold dry air of this periodic cold wave, which brings extraordinary changes of temperature, we owe much of the keen, alert mind, the incessant, unremitting energy of our American race. . . .

"The cold wave is born in the heavens miles above our heads, usually over the Rocky Mountains plateau. Suddenly a mass of bitterly cold air will tumble down upon Montana. It rushes down as though poured through an enormous funnel. As it falls it gains momentum, and, reaching the earth, spreads over the Mississippi Valley and then over the Atlantic States, covering them like a blanket. It scatters the foul, logy, breath-soaked atmosphere in our towns and cities, and puts ginger into the air. We fill our lungs with it and live. New waves are always coming, following each other in regular procession like the waves on a seashore."

On the Atlantic and Pacific coasts there are numerous good harbors; on the Southern coast from Hatteras around Florida to Mexico, there are fewer ports. "Despite the imperfection of the harbors from Hatteras southward, the coast of

North America is, on the whole, the most completely maritime of any continent except Europe. Its landlocked waters, including the Great Lakes, are of vast extent; the total number of excellent ports possibly exceeds that of the Old World."[1] Rainfall, except in the arid and subarid regions of the West and Southwest, is generally distributed, and the average precipitation is of sufficient volume to nourish the soil and produce abundant crops. The great climatal variations make it possible for all cereals and fruits found in the temperate zone to be grown, and in those regions where the temperature is subtropical the products of the soil show their exotic origin. Vast plains are the breeding-grounds of the animals that man needs for food and his convenience; forests and fields are the habitation of birds and game; the waters, both coastal and inland, teem with many varieties of edible fish; mineral wealth is inexhaustible. These things — the size of the continent, the climate, the rainfall, the abundance of food — are the elements that go to make a race what it is and produce their clearly defined psychological characteristics.

[1] Shaler, *op. cit.*, p. 217.

CHAPTER V

THE OLD IN THE NEW ENVIRONMENT

THERE came in the first place to America Englishmen from a small, compact country to whom the extremes of heat or cold were unknown, who had been accustomed to an almost stable climate, so that it justified the saying of Charles II that it "invited men abroad more days in the year and more hours in the day than another country." Its soil was fertile and yielded its reward to effort intelligently directed, and yet not so luxuriant that it did not demand persistent industry. Remote as the villages of Nottinghamshire and Lincolnshire and Yorkshire were from London in those days, they were still not isolated from the capital, and their people enjoyed that sense of security that comes from contact with the great world. England in the beginning of the seventeenth century was a land of cities and towns and villages, whose people tilled their farms and went about their ordained tasks in an orderly manner and whose civilization and conventions had come to them as a natural growth.

The Englishmen in America faced an unbroken wilderness, stern, harsh, forbidding. Of the immensity of the country they knew nothing, and not being gifted with the vivid imagination of the

Southerner they dreamed still less. What they confronted was Nature in her most savage mood.

"In similar circumstances Popham's settlers had despaired and fled; but the Plymouth Pilgrims were strong in religious faith, and in the sense of a divine mission." These Englishmen, as Fiske tells us, had heard of warm countries like Italy and cold countries like Russia; harsh experience soon taught them that there are climates in which the summer of Naples may alternate with the winter of Moscow. As if to forbid them entrance the water froze when the Pilgrims landed; consumption soon reaped its rich harvest. These intrepid adventurers learned then that truth which not until nearly three centuries later did science establish—that between Nature and man wages a never-ending war, and only man fit to survive lives. There at the very beginning the choice was forced upon them either to subdue Nature and make of her their slave or surrender to her. They conquered, but the far-reaching consequences of that struggle between man and Nature we are only now beginning to appreciate.

These Englishmen, these pioneers of their race, must subjugate Nature, who assumed a form hitherto unknown to them, and whose moods were so varied. It was from the beginning a savage, brutal, unrelenting fight; and it would result in making men morose, taciturn, harsh, weighed down by the immensity of the struggle, despairing, hopeless almost of overcoming their gigantic adversary; or it would make them self-reliant, determined to the verge of obstinacy, full of hope, supremely confident in their ultimate success. If the weight of Nature did not press upon them and crush them and deaden all power of imagination,— and imagination is only another name for hope, — then it would make them take everything in the spirit of a rude jest, a Gargantuan practical joke, that was not enjoyed, but pride forbade that they should wince. And that was their attitude. They jested with Nature, they gave back to her what she gave to them, and it made them rough, boisterous, fond of horseplay and the commonplace, and yet — could it be otherwise? — it produced a certain gravity and melancholy. This has left its ineradicable impress on national character. We have to-day the American love of fun, which must be obvious and broad without being coarse. Dainty humor, that lightness and delicacy of touch for which the French are famous, does not appeal to them; and of wit, as distinguished from humor, there is almost no national appreciation. The screaming farce rather than the gossamer comedy, whose words are as elusive almost as the intangible essence of the perfume of the forest, is their measure of enjoyment.

It has come to be believed that the Americans have a livelier sense of the ridiculous than any other people, but this is one of those cases of endowing a race with mythical qualities. Exaggeration, rough caricature, they understand, but they have no nice perception of proportion or perspective, and without that a fine discernment of the absurd is impossible; it is their extravagance of emotion that makes them so prone to the use of the superlative. At one time I believed that this national weakness for the superlative was simply *blague*, but I now know that it is constitutional. As deficient in the power to estimate true values as certain persons are wanting in the ability to differentiate colors or recognize harmony, their reflection of life is one of those convex mirrors so mirth-provoking to the yokel, who sees his features enormously distorted and grins back in delight at the exaggerated likeness. It is this constitutional tendency for exaggeration and the inability to measure men and things for what they really are that is responsible for the American belief, which is the cardinal doctrine of their faith, in the swanlike attribute of American geese, in the "bigness" of their country and the extraordinary ability of their men; in this respect similar to little children who, having mastered the elementary multiplication table, talk of millions and think, to their limited capacity, in billions. There is seldom a man elected to an office (immediately after his election), whether it be constable or President, who is not either in intellect or virtue without a peer, whose genius is not the admiration of all the world; without discriminating whether his place was the gift of a boss or the recognition of real merit. If the Americans had a keener appreciation of the ridiculous, their newspapers would be less amusing, but they would also be more informing. No newspaper, for instance, with a sense of proportion would attempt seriously to defend its cartoonist by bracketing in the same sentence the name of a quite unknown and crude amateur and Raphael, Michael Angelo, and Phidias![1] Yet the incongruity and absurdity of the juxtaposition does not make the paper the laughing-stock of the country. But it is a dangerous pastime for the inmates of glass houses to throw stones, and as hardly any newspaper excludes the superlative from its vocabulary there is reason why criticism is hushed.

In a democracy man is much given to the contemplation of himself, and there is tendency to exalt the individual and minimize the force of organized society. Where classes exist the person is of less consequence than the class he represents, the order whose champion he is, the traditions he defends. What gives weight to the utterance of the possessor of a historical name in a monarchy is not alone his talents or his virtues, but the feeling that through him speaks the historic past, that he voices not merely his own opinion but that of his class. Democracy undoubtedly is a spur to individual initiative, but man becomes so proud of what he has accomplished that he is apt to forget the obligation he owes the state.

[1] San Francisco *Examiner*, July, 1908.

It was an acute English observer who was over-impressed by the seeming gravity and melancholy of the Americans. He observed them at work, on the streets, in traveling, at play, and it was his conclusion that they were a sombre race. Compared with the volatile Latin untempered by the restraining influence of the Saxon strain, or the mercurial Celt, or even the phlegmatic Teuton, whose phlegm is partly the conventional habit of controlling emotions, the American appears markedly more quiet and as if weighed down by the burden of life, and yet distinguished by alertness that sets him apart. Had the original English stock spread across the continent undiluted by the blood of Europe, we should to-day have in the United States not a new race but simply a variation of the parent stem. It is this foreign element absorbed into the native stock (meaning by this not the indigenous race, the Indians, but the English, who in the second generation became native to the soil) that has been one of the causes to produce the new race, and that, in addition to the influence of environment and a political code that is not less a moral and social law, explains the many contradictions in the American character. The gravity, the melancholy, that feeling of national despair that finds its expression in the savage attacks of the press on the motives and integrity of public men, which is almost the agonized cry whether anything is worth while, is the spirit of the Puritan, which for three centuries has quickened the conscience of America and still lives. And the cynical indifference so often displayed, the levity with which things spiritual are treated, the sudden flaming emotion frequently akin to hysteria, the balance and sound judgment after the first gust of passion has spent itself, the feverish haste and the dogged persistence, the selfishness and the altruism, the suspicion and the almost childlike confidence, the self-consciousness and the poise, — these are the product of environment, of blood, and political and social institutions.

It is only the superficial observer who can dogmatically assert what the American temperament is. It is as true to say that the American is grave as it is to say that he is volatile; as true as it would be to say that America has mountains and plains; as misleading as it would be to say that its striking physical characteristics are mountains and to ignore the fact of its plains or rivers; as to say that the soil is influenced by the heat and to disregard the fructifying effect of cold. The American volubly strikes up a chance acquaintance with a man he may happen to meet in a railway carriage, while the Englishman retains his reserve and is oblivious of his fellow passengers, and the Englishman insists that the American is obtrusive and has no conception of dignity or reticence, forgetting that a social and political system that recognizes caste has a manner of expression entirely different from that in which labor may occupy the throne; that, as was said of the Florentines, the consciousness of having not simply the right to vote but the chance of being voted for must make every man feel within himself the power of sovereignty. A people cannot be deliberately guilty of national hypocrisy and not degenerate. The American must either believe in his articles of faith — the universal equality of man — or else go to destruction; for faith, a profound conviction, a belief in something, whether in the divine right of kings or the majesty of the will of the people, is necessary to hold society together. "Hypatia had taken away the living God and given him instead the four elements." It does not compensate, for the elements are unstable and society must anchor itself to a rock. The American no more than the Englishman is a conscious national hypocrite. Each recites his creed and believes it, but in this as in other things a definition of terms is necessary.

The struggle in which the founders of a new race engaged developed them physically and materially, but it dwarfed them spiritually. I do not use this word in the sense it is commonly employed. It connotes neither religion nor the spirit of religion, although the deep-seated devotion to religion, which was the essence of the Puritan character, was later bruised by the struggle. By spiritual I mean what Carlyle terms "our thinking." "In our inward, as in our outward world, what is mechanical lies open to us; not what is dynamical and has vitality. Of our Thinking, we might say, it is the mere upper surface that we shape into articulate thoughts; — underneath the region of argument and conscious discourse, lies the region of meditation; here, in its quiet mysterious depth, dwells what vital force is in us; here, if ought is to be created and not merely manufactured and communicated, must the work go on. Manufacture is intelligible, but trivial; Creation is great, and cannot be understood."[1]

This vital force lying in its quiet mysterious depths, latent but to be quickened into life by the spark of genius, remained inarticulate. "Why did poetry appear so brightly after the battle of Thermopylæ and Salamis, and quite turn away her face and wings from those of Lexington and Bunker's Hill?" Carlyle asks, and inadequately answers, "The Greeks were a poetical people, the Americans are not; that is to say, it appeared because it did appear!"[2] It would have been more scientific and more in consonance with the truth of race development had Carlyle explained that the Greek, living under soft skies and in the midst of color, which was a background to his domestic life, in whom the sense of the æsthetic had been highly cultivated, was stimulated to write poetry; he felt the imperious demand of his nature, and knew that he could command his audience; while the American, pioneering into the unbroken wilderness, wresting from the

[1] Carlyle: *Critical and Miscellaneous Essays*, vol. xiv, p. 347.
[2] Carlyle: *op. cit.*, p. 255.

soil his precarious existence, awed by the immensity and savagery of creation, felt his own insignificance. And all wares, even intellectual wares, are produced in the hope of finding a market. After Thermopylæ and Salamis there was an audience and a market for poetry and there was a profit or money in producing it; but those embattled farmers who were called from the plow to the battlefield, and from the battlefield returned to the plow, whose shot fired at Lexington was heard round the world, had no time to write or think poetry. There were sterner things to do, and they were done. Had these people, as Campbell says of the Dutch, also produced a Homer, a Dante, or a Shakespeare, they would have been a miracle and not a growth; and the American people, we cannot too often repeat, are not a miracle but a natural growth.

It is a well-established fact that the more primitive a people the higher the birth rate, and New England demonstrated the truth of this law. Men and women married early and bred fast. Of Mrs. Sarah Thayer, who died in 1751, a local bard recorded:—

> "Also she was a fruitful vine,
> The truth I may relate, —
> Fourteen was of her body born
> And lived to man's estate.
>
> "From these did spring a numerous race
> One hundred thirty-two;
> Sixty and six each sex alike,
> As I declare to you.

"And one thing more remarkable,
Which here I shall record:
She 'd fourteen children with her
At the table of our Lord." [1]

But before Mrs. Thayer's time, in the previous century, although the birth rate was very high, the mortality, especially among children, was equally great, and the population was at once abundantly replenished and ruthlessly weeded. "Like a tribe of savage men or wild beasts, it was exposed to a pitiless process of selection. Such a process must conduce to the physical vigor of a race; it would develop those qualities which accompany physical vigor and depend on it. But there are other qualities to which it would prove fatal. That the spirit of a Shelley could ever have shaped itself in the life of New England was impossible. But the impossibility dated from a stage earlier than that of training and culture. The birth of a possible Shelley in a Puritan household would have been a striking instance of what physiologists call atavism. But even if the portent had occurred, we may be pretty sure that 'died in infancy' would have been the only record of it in the family register. Physical selection was part of the process which was forcing the character of the American Puritan into a narrow and rigid mould." [2]

Wordsworth could sing of Nature and thrill to the carol of feathered songsters where all around him was orderly cultivation and birds nested in

[1] Adams: *Three Episodes of Massachusetts History*, vol. ii, p. 610.
[2] Doyle: *English Colonies in America*, vol. iii, p. 7.

the eaves of barns, and church steeples softened into the beauties of graceful age by time. The pioneer — and the whole people were pioneers — saw in the sunrise only the call to another day's toil; there was to him no music in the joyous note of the birds; it was simply a warning to protect his crops from their ravages and to mark the changing seasons. He looked on neither eaves nor steeples.

"I have been thinking all day," said gently the Puritan maiden,
"Dreaming all night, and thinking all day, of the hedge-rows of England, —
They are in blossom now, and the country is all like a garden;
Thinking of lanes and fields, and the song of the lark and the linnet,
Seeing the village street, and familiar faces of neighbors. . . .
You will say it is wrong, but I cannot help it; I almost
Wish myself back in Old England, I feel so lonely and wretched." [1]

From Nature savage and spiteful as he knew it the pioneer turned to Nature idealized as the literature of his youth pictured it and found there his solace, regretting what he had lost, perhaps, but animated by that spirit of hope and determination that had sent him forth fearlessly to find liberty; resolute, courageous, unafraid, but with no desire to sing the praises of the Great Mother, stern, forbidding, revengeful.

[1] Longfellow: *The Courtship of Miles Standish.*

CHAPTER VI

NEW ENGLAND THE CRADLE OF RACE

The history of the United States has been a defiance of precedent and the blazing of a new path in the trackless wilds of social progress. The impulse that led to the English colonization of America was different from that which had controlled other nations in their attempts to found colonies. "The dawn of the seventeenth century rose on a somewhat changed England. Englishmen filled with the new wine of the Renaissance and united under a queen whose rule, despite all its craft and meanness, appealed intensely to their imagination, had dreamt dreams and seen visions. A generation succeeded, not less enterprising, but more patient, more self-denying, more sane. The conception of colonies as centres from which Christianity might be spread through savage lands did not altogether disappear, nor did English emigrants at once give up the idea of rivaling Spain in the race for gold. But these ideas fell into the background. Colonization designed to provide home for surplus population, to expand alike the imports and exports of England, and thereby to develop her naval resources, now became the dominant motive."[1]

[1] *Cambridge Modern History*, vol. vii, p. 4

Remembering this, bearing clearly in mind the dominating motive that led to the English migration to America in the seventeenth century, we shall be able to understand why it was inevitable that these pioneers of a new race should absorb the characteristics of their soil and the land which it was their mission to subjugate. Whether they were divinely inspired, as some writers would have us believe, whether it was merely one of those accidents with which the pages of history are crowded that brought the storm-tossed Mayflower to her haven in Cape Cod Bay instead of finding refuge in the Delaware as had been planned, is of all things the least material. What is vital to grasp is that this little band came to America as "adventurers," as the word was then used, which corresponds to the sense in which we use the word "exploiters" now; not as "promoters," not as mere transients, but as settlers. England, France, Spain had hitherto sent their sons to cross the sea with a twofold purpose in view: God was to be glorified and the might of the nation magnified by the cross of Christ upraised before savages, who incidentally were to be spoiled of their gold. Nothing is more delightful than the delicious *naïveté* of the early chroniclers, who in their unconscious simplicity give themselves away at every opportunity and are as obvious as children.

"Then we demand farther what was the cause of his being in this place [Dominica], and how he came thither; he answered, That the King of

Spain did every yeere, send out of every great monastery certaine Friars into the remote parts of the Indies, both to seeke to convert the Savages, as also to seeke out what benefits or commodities might be had in those parts."[1]

But neither England, nor France, nor Spain understood the philosophy of colonization as colonization, beginning with the settlement of America, has expanded to the present day. Colonies separated from the mother country by oceans, where the power of government quickly went into the hands of the people instead of being autocratically retained by civil or military governors, where from the beginning the spirit of self-government, and self-reliance, and independence was the spirit of institutions, — this conception of colonization, I repeat, was unknown to political philosophy until the settlement of the New World by Englishmen.

In tracing the different methods by which nations have been made, Fiske contrasts the Roman and the English. The former, he says, may be briefly described "as conquest with incorporation, but without representation," the latter differing "in a feature of most profound significance; it contains the principle of representation."[2] Mr. Fiske with his lucid insight has explained one of the reasons why England succeeded where Rome failed, but I am inclined to believe that even more important than the

[1] *Challon's Voyage*, 1606.

[2] Fiske: *The Beginnings of New England*, p. 12 *et seq.*

principle of representation — great as that principle is, and I would by no means be understood as holding it lightly or detracting from its true value in colonization — is the spirit of the Englishman, whether inborn or acquired no one can say, that leads him as a colonizer to look upon his migration not merely as a temporary sojourn, but as the beginning of a new life and the founding of a home in a new land that henceforth is to be his land. One reason offered for the failure of the French as colonizers in our day is the intense sentimental longing of the Frenchman for his own country, which is so much a part of himself that he cannot be content anywhere else.[1] The English may be less sentimental than the French — there is no scientific instrument yet devised for the measurement of emotions — or more easily adaptable to new environment; whatever the reason, the colonizer in the early days went forth with the firm purpose to bide in the land of his promise, as his descendant of to-day, the emigrant, turns his back on the land of his birth to find a new home across the seas. To employ a modern simile, colonizers before that historic departure from Plymouth in 1620 were always careful to provide themselves with return tickets, while beginning with that day men concerned themselves only with the means of reaching their destination and gave no thought of how they were to come back.

[1] "A Briton, while he has an abstract reverence for the island of his origin, has rarely the clinging attachment to its soil which a Frenchman has to the land of France." — Bodley: *France*, vol. i, p. 233.

We are impressed by another extraordinary circumstance in connection with this establishment of the first colony founded under the new philosophy. Hitherto England and France and Spain had sent out expeditions whose members were either soldiers or priests, frankly for conquest; and the sword and the cross were so frequently found on the same hilt that it was not always easy to determine whether its owner was habited in coat of mail or cassock. The passengers of the Mayflower were drawn from a different class of society. They were neither soldiers, buccaneers, freebooters, licensed pirates, nor priests. On the roll we find the name of only one man who had made arms his profession, that doughty old captain, Miles Standish, whose military knowledge served the colonists in good stead when they fought for their existence against the Indians; but who is better known to fame as the romantic hero of a mythical incident that Longfellow created and the world generally has accepted as history. Of priests there were none. To minister to their spiritual welfare they had only one "lay reader."

They were neither soldiers nor priests, these founders of a race; what, then, were they? They can best be described, in terms that are easily intelligible to-day, as members of the middle and lower middle classes; men from the shop and the farm; men not without education and culture, but who were not readily to be distinguished from the great mass of their fellows, some of whom might perhaps gain fame in the narrow field of established routine, but who had not yet arrived. They were "used to a plain country life and the innocent trade of husbandry," one of their admirers has written.[1] But what was common to all of them, which was the dower of inheritance and the unconscious influence of their environment, was a sense of order and system, of thrift and prudent management, of that bent of mind, in fact, that is commercial rather than artistic. These men had in them the qualities that everywhere, at all times, under all circumstances, make good men of business, and this faculty was given almost instant expression. The systematic methods that were adopted in the establishment of the settlements and their governments, that began with the drawing up of the compact in the cabin of the Mayflower, which in its phraseology and purposes suggests the scrivener rather than the soldier, that later expanded into a more complex social and political code as the needs of the colonists made necessary, indicated that form of executive ability which is the special attribute of a commercial people. We find little evidence of military ability or the influence of militarism in the first century of the American colonies. There was a savage foe to fight, and from the beginning measures had to be concerted for defense and offense, but they were incidental; they were necessary for the preservation

[1] Byington: *The Puritan in England and in New England*, p. 53.

and protection of society; they were part of the day's work, but they were not undertaken for the pure love of fighting.

Even less do we find any evidence of an artistic spirit or a love of art pervading the people. Either they were people to whom art in their former surroundings had made no appeal or in whom the artistic feeling was checked and stifled by the intense concentration of all their faculties on the problem how to solve the struggle for existence. It is difficult, impossible in fact, to determine to which cause we must look for the true explanation, and while, of course, we must not forget the underlying influences of the Puritan character and the foundation on which the Puritan state was laid, it seems almost incredible that a body of English men and English women of that day, of intelligence and not without education, could be almost primitive in having no appreciation of art or content not to attempt to give it expression. The true explanation, I believe, is the one that has already been advanced: the material struggle was too insistent to afford opportunity for anything else. If this reasoning is sound, it is psychologically of great importance, for it proves that the æsthetic civilization of England, at that day highly developed, was not transplanted and did not put forth new roots in the new soil, but for a time withered and only came to life again at a later period. And perhaps more important than all, we see why the American comes naturally by his love of and aptitude for business. He is simply fulfilling the law of heredity. It is not alone the sins of the father that are visited upon the children of unborn generations, but also the bent of the father's mind which is transmitted. The fathers of the race were men of business, men who were fond of trade and to whom commerce was a passion, and their children have followed in their footsteps. We shall have occasion later to examine into this question more in detail.

It is proper here to call the attention of the reader to what thus far may have appeared an anachronism. In logically studying the development of the American character, I have begun with the Pilgrim migration, ignoring, for the present, the earlier settlement of Virginia. Were this a history of the American people instead of a study of race growth, it would be proper to begin at the beginning with the first settlement of the English in America, at Jamestown, and, using that as the foundation on which was reared the superstructure of an enduring civilization, employ the chronological method to show how stone was laid on stone until the completed edifice crowned the labors of the master builders. But the coming of the English to Virginia in the first decade of the seventeenth century was a thing trivial compared with the momentous consequences that followed from the landing of that little band of pioneers on the bleak shores of Massachusetts fourteen years later.

Had the English occupation of America proceeded along the lines that were first established, there would have been indeed a Nova Albion to redound to the glory of English conquest and fulfill the dreams of Raleigh and Gilbert and those other adventurers of undaunted courage and splendid audacity and superb imagination who laid the foundation for England's greatness, commercial prosperity, and peculiar genius for the development and government of alien lands and peoples, but the psychological results would have been different. The English went to Jamestown as up to that time they had gone elsewhere, with two distinct objects in view. They went to find wealth, the fabulous gold that they believed was to be obtained without effort, and to provide an outlet for a population that even then pressed upon the limits of subsistence.

"Their principal reason for colonizing these parts is to give an outlet to so many idle and wretched people as they have in England, and thus to prevent the dangers that may be feared from them," Don Alonso de Velasco, the Spanish Ambassador, wrote from London in March, 1611, to His Catholic Majesty. Spanish testimony of that day cannot be accepted without due allowance being made for prejudice and jealousy, but no such motives governed the English in their own frank admissions. In "A Letter from the Council and Company of the honourable Plantation of

Virginia to the Lord Mayor, Alderman and Companies of London" (probably written in 1608), we find the first suggestion of that vicious scheme of "assisted immigration" that so seriously embarrassed the United States two centuries and a half later.

"Whereas the Lords of his Majesties Council," the Virginia Company writes, "Commissioners for the Subsidy, desirous to ease the city and suburbs of a swarme of unnecessary inmates, as a contynual cause of death and famine, and the very original cause of all the Plagues that happen in this Kingdom, have advised your Lordship and your Brethren in a case of state, to make some voluntary contribucon for their remove into this plantation of Virginia, which we understand you all seemeth to like as an action pleasing to God and happy for this Common Wealth."[1]

The English in the beginning of their colonization had to serve both God and Mammon and appeal to the spirit of the age by a judicious mixture of theology and greed.

"And thus, as an action concerning God, and the advancement of religion, the present ease, future honor and safety of the Kingdome, the strength of our Navy, the visible hope of a great and rich trade, and many secrett blessings not yett discovered; wee wholly comend the cause to the wisdome and zeal of your self and your Brethren,

[1] Brown: *The Genesis of the United States*, vol. i, p. 252.

and you and it, and us all to the holy proteccon of the almightie."[1]

"The eyes of all Europe are looking upon our endeavors to spread the Gospell among the Heathen people of Virginia, to plant our English nation there, and to settle in those parts which may be peculiar to our nation, so that we may thereby be secured from being beaten out of all profitts of trade, by our more industrious neighbors."[2]

This, then, was the controlling motive of the men who established the first English colony in Virginia — the greed for gain and a convenient way of disposing of "a swarme of unnecessary inmates." But far different were the motives that animated the Pilgrims. They embarked on the unknown not in quest of gold, not for the glory of God, not even "for the future honor and safety of the Kingdome," but simply that they might be permitted to live their own lives in their own way unhampered by fanatical or tyrannical rulers.[3]

[1] "A Letter from the Council and Company of the honourable Plantation in Virginia to the Lord Mayor, Alderman and Companies of London," probably written in 1608 or 1609.

[2] Brown: *The Genesis of the United States*, vol. i, p. 463.

[3] In accordance with the spirit of the age the propitiation of God must be sought to bring success to a commercial venture, and the governor and council of the Massachusetts Company, writing to Endicott, tell him "that the propagation of the Gospel is the thing we do profess above all to be our aim in settling this Plantation"; and the pious hope is expressed that "the Indians may, in God's appointed time, be reduced to the obedience of the Gospel of Christ." The charter avers that "to win and invite the natives of the country to the knowledge and obedience of the only true God and Saviour of Man-

It was the difference in character between the adventurer, the rover, the soldier of fortune, the man with the insatiable *Wanderlust*, who, with childish credulity, despite his experience of the world, always believes in the pot of gold at the end of the rainbow, and the austere man of narrow conscience, who is compensated for his lack of imagination by the gift of steadfastness that produces results because he cannot be swerved from his purpose. It is often said that men are ruled by their imagination; but it would be truer to say that they are governed by the weakness of their imaginations.[1] But, curiously enough, the foundation of the American character—the love of gain and the acquisition of wealth in commerce — was laid by the men whose outlook on life was narrow and dwarfed by the barriers of over-refined intellectual development rather than the wider imagination of the adventurer whose one thought was the pursuit of fortune. Later I shall subject these qualities to more

kind and the Christian faith, is our royal intention, and the principal end of this plantation."

Always this extreme solicitude for the spiritual welfare of the Indian. It is touching. "If we were once the masters of their Countrey and they stood in fears of us (which might with few hands imployed about nothing else, be in short time to passe) it were an easie matter to make them willingly to forsake the divell, to embrace the faith of Jesus Christ, and to be baptized. Besides, you cannot easilie judge how much they would be availeable to us in our discoveries of the Countrey, in our buildings and plantings, and quiet provisions for ourselves, when we may peaceably passe from place to place without neede of arms or guarde." — Whitaker, *Good Newes from Virginia*, 1613. *Cf.* Brown: *Genesis of the United States*, vol. ii, p. 585.

[1] Bagehot: *The English Constitution*, p. 101.

minute analysis and explain the reasons for this seeming contradiction; for the present it is necessary only to state the fact and to ask the reader to bear in mind that, from the very first, civilization in America was composed of two elements almost antagonistic, which like two chemical elements can only be fused in combination with a third. That agent was found in the flux of common resistance to oppression, and the States, which Rufus Choate compared "to primordial particles of matter, whose natural condition is to repel each other, or, at least, to exist in their own independent identity," became homogeneous.

These considerations, I hope, will make it sufficiently clear why the writer has found it necessary to begin this investigation in New England rather than in Virginia.

CHAPTER VII

THE PURITAN

It is impossible to have a proper comprehension of the character of the American people, or intelligently to examine into the causes that have produced this race and made them what they are in mind and spirit, unless at the outset we have a clear conception of the men from whom the race sprang. The psychological student of America must study the Puritan and subject him to as minute analysis as the student of anthropology gives to his study of the caves of a prehistoric age, or the physiologist to learn the vital relation of the heart to the body. The Puritan is the heart of American civilization.

In attempting to bring back to life the figures of the dead, in revisualizing lineaments that are shadowed by the haze of time, in putting a historical character upon the modern scene, there is always the danger of interpreting motives and the play of forces by the light of the present instead of the obscurity in which men then moved.

Excellent indeed is the perspective of history; it has made many things clear that at the time they happened were vague; but the farther we are removed from a great event the more it is softened and often distorted by distance; just as the majestic fane viewed by the traveler from afar impresses him with its bulk; but to appreciate the soul of the artist who created it, to be touched by that spirit of religious devotion, it must be seen close at hand.

Correctly to understand the seventeenth century, it must be read not through the eyes of the twentieth century, but the focus must be readjusted; the mind must throw off all the progress and humanizing influences that are the gifts of each century to the next and reincarnate itself. Unless that is done, unless we approach the subject with that intrinsic detachment, we bring on the stage not men but puppets, lay figures properly proportioned, perhaps, but clothed in anachronism.

In the first place we are to remember that in the seventeenth century life and religion were one. They were so inseparably interwoven that they could not be dissociated. Religion was a part of the conduct of life, of all life, of all society; the respect and obedience that were given to constituted authority were founded on the acceptance of religious belief and practice. In the twentieth century life and religion are apart; powerful though the influence of religion is to-day, it does not control life or society. Unless we clearly bear this in mind it will be impossible justly to estimate the Puritan character or to find an adequate explanation for the many seemingly inexplicable things done by the Puritan.

The Puritan, idealized, sublimated, painted in monochromes against a colorless background, emblem of passionless existence and dead to human emotions, his character distorted by injudicious and over-zealous admirers and defenders, his motives misunderstood, — it is this figure that obscures the founders of the race; and we have been made to think of the Puritan as slow of speech, perpetually sunk in the gloom of his own conscience, too solemn to see that life is ever a farce even when tragedy, lingering on earth but longing for heaven. Now as a matter of fact these progenitors of a lion's breed, these pioneers who fought for the right as they fought against Nature, to whom life was something more than the antechamber to hope, were a practical people not without a sense of rational pleasure.

It is not necessary to trace the causes that produced Puritanism in England; they are known to every schoolboy who has studied in even an elementary form the history of England or the United States, but it is necessary for an intelligent comprehension of one of the greatest social movements in the world's history to clear away some of the misapprehensions, the false impressions, the romance that in the course of three centuries have grown up around the majestic figure of the Puritan, which, like the weeds about a temple, dwarf its beauty and distort its proportions.

To begin with, we must destroy the very common idea that the Pilgrims and the Puritans were intellectually and spiritually blood of the same blood and flesh of the same flesh. They were no such thing. In everything that makes for character — in the concept of life, in the relation of man to man, in the code that governed the family and the family magnified, the state — "the Puritan differs from the Pilgrim as the Hebrew prophet from Saint John," the late Senator Hoar of Massachusetts, himself a descendant in direct descent from three centuries of Puritan ancestors, said on one occasion.[1] And he elaborated his theme in this striking passage: —

"The Puritan differs from the Pilgrim as the Hebrew prophet from Saint John. Abraham, ready to sacrifice Isaac at the command of God; Jeremiah, uttering his terrible prophecy of the downfall of Judea; Brutus, condemning his son to death; Brutus, slaying his friend for the liberty of Rome; Aristides, going into exile, are his spiritual progenitors, as Stonewall Jackson was of his spiritual kindred. You will find him wherever men are sacrificing life or the delights of life on the altar of Duty.

"But the Pilgrim is of a gentler and a lovelier nature. He, too, if Duty or Honor call, is ready for the sacrifice. But his weapon is love and not hate. His spirit is the spirit of John, the beloved Disciple, the spirit of Grace, Mercy, and Peace. His memory is as sweet and fragrant as the perfume of the little

[1] Speech at the banquet of the New England Society, Charleston, S. C., December 22, 1898.

flower which gave its name to the ship which brought him over."

There are few more romantic episodes on the great canvas of history than the sailing of the Pilgrims and their arrival in the land of promise and hope. There are few that so vividly thrill the imagination and appeal to all that is best in man as the recollection of that day when the Pilgrims set foot on the rock that Americans hold sacred. There are few that have so admirably served as the inspiration for painter and poet and story-teller. It is background perfect in its composition and detail to make that gentle figure of the Pilgrim stand forth in all its majesty. Painter and poet and story-teller have labored with rare devotion to exalt his virtues and with loving hands have hidden his vices. He stands in imagination the progenitor of a race and the founder of a new social system. And all the labor has been in vain.

The Pilgrim made only the very slightest impress upon the American character. He founded no social institution. He gave birth to no political system. So far as the America of to-day is concerned, it is as if he had never existed. It is to the Puritan and not to the Pilgrim that America owes what she is.

The Pilgrim stands in the same relation to present-day America as the Saxon Heptarchy does to present-day England. What the Norman Conquest wrought we all know; and it was the Puritan who played the part of the Norman in American race development. The Pilgrim simply became merged into the Puritan as all cities were absorbed into the Roman state; and in a very short time the Pilgrim no longer existed. But the Puritan lived; he lives to-day. The difference between the Pilgrim and the Puritan is not of the greatest importance historically, but psychologically it is of the utmost importance that the distinction should be made.

The Pilgrims were not virile enough to found a race; the Puritans were. When the Plymouth Colony was fifteen years old it numbered only five hundred people. Twelve years after the Puritans had first settled in Massachusetts they counted twenty thousand souls. They had founded Harvard College; with that insatiable land hunger that was in the blood they had planted colonies in Connecticut and Rhode Island and New Hampshire; they had built churches and provided for their ministers; they were even in that early day living in comparative comfort. It staggers the imagination when one recalls all that had been accomplished in so short a time. The mother colony, its people influenced by the easy-going characteristics of the Dutch, which they had, perhaps, unconsciously assimilated, slowly, very slowly, gained in strength, but gave no promise of developing into a nation. The younger colony, almost at a single bound, displayed its potential power and showed that its people had in them the spirit of the nation builders. One would like to let poetic fancy dwell on the

Pilgrims, for there is no period in history more alluring than this, and no people more entrancing to the lover of the poetic and the imaginative than these simple but courageous folk who loved God and their fellow men; who with such perfect trust committed themselves to the benign protection of their Ruler and Guardian; who under adversity were patient, and who in all things had faith. Sublime qualities these, a much-needed inspiration in a day of gross materialism and little faith, but, alas, not the qualities that make a living race. I must not be understood as implying that the Pilgrim served no useful purpose. He did. He was an instrument in the hands of fate, and fate has never misused an instrument. He had a mission to perform, and he performed it successfully within the limits of his capacity. He moved across the rough stage, but the great drama of life in the New World, with all its pathos and struggle and triumph, was played by men cast in a sterner mould and with a grimmer appreciation of tragedy. That the Pilgrim never had.

Mr. Hoar has poetically compared the memory of the Pilgrim to the sweetness and fragrance of the perfume of the little flower which gave its name to the ship which brought him over. True, indeed, is the characterization, which unintentionally reveals the limitations of the Pilgrim and explains why he made no mark on the continent that lay at his feet. Before men can appreciate the delicate beauty of the coloring of the hidden flower and its exquisite odor, they must go into the forest and fell great oaks to shelter them. Men, men made resolute, obstinate, courageous by the fierce spirit of persecution and the determination to meet oppression with resistance, were required to bring forth a new life, not the men "of a gentler and lovelier nature" whose "weapon is love and not hate." Hatred, the thirst for revenge, is a very detrimental quality in the individual and, as a rule, does more injury to him who nourishes it than to its victim, but in a race or a people it has often had beneficial results. It has hardened the mould of character, it has made even the timid bold, it has made the weak face peril and death. The great sweep of history is the record of men who have had a grievance and dared to redress it, not the chronicle of men whose weapon was love. In the ultimate the tyrants have done more for mankind, by involuntarily giving impetus to the qualities of self-reliance and a love of liberty, than the beneficent rulers whom their subjects called the just and the merciful.

The Pilgrims, the men who left England and found a temporary asylum in Holland before their great hegira to the New World, were Church of England men, who separated from the faith of their fathers because they objected to the union of Church and State; and the corruption into which the Church had then fallen was to them abominable.

Hence they were called Separatists or Brownists, from the name of their founder, Robert Browne, a man of gentle birth, a Cambridge graduate, and a relative of Lord Burleigh, one of Queen Elizabeth's great ministers of state. This is so well known that it seems almost unnecessary again to restate it; but so many persons have such vague ideas about the origin of the Pilgrim movement that the salient facts must be emphasized for the better understanding of subsequent events.

The history of the Church, of all churches, until humanity and religion became one (and they were far apart in the early days of religion), has always been the fierce persecution of those who questioned its authority or would attempt to make its practices more nearly conform to its spiritual teachings. Itinerant preachers in the Church of England who urged upon the simple country folk to live better and purer lives fell under the persecution of the Established Church, and to escape their enemies fled to Holland, where men might without interference worship their God in their own way. Those who remained suffered for the sake of conscience. "For some were taken and clapt up in prison, others had their houses besett and watcht night and day, and hardly escaped their hands; and yet most were faine to flie and leave their houses and habitations, and the means of their livelihood. Yet these and many other sharper things which afterward befell them, were no other than they looked for, and therefore were ye better prepared to bear them by ye assistance of God's grace and spirit."[1]

Nothing more concisely typifies the character of the Pilgrim, his whole conception of life, his softness, his almost passionate prayer to be let alone, than his circumlocutory flight to America; and nothing more vividly contrasts the character of the Pilgrim and the Puritan than the reasons which made the latter leave the land of his birth.

When the Pilgrim found that he was an object of persecution because his worship of God was not that of the great majority of the nation, he went to Holland — and this is to be noted — not as a rebel against his sovereign or to be a thorn in the side of the kingdom that had thrust him out; he went not to found a new state or to lead in a reformation. Peace and quietness he craved, and he believed he would find them among those tolerant Dutch folk to whom sects and formularies meant less than they did to any other people of Europe at that time. He prayed and he worked, for he was always industrious and work seemed the natural condition of man, but he was a stranger apart from the people among whom he tarried. And it was this feeling of isolation and of being a stranger in a strange land that led to the greater flight.

That insularity of the English that has made the race what it is was in the blood of the Pilgrims.

[1] Bradford's *History of Plymouth Plantation*, p. 14.

The little children they had brought with them were growing up and other children were born unto them, and they wanted these children to be English-speaking and English-thinking and not half-English and half-Dutch. The motives that inspired their flight, as one of their historians tells us, were that they might enjoy liberty of conscience, and keep their own language and the name of Englishmen, and train their children as they were trained, and enlarge the Church of Christ.[1] Beyond the seas was a country in which Englishmen were settling, a country that promised rich rewards to the industrious and God-fearing, in which God might be worshiped without the fear of persecution of king or clergy. There was to be found that freedom and liberty, that perfect right to live according to the dictates of their conscience, that was denied them in the Old World. And they went.

Now see how differently the Puritan faced the problem that so vexed the soul of the gentler Pilgrim. The Puritan was no separatist. He was a Church of England man, but he was at one with the Pilgrim in demanding reformation. Christ's vicar on earth was no longer Christlike. The Church was rotten with corruption; its ministers, instead of setting the example of holy living and holy dying, were a stench in the nostrils of men who lived decently and died in the profound consolation of a just but merciful Creator; the ceremonies of the Church, the

[1] Young's *Chronicles*, p. 381.

vestments of its priests, its prayers and forms, savored of the mockery of Rome and were abhorrent to men who had drawn a new inspiration from the stern morality of Calvin. "Some men of the greatest parts and most extensive knowledge that the nation at this time produced, could not enjoy any peace of mind, because obliged to hear prayers offered up to the Divinity by a priest covered with a white linen vestment."[1] Yet the Church was their Church, not to be destroyed but to be brought back to its old ways, to be reformed, but to be reformed from within and not from without. The Puritans in England stood up manfully to the fray. They had no thought of going to Holland or elsewhere to establish a Church more in consonance with their idea. The Church they had to reform was in England, and it was there the battle was to be fought. And fight they did with all the zeal and courageous determination that men display only when they are fighting for a principle; how well they fought is told in the story of Cromwell and his psalm-singing Ironsides at Marston Moor and Naseby; and their vengeance went unsatisfied until the king they fought laid his head on the block and the great principle of free speech and a free parliament was forever established. These were the men who went forth to found the Massachusetts colony. They brought their religion with them, they brought the same spirit of resistance to the evil practices that

[1] Hume: *History of England*, p. 526.

the Church sanctioned, and the same determination to purify the Church. The Church was still to them their spiritual mother whose blessing they invoked. "We separate not from the Church of England, but from its corruptions," they said.

A nation to endure must be animated by higher and nobler reasons for its existence than the mere material desires that have led to the propagation of the animal species. Ease, mere wealth, the support of life under the most favorable conditions are all insufficient, and in the end they destroy. A race to live, a nation to grow and become truly great, must have implanted in its breast aspirations and ideals; it is of no consequence what form those aspirations and ideals take, but they must be a beacon light toward which the eyes of men forever turn. One reason why savage races have become extinct is that they were content with their material surroundings and were not quickened by the prompting of the higher things. They were deaf to the spiritual voice. The great nations who have moulded civilization have felt the ennobling influence of the infinite mystery; they have yearned for that something that would lift them above their sordid surroundings. It is immaterial whether the ideal for which they strove was personal liberty or liberty of conscience; religion, which often assumed a form material rather than ideal; the betterment of mankind. Whatever form it assumed, it was for the moment an idealistic conception, an effort to lift the race to a higher plane, mistaken as were the methods so often employed. But the men who fought for what they believed to be right were men who were not afraid to shed their blood in defense of the right. They fought because the path to the ideal had to be hewed out with the sword, and in its making many men must be overcome by the heat and burden of the fray. They did not run away.

The Puritans were men with ideals and aspirations. Their ideal was a state in which the word of God was the law of man, — "a practical world based on Belief in God," Carlyle says. Their aspiration was to found a state with the Bible as their constitution.

CHAPTER VIII

PURITANISM GIVES BIRTH TO DEMOCRACY

At the time when the great Puritan migration took place from England to Massachusetts, between the years 1620 and 1630, England was at heart Puritan and the Puritans were in the majority. Puritanism had its adherents and supporters in all ranks of life. Great nobles, leading members of the House of Commons, city merchants who with splendid audacity were financing ventures and expeditions to all parts of the world and laying the foundation for England's incomparable commerce; landed squires, the men who have always been the backbone of English solidity and conservatism; country preachers, the common people, the dwellers in villages as well as those in London and the other large cities, were in favor of the reformation of the Church and a wider political liberty.

It is important that the position and strength of the Puritan party in England should be clearly understood; but it is perhaps even more important to dwell with emphasis upon the truth that the Puritan movement, born in the throes of religious conviction, matured into a political party. It was a protest against the existing order.

The pictures and stories of the Pilgrims setting sail in their frail bark, their landing amidst surroundings so strange and forbidding, their trials and sufferings, their scanty supplies, convey to the modern mind that the Puritans — and this confusion of idea between the Pilgrim and the Puritan seems almost impossible of rectification — were the prototypes of that stream of emigration that for three quarters of a century has flowed through the gates of America in ever-increasing volume, and that, like the modern emigrant, the Puritan came to his new home with a pack on his back, unkempt, friendless, and poor. These hardy pioneers — Pilgrims as well as Puritans — had to bear the brunt of discomfort as the vanguard of every army of civilization always must; but it was not an army of tatterdemalions without stores or provisions. The Puritans were much better provided than the Pilgrims, but even they had some things that make for comfort rather than solely for necessity. Mourt in his *Relation* tells of "a green rug and three or four cushions" that were used by the Pilgrims in the ceremonies attending the state reception given to Massasoit, which "were, of course, necessarily brought in the *May-Flower*," Ames says.[1] In case the reader may have overlooked it, I call his attention to the fact that the rug was green, which is evidence that the mythical belief in the Pilgrim and the Puritan hatred of bright colors has no existence.

[1] Ames: *The May-Flower and her Log*, p. 221.

From the beginning the Puritans were well provided. They were backed by strong interests in England, who had the money to charter ships and furnish them with all that was needed to support a colony until it could stand alone. In the twelve years of Archbishop Laud's administration, Neal tells us, about four thousand planters left England, "who laid the foundation of several little towns and villages up and down the country, carrying over with them in materials, money and cattle, etc., not less than to the value of one hundred and ninety thousand pounds, besides the merchandise intended for traffick with the Indians. Upon the whole, it has been computed, that the four settlements of New England, viz. Plimouth, the Massachusetts Bay, Connecticut and Newhaven, all of which were accomplished before the beginning of the civil wars, drained England of four or five hundred thousand pounds, (a very great sum in those days) and if the persecution of the Puritans had continued twelve years longer, it is thought that a fourth part of the riches of the kingdom would have passed out of it through this channel."[1]

Not only were they well provided with the things necessary to set a young colony on the road to material success, but they were captained by men of strength and ability and standing. They were not men to whom life had been a failure and who, having nothing to lose, could afford to risk much for

[1] Neal: *History of the Puritan*, vol. i, p. 546.

great gain. In 1630, only ten years after the little company of the Mayflower had for the first time laid eyes on their new home, John Winthrop and seven hundred companions set sail in eleven ships. "It was more than a colony, it was the migration of a people." The managers of the expedition were Winthrop, a lawyer in the prime of life, of good family and comfortable estate, and worthy; John Humphrey and Isaac Johnson, sons-in-law of the Earl of Lincoln; Thomas Dudley, manager of the Earl's estates; Theophilus Eaton, a London merchant who had served the king as minister to Denmark; William Vassall, an opulent West India proprietor. "The principal planters of Massachusetts," Chalmers says, "were English country gentlemen of no inconsiderable fortunes; of enlarged understandings improved by liberal education; of extensive ambition concealed under the appearance of religious humility." Their concealed ambition was to lay the foundations of "a renovated England, secure in freedom and pure in religion."

Before sailing, Winthrop issued an address "to the rest of their Brethren, in and of the Church of England." It gave assurance that "we desire you would be pleased to take notice that the principals and body of our company esteem it our honor to call the Church of England from whence wee rise, our deare mother, and cannot part from our native countrie, where she specially resideth, without much sadness of heart and many tears in our eyes, ever acknowledging that such hopes and parts as we have obtained in the common salvation, we have received in her bosom and sucked it from her breasts. We leave it not therefore as loathing that milk wherein we were nourished there, but blessing God for the parentage and education, as members of the same body, while we have breath, we shall syncerely indeavour the continuance and abundance of her welfare."

The rank and file in the earlier days of the migration were men of sterling character and correct morals, many of them of substance and well educated, and all of them, rich and poor, animated by a very high and noble purpose. They were unlike the earlier colonists who went to Virginia, who were a mixed company of adventurers, bankrupts, and criminals; they were of a different social class from the Mayflower's Pilgrims. The leaders who urged upon their followers to leave England and begin life anew "were the puritan ministers, who being hunted from one diocese to another, at last chose this wilderness for their retreat," Neal records, and he adds: "I have before me a list of seventy-seven divines, who became pastors of sundry little churches and congregations in that country before the year 1640, all of whom were in orders in the Church of England." He bears this tribute to their worth: "Though they were not all of the first rank for deep and extensive learning, yet they had a better share of it than most of the neighboring clergy; and which is of more consequence, they were men of strict sobriety and virtue; plain, serious, affectionate preachers, exactly conformable in sentiment to the doctrinal articles of the Church of England, and took a great deal of pains to promote Christian knowledge, and a reformation of manners in their several parishes."[1]

Later the tares were mixed with the wheat, but Longfellow was not giving rein merely to the fancy of his poetical imagination when he wrote: —

"God had sifted three kingdoms to find the wheat for this planting,
Then had sifted the wheat, as the living seed of a nation;
So say the chronicles old, and such is the faith of the people!"

The Puritans had a twofold purpose in coming to America. One was purely commercial, the other was religious. It was the religious element in the Puritan that gave birth to American democracy and American political institutions, that turned the current of English civilization when the drift of events carried it against the shores of the New World. History affords no parallel instance of a political system resulting from an attempt to reform a church polity by men who were members of that church and who believed in it as their spiritual guide. In all the determining factors that go to make a race, the influence of religion on national character is one of the most important and one of the most difficult scientifically to estimate. The religion of Rome and Greece, of Egypt

[1] Neal: *op. cit.*, vol. i, p. 546.

and Asia, of Protestant and Catholic Europe, of tribes so barbarous that they had not the faintest conception of civilization but to whom religion was the essence of life, profoundly modified national character and institutions.

Elizabeth came to the throne when the embers of the fires of Smithfield were still smouldering. Mary had sent to the stake more than three hundred martyrs who counted their lives as nothing in defense of the faith. Hundreds fled to escape imprisonment and death. The executioner and the torturer reaped their rich harvest and spared neither young nor old. Cranmer, the Archbishop of Canterbury, beloved of his people, venerated for his saintly character, faced the fagot unflinchingly, and his ashes were a greater inspiration to the cause of Protestantism than his living voice. Latimer, with prophetic vision, as the executioner applied the torch, looked beyond the flames and saw an even greater light, and delivered this last message of cheer: "We shall this day light such a candle, by God's grace, in England, as, I trust, shall never be put out." It was a pillar of fire rather than a candle, and it lighted the people of England to their liberty.

A new life was beginning in England. It was a day of great deeds. A new spirit entered into the nation. The deathless voice of English literature was born. The seas swarmed with English captains, who knew no fear, who fought the elements as they fought their foes, who laid virgin continents and the spoils of Spanish galleons at the feet of the Virgin Queen. The world rang with the achievements of the English, and the whole people felt the thrill of power and rejoiced in the terror that the name of England inspired.

The people were beginning to make themselves heard; in a dim way they were beginning to appreciate their own strength that ninety years later manifested itself when they sent their sovereign to the block. Protestantism had taken deep hold of the English people, and it grew with Catholic opposition that saw in a reformed England a menace to the political supremacy of the Pope. Henry VIII assumed the title of Defender of the Faith for political rather than religious reasons and for the increase of his authority with his own subjects; the motive being not unlike that which influenced Queen Victoria to add to her other titles that of Empress of India. With Elizabeth it was different. No sooner had she taken her seat on the throne than her right to it was challenged by the Pope; when she declared herself a Protestant, to satisfy the conscience of a majority of her subjects, the Pope issued a bull of excommunication, declared the throne vacant, and released the people of England from allegiance to their sovereign. It was the one thing needed to make Protestantism a political force. Catholic nobles raised the standard of rebellion, plots to assassinate the queen were traced to the Catholics, and it was the alleged complicity of Mary Queen of Scots in one of these plots that finally gave Elizabeth the pretext to send her rival to the scaffold. As the last desperate effort of the Pope to make Elizabeth bend to his will and restore the old faith in England, there occurred that most picturesque and glorious sea fight to prove the valor of Englishmen,—

> "When that great fleet invincible
> Against her bore in vain
> The richest spoils of Mexico,
> The stoutest hearts of Spain."

The Invincible Armada was sent forth by Spain in the hope not only that it would destroy England's command of the seas, but with England's ships flung to destruction and England crushed and humiliated and her shores defenseless, the Catholics would rise, Elizabeth would be deposed, and the Holy Inquisition would engage in its pious work of teaching the love of Christ with the rack and the fagot.

Medina Sidonia's defeat was one of the turning-points in history. It is a fascinating speculation to theorize on what might have happened if at one of those critical historical junctures defeat had been turned into victory; if a grain of sand had fallen into the machinery of fate and brought destiny to a standstill. It is easy enough to grasp what the consequences would have been had Howard and Drake been defeated in the Channel, and if the

Spaniards and not the English had made that day their triumph. But in the English victory was something more than a victorious battle; it had deeper and far more enduring consequences. It made Protestantism a living, vital force to safeguard the liberties of England against the menace of Romanism; it caused Romanism to be looked upon as a threatening foe always to be guarded against.

It is necessary to refer only incidentally to similar causes on the Continent that deepened the conviction of English Protestants. The massacre of the Protestants in France on Saint Bartholomew's Day and the unspeakable cruelties practiced by the Duke of Alva in the Spanish war against the Netherlands, in which he boasted that exclusive of those who fell in battle, siege, and massacre, he had executed eighteen thousand six hundred heretics and traitors,[1] aroused the horror and pity of their English co-religionists and strengthened their resolve to yield nothing to Rome and to die in defense of the faith as Frenchmen and Dutchmen had done. Both from France and the Netherlands came refugees seeking an asylum in England, whose recital of the cruelties they had suffered and the persecution they had endured for the sake of conscience made the character of the English Protestant more militant and more than ever determined to revenge himself on his oppressors; more convinced that death were sweeter

[1] Campbell: *The Puritan in Holland, England, and America*, vol. i, p. 212.

than life in the iron grip of Rome; better an end with terror than terror without end. It is interesting as noting that constant revolution of the wheel of history and social progress to which I have referred in a previous chapter, that these Dutch refugees, driven by persecution from their native land, fled to England, where they settled in the eastern counties, and a few years later, when Englishmen, to escape religious persecution, fled from England to Holland, the migration began in the eastern counties, and it was from these counties there went forth the first settlers of New England.

And now the great power of the printed word was exercising its influence. Few books have so swayed a nation as Foxe's *Book of Martyrs*, which told with all the direct force of Elizabethan English how men had died under the hand of the torturer rather than renounce their faith. By order of Queen Elizabeth a copy was placed in every parish church, and the people read it and were moved by the pity and the horror of that grim tale of religion run mad. It was a time when the Bible was much read; it was a day when there were no newspapers and no circulating libraries, when books were rare and expensive, and when the common people read the Bible because it was the only literature of which they knew. One does not have to be a great scholar to understand the simple and short words in which the Bible is written, or to be thrilled by the melodious beauty of its matchless diction; and even the poorest intellect can grasp its great lesson of love and sacrifice and duty. If there is one lesson more than another that the Bible teaches, it is the duty of man to resist oppression, to count suffering as naught in defense of the right, to cast down idols and drive forth those who bend the knee to Baal. The Bible left its impress upon the English. It moulded their thought as it influenced their actions, it colored the language and found its expression in the common talk of the people. In piecing together the causes that produced Puritanism, much weight must be given to the deep knowledge the English people had of their Bible and the hold it exercised over them.

"The Bible was as yet," Green says in his peculiarly vivid style, "the one book which was familiar to every Englishman; and everywhere its words, as they fell on ears which custom had not deadened to their force and beauty, kindled a startling enthusiasm. The whole moral effect which is produced nowadays by the religious newspaper, the tract, the essay, the missionary report, the sermon, was then produced by the Bible alone; and its effect in this way, however dispassionately we examine it, was simply amazing. The whole nation became a church."[1] And in another striking passage he says, "the mighty strife of good and evil within the soul itself which had overawed the imagination of dramatist and poet became the one

[1] Green: *A History of the English People,* vol. vi, pp. 190–191.

spiritual conception in the mind of the Puritan. Religion had to do not with churches, but with the individual soul. It was each Christian man who held in his power the issues of life and death. It was in each Christian conscience that the strife was waged between heaven and hell. Not as one of a body, but as a single soul, could each Christian claim his part in the mystery of redemption."

While Calvinism led to democracy, which in its spirit is the merging of the individual in the mass, contradictorily it produced an intense individualism, the like of which the world had never before known. All other religions, the Catholic religion especially, either shifted the burden from the individual to the mass, or else made it possible for the individual to relieve himself of the weight of sin by sharing it with the Church. Calvinism offered no such hope. The Calvinist himself must make his peace with God and his own conscience without an intercessory mediary. He fought always with the powers of darkness in single combat, and it requires more courage to fight alone than with the exhilaration that comes from touching shoulders in the ranks. Calvinism has had much to do in producing the individualistic nature of the American, even among Americans who subscribed not to the doctrines of Calvin. It laid the foundation of American character in the first days of America, and by a natural development the social influence of Calvinism became part of the temper of the American people when the religious side of Calvinism had expended its force. To Jefferson and Franklin and Charles Carroll — one mentions at random merely a few of the signers of the Declaration of Independence — Calvinism meant nothing, but the spirit which it created, the passionate belief in the individuality of man, was the legacy of the Puritanism that had descended to them from the settlers of Massachusetts Bay

" By making man sole sponsor of himself."

CHAPTER IX

PURITANISM BECOMES A POLITICAL FORCE

ALTHOUGH Elizabeth was a Protestant, the Church was still filled with the practices of Rome, and as the Pope regarded himself as the spiritual head of the Catholic world, so Elizabeth constituted herself the head of the Church and would permit no interference in its direction by her subjects. Elizabeth understood the temper of her people better than did her successor, James I, and had more tact than to put into words what he expressed,—"as it is atheism and blasphemy to dispute what God can do; so it is presumption and a high contempt in a subject to dispute what a king can do,"— but she was fully as strong in her faith in the divine right and omnipotence of kings. This was abhorrent to the reformers, who wished to see the Church entirely divorced from Rome. They objected to the use of the sign of the cross in baptism, of the ring in marriage, of bowing at the name of Jesus, of the use of certain vestments; they demanded a more strict observance of the Sabbath. The Church had fallen into a low estate and many of its ministers were unworthy to be its servants. In 1571 the reformers presented a petition to the queen alleging these grievances:—

"Great numbers are admitted ministers that are infamous in their lives, and among those that are of ability their gifts in many places are useless by reason of pluralities and non-residency, whereby infinite numbers of your majesty's subjects are like to perish for lack of knowledge. By means of this, together with the common blasphemy of the Lord's name, the most wicked licentiousness of life, the abuse of excommunication, the commutation of penance, the great number of atheists, schismatics daily springing up, and the increase of papists, the Protestant religion is in imminent peril."[1] Another petition complained that the ministers who were competent had been silenced for non-conformity, and that such as were left were unfit for the office, "having been either popish priests, or shiftless men thrust in upon the ministry when they knew not how to live, — serving men, and the basest of all sorts, men of no gifts. So they are of no common honesty, rioters, dicers, drunkards, and such like, of offensive lives."[2]

But Elizabeth, as Campbell points out, was unmoved. She did not believe in freedom of speech on any subject. She was the head of the Church, and it was her province alone to decide such questions and not to have them decided for her by Parliament. As the law prohibited a Catholic from sitting in the House of Commons, the Puritans were

[1] Campbell: *The Puritan in England, Holland, and America*, vol. i, p. 466.

[2] Byington: *The Puritan in England and New England*, p. 53.

in a majority in that body during the reign of Elizabeth, but the power of the Crown was greater even than that of the Commons. The independence of members was stifled by bribe and imprisonment, and legislation was throttled by the lords spiritual and temporal. Reforms which the people demanded, the queen, by the exercise of her great power, was able to prevent.

Unconsciously a religious movement was now about to become a great popular movement in protest against the arbitrary exercise of power by the sovereign. The word "unconsciously" is used with deliberation, for the great historical movements in the life of a nation take hold of a people long before they are discerned; they exercise their influence imperceptibly and without any external indication of the change of character that has taken place. Sometimes a people flash into revolt or rebellion with as little warning as a volcano throws out its molten lava, and in the one case as in the other the damage may be swift and terrible; but seldom is the damage so great that it cannot be repaired by time. The agencies that change the character of a race are as gradual and as unperceived as the conversion of wood and swamp land into coal, hidden for centuries and then changing the destinies of mankind.

The Church, not any particular sect, but the Church as an institution, has always been an aristocratic fellowship. Professing the principles of equality, recognizing the universality of man, it has depended for its existence upon caste. Popes and sovereigns, cardinals and bishops, priests and pastors, constitute the hierarchy of the Church, elevated according to their degree over the heads of the masses to whom they minister. In this is to be found one of the secrets of the perpetuation of the Church and its power, for man needs a master, and men are willing to obey those set over them until the pressure from above becomes too severe.

The English, Campbell says, are little influenced by theories; they respect hard facts and not ideas; and Boutmy's deduction is that the Englishman "has no time to follow vain phantoms; they are too far removed from earth, too alien to life here below, to its conditions and necessities." In other words, the Englishman is not metaphysical like the German, nor imaginative like the Latin, and what is known as the deep-rooted conservatism of the English character is simply an acceptance of the established order — the facts of society — and a reluctance to indulge in experiments that may overturn the established order; and it is only when that order is threatened, when liberty is in danger or the freedom of conscience is denied, that he can be induced to offer resistance. Compare, for instance, the English and French revolutions. The English had a definite purpose to accomplish. The rights of the people, rights which had been theirs from time immemorial and had become indefeasible and constituted the basis on which society was organized, were menaced by Charles I, who attempted to subvert the Commons and magnify the power of the Crown. There was only one thing to do, and that was to resist encroachment, then to fight against it, finally to remove the sovereign whose existence threatened the destruction of society. It was all done in a grim, stolid, rather matter-of-fact way, with as little noise and disturbance as possible. It was reform from within and not from without; it was not necessary to overthrow the social order to correct abuses; it was folly to burn down the mansion to purify a single room. In England the revolution was not accompanied by a reign of terror, and an incautious word did not sign a death warrant. Now, the French are differently constituted, and they resisted oppression and brought their king to the guillotine in quite another fashion. They must needs do their killing to the accompaniment of the sham philosophy of the encyclopædists, to "deluges of frantic Sansculotism," as Carlyle says; they prate much of liberty and equality, and they wear the *bonnet rouge* as symbolic of that liberty upon which they trampled.

In the reign of Elizabeth those Englishmen who had broken away from the Church of Rome were Calvinistic in their theology — and Calvin has been described as "Half Old Testament prophet, half Republican demagogue" — but still aristocratic in their church system. The bench of bishops, created by the king, naturally believed in the divine right of kings and preached obedience and submission to the spiritual and temporal head of the Church. The Reformation had wrought many changes in the outward observance of religion and religious forms, but it had left untouched the great system of caste in the Church. No stronger incentive than that was needed to make men imbued with the tenets of Calvinism unconsciously drift toward democracy.

Calvinism was in essence democracy. In the Parliamentary party there were men who were in religion Independents, who were, "to use the kindred phrase of our own time, radicals," as Macaulay says.[1] "Great as were the faults of Puritanism, it may fairly claim to be the first political system which recognized the grandeur of the people as a whole."[2] Green dwells on "the new conception of social equality" that was the product of Puritanism and shows how it led to democracy. "Their common call, their common brotherhood in Christ, annihilated in the minds of the Puritans that overpowering sense of social distinction which characterized the age of Elizabeth. The meanest peasant felt himself ennobled as a child of God. The proudest noble recognized a spiritual equality in the poorest 'saint.'"[3] Thus it will be seen that democracy did not spring from the virgin soil of

[1] Macaulay: *History of England*, vol. i, p. 58.
[2] Green: *History of the English People*, vol. vii, p. 150.
[3] Green: *A Short History of the English People*, p. 451.

Massachusetts; the seed had been sown on English ground, and it brought forth its harvest long before that great hegira which gave a new impulse to individualism.

The growth of Protestantism, of Calvinism especially, made the masses appreciate their power. "For the first time in British history, the common people had become a power in the land. They cared nothing for their leaders and little for their king. They worshiped a heavenly monarch, so far above all earthly rulers that to them terrestrial potentates seemed puppets. Narrow-minded these men were, of course, ignorant, and like their preachers, superstitious, rude in manner, often brutal in action."[1] But they were no more sensible of their power at first than the growing, healthy child knows his strength, the full realization of which comes to him only when in a moment of resistance against the authorities of the home he rebels and finds he has that within him that makes him feared. Under the influence of religion the people of England had been slowly acquiring moral strength, courage, purpose, the importance of which the world was first to see on a new continent where there was space to build new political institutions, where the ground was unencumbered with the *débris* of institutions become obsolete, and where the foundations could be laid so deep that neither the storm of passion nor the folly of man could destroy them.

[1] Campbell: *op. cit.*, vol. ii, p. 12.

CHAPTER X

THE AMERICAN HAS ALWAYS BEEN A REBEL

In previous chapters I have shown how the character of the English people had been slowly changing, developing, and broadening from the time of the Reformation until the Commonwealth. The transition was logical. Serfdom had given way to freedom, the power of the barons had been curtailed until at last the feudal system was broken down; as the power of the nobles declined that of the people rose, and with every fresh extension of their liberties they demanded still more. Long had they lain under the thrall of the Church, and long had they felt an insistent desire to escape from it and to come into their spiritual and moral freedom, which at last they won because they had the courage to fight for it.

In an age that has long ceased to believe in miracles one miracle has still survived, and with an industry worthy to be devoted to better things teachers have endeavored to impress on their students a belief in the miraculous. A very simple explanation has been offered for the genesis of American institutions, those institutions that Campbell, in his intense desire to trace back to Rome and to Holland, to Scotland and to Spain, to anywhere, in fact, except to England, so curiously terms "un-English." In some mysterious way those seers of New England drew their inspiration from the air, and like Jonah's gourd their civilization sprang up overnight. Never has the world witnessed a miracle more wonderful than this. The carpenters and the coopers, the fustian-workers and the hatters, the smiths and the wool-carders,[1] these plain and simple folk who were the passengers on the Mayflower, who in England were content to pursue their humble callings and had given no evidence that they were superior in intellect to their fellow workers, in their passage across the ocean had been transformed and become endowed with the gift of genius. If so, the voyage of Jason and his fellow Argonauts was no more marvelous than this.

But alluring as it would be to the imagination to think that at the moment when the sails of the Mayflower were furled the law of causation ceased and like the magnetic needle at the North Pole no longer pointed to the true north, there is neither justification nor reason for dismissing the truth to seek an explanation in the fantastic. The causes are quite simple and perfectly rational. They are to be found close at hand if the trouble is taken

[1] Ames: *The May-Flower and her Log*, p. 194. Ames gives this list of the vocations of adults so far as known (except wives, who are presumed housekeepers for their husbands): Carpenters, 2; Cooper, 1; Fustian-worker and silk-dyer, 1; Hatter, 1; Lay Reader, 1; Lady's-maid, 1; Merchant, 1; Physician, 1; Printers and publishers, 2; Seamen, 4; Servants (adults), 10; Smith, 1; Soldier, 1; Tailor, 1; Tradesmen, 2; Wool-carder, 1.

to search for them. Nor do we have to go back to Rome, which has been the fad of some writers, to find there the inspiration for American institutions, except as Rome colored English civilization. And it is equally absurd to think that the short time spent by the Separatists in Holland so altered their whole concept of life that they cast off the influences of English descent and training and traditions and became Dutch in spirit and in everything else except in language. That were a miracle second only to the first and greater phenomenon. "The whole world was their quarry, and all the past their architects." Most accounts of the origin of American institutions have been so colored by the prejudices of their writers that although they conscientiously endeavored to write history they succeeded in producing hagiology, which may be entertaining reading, but is never accurate.

It is worth noting here that although the Dutch planted New York, and the Swedes Delaware, and the Spanish Florida, and the French Louisiana; "the Dutch, the French, and the English made a simultaneous sowing of the great struggle for commercial and political supremacy in North America"; and since that day the Irish, the Germans, the Italians, the Jews, the Scandinavians have flowed in never-ending stream to swell the flood of the American race, they have all been absorbed into and have not absorbed the English. The law, the speech, the institutions of America are English, and modified only by conditions peculiarly American. Neither the Dutch nor the French nor the Spanish left a single enduring law nor a single institution that has survived.[1] The immigrant since their time has brought with him his own customs, and he has cast them off as he discarded the garments of the Fatherland when with American money he purchased American clothes. Whence came this extraordinary power of assimilation? We cannot answer that question now; it will answer itself in the succeeding pages as we trace the growth of American nationality.

No, the Puritan — for the Pilgrim need be only incidentally considered in the course of this investigation — came to Massachusetts an Englishman, a rebel at heart, a protagonist to be given for the first time full scope for the display of his powers, and a man of profound religious conviction who was to set up the theocracy in which he believed and which had been denied him in England. The Massachusetts man was not an American, for America in the early part of the seventeenth century was a geographical expression and not a political entity.

A race is not the product of to-day or yesterday; it is the result of all the influences that have made it. In England those influences had been at work for a hundred years before the Puritan set foot on American soil. The Puritan left England with

[1] That in Louisiana the code is based upon the Spanish law and the *Code Napoléon* does not contradict the general assertion.

bitterness in his heart not untinged with regret; the voyage across the Atlantic changed him not in the slightest, and he came to his new home full of courage but also full of determination, still ready to rebel against authority that should attempt to throttle his liberty. The American has always been a rebel. He is a living protest. His existence is a protest against usurped authority. To a rebel fighting is second nature. The American has always fought, against nature, against man, against government when that government sought to oppress him. That was the moral attitude of the Puritan. It displayed itself as early as 1635, when Massachusetts contained a mere handful of struggling colonists. The fear that Charles I would seek to exercise arbitrary power led them to prepare to resist the Crown. They fortified Boston Harbor, and the militia was placed on a war footing. The spirit of 1776 did not suddenly flash into life. It was born nearly a century and a half before.

A digression for a moment is necessary. In reading history backward the mind overleaps the ages. Certain great events in the life of races or nations stand out so prominently that they cannot be overlooked, but the causes that produced them are often obscure and their significance is hidden. Many writers have found it convenient to ascribe the beginning of Americanism to the Declaration of Independence, as if that had made articulate an invertebrate people. Now that were absurd. The

Declaration of Independence was not cause but effect. "It was only the first unanswerable assertion that this new people had come into existence." [1] The defiance of England by Jefferson and Hancock and Franklin and the other men who appended their signatures to the great charter gained no strength from their written declaration. This defiance had for years been slowly growing. It followed, it did not precede, the liberty that Patrick Henry so passionately invoked. Long before the parchment was made on which the Declaration of Independence was written, long years before that shot was fired which echoed in the heart of freedom, long before the guns of Lexington and Concord spoke, men had heard the voice that called them to resist. Lexington and Concord were the outward and visible signs of the spiritual teachings that began in England two hundred and fifty years earlier, that buried their roots deep in the soil of New England, and were fed by the immanent conviction in the divine inspiration, and a profound belief that there was only one law — the law of God — and that as God had taught His people to resist oppression, so it was the duty of those who would walk in the light of His countenance to hearken to the voice of Sinai.

The beginning of America we may really date to 1604. In that year met the first Parliament of James I, in which the Puritans had a majority;

[1] Wendell: *Liberty, Union, and Democracy*, p. 81.

and one of the first acts of the House of Commons was to enact measures to redress certain ecclesiastical grievances, which the Lords, backed by James, rejected. This put the Commons on their mettle, and they boldly told the king that he had no more power to change religion than he had to alter any laws without the consent of Parliament. James, with all the obstinacy and short-sightedness of the Stuarts, would listen to no advice; reformers were declared guilty of sedition and rebellion and punished; the Church enunciated anew the doctrine of the divine right of kings and the duty of obedience to those placed in authority. And observe again how the great wheel of life forever revolves and the seeming impossibility of men to profit by the experience of the past. The contest between James I and his people ought to have been a warning to Charles I, but it went unheeded, and Charles lost his head, just as George III, for the same reason, lost his American colonies. Had the grievances of which the Puritans complained been redressed by James, there would, in all probability, have been no civil war, no flight to Holland and thence to America, no tragedy at Whitehall; America would have been settled by Englishmen, but they would, one is inclined to believe, have remained Englishmen. It was the stupidity and vanity of an obstinate and narrow man that created a race.

The purpose of the Puritan in leaving England

and coming to Massachusetts was to create a theocratic state which, as Fiske says, should be, under the New Testament dispensation, all that the theocracy of Moses and Joshua and Samuel had been to the Jews in Old Testament days.[1] "It was one great design of the first planters of the Massachusetts colony to obtain for themselves and their posterity the liberty of worshiping God in such manner as appeared to them to be most agreeable to the sacred scriptures."[2] They came with that distinct purpose, and it was one of the causes that made them rebel at heart from the beginning. They were prepared to render allegiance to their Heavenly King, but they were in no mood tamely to submit to the tyranny of Stuart monarchs. They had no use for man-made constitutions, or for experiments in government; to those speculations that later were so dear to the French philosophers they gave no countenance. Their way lay straight before them. The small book that has influenced the thought of mankind more than all the ponderous tomes of philosopher and reformer was their sole guide. If they were in doubt, they had only to look into the Bible and find all doubts removed. If there was any question beyond the finite capacity of man to solve, they had only to search and find the answer in the Word.

They were not tolerant men, they were not

[1] Fiske: *The Beginnings of New England*, p. 146.

[2] Hutchinson: *History of New England*, vol. i, p. 417.

liberal, as we understand the meaning of the term in this day of enlightened liberality. They purposed no asylum for the persecuted of other sects. They had not made themselves exiles, that they might prepare an arena where all kinds of beliefs might disport themselves. They had come three thousand miles, at a great cost of money and of feeling, that they might here make a better England according to their own convictions of that which was true and right.[1] They were fanatics, if you please, at a time when the world was either fanatical or full of scoffing doubt, and it was a time when the fanatic was more useful and played a greater part than the Laodicean. They stand accused of becoming more royalist than the king in their religious bigotry, and after having escaped from persecution they persecuted with even greater ferocity those who had the courage to disagree with their theology. Those historians who have built on this false premise must naturally reach an erroneous conclusion in their attempts to judge the character of the Puritans, but this error is to be attributed largely to the confusion of Pilgrim and Puritan. The former separated from the Established Church because their consciences led them to a form of worship that seemed more in keeping with divine commandments, and they could not, unless they were hypocrites, claim liberty

[1] McKenzie: Introduction to Byington: *The Puritan in England and New England.*

for themselves and deny it to all others. They asked religious liberty, and in equal measure they were prepared to grant it. The vagaries of the Quakers were to be sorrowed over rather than to be corrected in anger. Although the Quakers fell under the Pilgrim lash just as later they did under the Puritan, and although it was applied in a spirit of charity rather than vengeance, it scarred naked backs as much in the one case as in the other. The belief in witchcraft was universal, and the Pilgrims were no more superior to the teachings of their day than were the Puritans, but their natural benevolence stayed the hand of the executioner. With the Puritan it was different. He who was not of their faith was an evil-disposed person who was an enemy to the theocratic state, and there was no place for such in the community. There was no more room for heretics in Massachusetts than there was in Rome or Madrid, Fiske says. It was a day of swift trial and stern punishment. The heretic must recant or die for his heresy. Heresy was treason, and treason was death.

Bear in mind another fact. The Pilgrim had separated from the Church of England; the Puritan, at the time of his migration, when he laid the foundation of empire, was a member of the Church, and he resented the imputation that he was a schismatic. As the shores of England were fast receding, Higginson called his little band about him and thus addressed them: —

"We will not say as the Separatists were wont to say at their leaving of England, Farewell Babylon! Farewell Rome! but we will say, Farewell, dear England, farewell, the Church of God in England and all the Christian friends there. We do not go to New England as Separatists from the Church of England, though we cannot but separate from the corruptions of it; but we go to practice the positive part of church reformation, and propagate the Gospel in America."[1]

Typical of this same feeling, which finds its expression in numerous addresses and records, is the letter from Dudley, the deputy governor of Massachusetts, to the Countess of Lincoln; he writes in February, 1631:—

"Also, to increase the heap of our sorrows, we received advisement by letters from our friends in England, and by the reports of those who came hither in this ship to abide with us, (who were about twenty-six) that they who went discontentedly from us the last year, out of their evil affections towards us, have raised many false and scandalous reports against us, affirming us to be Brownists in religion, and ill affected to our State at home, and that those vile reports have won credit with some who formerly wished us well. But we desire, and cannot but hope, that wise and impartial men will at length consider that such malcontents have ever pursued this manner of casting dirt, to make

[1] Bacon: *Genesis of the New England Churches*, p. 467.

others seem as foul as themselves, and that our goodly friends, to whom we are known, will not easily believe that we are so soon turned from the profession we so long have made in our native country. . . . We are not like those which have dispensation to lie; but as we were free enough in Old England to turn our insides outward, sometimes to our disadvantage, very unlikely is it that now, being *procul a fulmine*, we should be so unlike ourselves. Let therefore this be sufficient for us to say, and others to hear in this matter." [1]

The Puritan has been called a fanatic, and fanatic he undoubtedly was, and yet his was a fanaticism unlike that the world had ever before known, and therefore it produced results different from other religious persecution. In an attempt to make men conform to a particular creed or form of worship, pope and king had claimed divine authority which men might not challenge, and so long as the creed they preached was accepted they cared little for the sincerity of professed belief. With the Puritan it was different. He would tolerate no mere lip service. Puritanism, as I shall show in the next chapter, was a polity as well as a religion; it was not only the life of the people but it was also the life of the state; it was a new trinity — the guide to morality, the guide to temporal obedience, the guide to the achievement of material welfare. Until the time when the Puritans settled in Massachusetts

[1] Force, vol. ii, 4. 16.

creeds were to be savagely defended and fought for, but they were always exotic; they were always something outside of men themselves, the meaning of which men only dimly comprehended.

"The passionately precise idealism" of Calvinism was the basis of the Puritan character. His theodicy was to him real. Forever tortured by doubt, forever striving to reach a higher spiritual plane, he must forever be vainly searching, struggling, asking; engaged in a perpetual conflict with himself; endeavoring with all his strength to overthrow the enemy and rise triumphant over sin. He was always questioning. The Puritan has been represented as a man of little and narrow imagination, but this misreads him. No man is unimaginative whose whole life is a spiritual conflict such as the Puritan was always engaged in; the struggle for freedom vividly awakens the imagination. The man who accepts everything as *fait accompli*, to whom the things of heaven and earth are a finality, who has never been moved to question the meaning of life or the mystery of death, who accepts whatever is, moves with narrowed vision and is deaf to the power of impression. The Puritan's whole training, his intense idealism, quickened the imagination, for had he not been gifted with the divine power of imagination, life would have lost many of its terrors and death promised fewer rewards.[1]

[1] "Those people believed. They never for one instant questioned"; thus Charles Francis Adams in *Massachusetts, its Historians and its History* (p. 36). They believed, yes; it was inseparable from their lives; but they

Puritanism was not a garment to be hastily slipped into on Sunday and to be forgotten for the other six days of the week. The Puritan wore his religion at all times as he wore his leather-lined doublet, for without it he would have stood ashamed in his own nakedness; and one was as necessary to him as the other. Whether he worked or played, whether he sat in meeting-house or in the general court, whether he tilled his fields or snatched up his musket at the sound of an Indian alarm, wherever he went or whatever he did, he took his creed with him, for it was the criterion of right living, the benison of divine grace.

never ceased to question. The difference between Puritan and Catholic was that while both believed, the Catholic never questioned, and the Puritan was always tortured by doubt. The Catholic believed with faith sublime, which brought peace; the Puritan believed, but was never at peace with himself. "I cannot imagine why the Holy Ghost should give Timothy the solemnest charge, was ever given Mortal man, to observe the rules he had given, till the coming of Christ; if new things must be expected." — *The Simple Cobler of Aggawam* (Force, vol. iii, 8). And Mather and Johnson and other Puritan theologues show how this fear, this doubt, this longing to believe, and yet always this eternal questioning, had possession of the Puritan mind; which was at once its weakness no less than its strength.

CHAPTER XI

THE BIBLE THE PURITAN CONSTITUTION

To the Puritan the ideal concept of society was a form of government in which the Word of God, as exemplified in the Bible, was the law of man. Grasping this basic truth, we see at once where it led him.

The Bible was the Constitution of the Puritan State.

All society, civilized or uncivilized, rests upon a body of laws. Among an uncivilized people, in a primitive or rudimentary state, those laws are the customs of the tribe or the traditions of the clan. As society escapes from barbarism and its intellectual faculties develop, customs and traditions are codified into fundamental constitutions and statutes, which are either precisely defined or, by the sanction of usage, become the unwritten law. In the New World, in his new environment, the Puritan began his social and political existence with a written constitution — the Bible. I make no apologies for reiteration. It is necessary that this should be emphasized if its significance is to be appreciated and its consequences understood.[1]

[1] "It was then requested of Mr. Cotton, that he would, from the laws wherewith God governed his ancient people, form an abstract of such as were

Every nomadic tribe, every clan, every people from whom has sprung a race, is not less influenced by its laws or customs than those laws or customs reflect the physical and mental state of their creators; and it is impossible to comprehend their view of life unless we have knowledge of the code to which they rendered obedience. The laws of Draco and the laws of Solon typify two stages in the life of Athens. You cannot enter into the Athenian mind if you are unable to see why those codes were enacted; with that understanding the Athenian social and moral philosophy is its own interpretation.

No writer with whom I am familiar has brought the Bible in this exact relation to the Puritan. And yet it is fundamental. It is because of his Biblical constitution that the Puritan was what he was. It is one of the chief explanations of the difference in character between the Pilgrim and the Puritan. It is the reason why the Puritan made America and the Pilgrim was merely an episode in historical evolution.[1]

of a moral and a lasting equity: which he performed as acceptably as judiciously. . . . Mr. Cotton effectually recommended it unto them, that none should be electors, nor elected therein, except such as were visible subjects of our Lord Jesus Christ, personally confederated in our churches. In these, and many other ways, he propounded unto them, an endeavour after a *theocracy*, as near as might be, to that which was the glory of Israel, the peculiar people." — *Magnalia*, vol. i, p. 243.

[1] *An Abstract of the Lawes of New England as they are now Established* (Force, vol. iii, 9), chapter i. Of Magistrates. First, All Magistrates are to be chosen, First, By the free Burgesses (Deut. i, 13). Secondly, Out of the free Burgesses (Deut. xvii, 15), and so on throughout, the warrant for the law being found in Scripture.

A writer usually so careful as Pierre Leroy-Beaulieu falls into the common error of regarding Pilgrim and Puritan as synonymous and interchangeable terms. "From the days of the Pilgrim fathers," he says, "who expatriated themselves in order that they might establish on the rude shores of Massachusetts a government resting on the principles derived from the Bible." [1] But this the Pilgrim did not do. He had no purpose to found a theocratic state. That was the self-appointed mission of the Puritan.

"And the elder Saints and Sages laid their pious framework right
By a theocratic instinct covered from the people's sight."

Agreed as men may be on principles, on details there will always be a wide divergence of opinion, and the greater their intellection the greater that divergence will be. Nothing is more enticing to flexible and subtle minds than to discuss the meaning of words capable of more than one construction by ingenious argument or adroit sophistication, and to convince themselves by their arguments of the correctness of their position and the weakness of that of their opponents. The Constitution of the United States has been in existence for one hundred and twenty-five years, and in that time it has been passed upon and interpreted by some of the clearest and most acute minds the world has known; it has been written on and expounded and discussed by men of great learning, great honesty, and great abil-

[1] Leroy-Beaulieu: *The United States in the Twentieth Century*, p. xvii.

ity at perhaps greater length than any other man-made code, and yet to-day we are as far from the last word having been said as we were almost at the beginning. What do a few simple words mean that are in every-day use, words so simple that the ordinary public-school boy in the lower grades has no difficulty in understanding them? But great lawyers, great jurists, great statesmen, great writers spend long hours in patient research endeavoring to give these simple words an interpretation that shall square with their own views, or what they believe to be the intent of their writers, or the purpose for which they were designed; which by that construction shall be for the good of the state or the benefit of the people. In the forum, in the courts, in the press, there is constant discussion of the Constitution of the United States. That is not merely an intellectual diversion, the luxury of idle minds, to whom academic, hair-splitting argument is an amusement as keen as it was to the Greeks and Romans, who, at the height of their intellectual development, sat enraptured under the spell of their great orators; nor does it bear any resemblance to "the subtilities and quiddities of mediæval theologians, who seriously discussed such silly questions as the digestibility of the consecrated elements in the eucharist." This discussion of the American Constitution has a deeper and more ennobling purpose. The Constitution of the United States is to the American people a code political as well as a code moral. It is the ark of the covenant. No impious hands may be laid upon it, for that were sacrilege; it would, if it were falsely construed, destroy political liberty and a moral standard that men regard as vital for their spiritual growth.

The Constitution of the United States is a comparatively short document and not more difficult to memorize than many other pages of prose that students have committed to heart. If, then, there is this wide difference of opinion as to the meaning of the words and purposes of the American Constitution, how inevitable that there should be even greater differences of opinion as to the meaning of that much larger and more complicated constitution of the Puritan, the Bible?

The Puritans had their constitution made for them not by man but by the inspired Word of God; but because they were men and not divinely inspired, it was necessary that they should seek its interpretation according to their own human limitations and the finite capacity of their understanding. That could not be done in a day or a month or a year. It was a matter that required the earnest devotion of serious and zealous men, who approached the study of their subject in a proper frame of mind, who must look upon it as the greatest of all duties, who, convinced of the correctness of their judgment, were like the champions of old, ready to enter the lists against all comers to defend their cause.

An effective but cumbersome weapon was the lance; much more convenient and deadly is the magazine rifle. The expounders of the Puritan constitution must needs use the means at hand. It was not a day of steam printing-presses that turned out their millions of printed words by the hour; the machinery of distribution was wanting. No man was driven by the spur of haste; society was not revolutionized between breakfast and dinner; reputations were not made or destroyed between dinner and bedtime by the facile pen of the morning newspaper leader writer. The controversialists of the Puritan constitution, the strict constructionists and the liberal expounders as we should term them to-day, relied on the tract and the spoken word to convince. Their tracts like their discourses were heavy, rambling, discursive, frequently involved. Nothing more strikingly marks the difference between the old and the new than our brevity, our conciseness, our horror of circumlocution or the unnecessary use of mere words. We have simplified the expression as well as the method of expression; we have substituted the typewriter for the quill pen, and thrown into the limbo of forgotten things the grandiloquent and meaningless phrases that require too much time to form into thought and too much space to shape into words.

It was a day of controversy, a day when men delighted in argument, for controversy and argument were the means by which the people were educated, but it was not a day of little things. Men of mature years did not, like Didymus, waste their time in inquiries as to the relative ages of Hecuba and Helen, or the name of the mother of Æneas, or the character of Anacreon or Sappho.[1] Argument brought home to the people in the quickest and most direct way the truths that it was essential for them to know. For knowledge they were eager. They avidly read what was written, they listened with absorbent minds to what they heard. To them that was a pleasure no less than a duty.

Much has been written of the gloom of the Puritan Sunday, of the long sermons and services at the meeting-houses, of the peculiar institution that was native to the soil of New England. Now in the first place the Puritan Sabbath was not indigenous to the soil of Massachusetts, but was one of the things that Englishmen brought with them. "And to the end the Sabbath may be celebrated in a religious manner, we appoint that all that inhabit the Plantation, both for the general and particular employment, may surcease their labor every Saturday throughout the year at three of the clock in the afternoon; and that they spend the rest of that day in catechising and preparation for the Sabbath, as the ministers shall direct," were the instructions given to Endicott and his council in 1629 by the New England Company in London.[2]

[1] Dill: *Roman Society from Nero to Marcus Aurelius*, p. 300.

[2] Young: *Chronicles of the First Planters of the Colony of Massachusetts Bay*, p. 163.

It is easy enough to understand how the custom originated. Warrant for it was found in the Puritan constitution, where precise injunctions were laid down for the observance of the Sabbath. Thus in Leviticus xxiii, 32, the Jews are commanded, "from even unto even, shall ye celebrate your Sabbath." Mather says that John Cotton began the Sabbath the evening before; "for which keeping of the Sabbath from evening to evening, he wrote argument before his coming to New England: and I suppose, 'twas from his reason and practice, that the Christians of New-England have generally done so too."[1] Hutchinson says it was some time before this custom was settled. Hooker, in a letter written about the year 1640, says, "The question touching the beginning of the Sabbath is now on foot among us, hath once been spoken to, and we are to give in our arguments each to the other, so that we may ripen our thoughts concerning that truth, and if the Lord will, it may more fully appear"; and in another letter, March, 1640, "Mr. Huit hath not answered our arguments against the beginning the Sabbath at Morning."[2]

Through the mist of long years we look back on the Puritan Sabbath and we see nothing but darkness and gloom, a day in which the austere soul of the fanatical Puritan could sink itself in the dread of eternal punishment and rejoice in the thought

[1] Mather: *Magnalia*, vol. i, p. 253.

[2] Hutchinson: *History of Massachusetts*, vol. i, p. 428.

of everlasting damnation. Malice aided by ingenuity has heightened this mirage. Not content with imposing an all-day religious observance on these unfortunate progenitors of a race, natural emotions and sympathies were crushed out as abominable in the sight of the Lord. We know of course now that the celebrated Blue Laws had no existence in fact and were the creation of malicious imagination, but generations have believed in all sincerity that the code of the Puritans forbade a husband to kiss his wife on Sunday, that Sunday was to little children a day of torture and torment, and that the Puritan father found pleasure in making them suffer.

"Home, as we conceive it now," Green says, "was the creation of the Puritan. Wife and child rose from mere dependents on the will of husband or father, as husband and father saw in them saints like himself, souls hallowed by the touch of a divine spirit and called with a divine calling like his own. The sense of spiritual fellowship gave a new tenderness and refinement to the common family affections."[1] Instead of Sunday being to the Puritan a day to be dreaded and to be approached with a feeling of repugnance, it was a day to be looked forward to with delight. Campbell has well said that "the Puritan took as keen a pleasure in his four hours' sermon from a moving preacher as ever did the most ardent admirer of the drama

[1] Green: *A History of the English People*, vol. vi, p. 199.

at the first night of a great play,"[1] It was a day of quiet and rational enjoyment according to the Puritan idea of what was rational and meet to be enjoyed by the godly.

Puritanism, it cannot be too often repeated, was a political-social movement as much as it ever was a religious; it was the sowing of the great seed of democracy that has overrun the earth. The life of the common people of England, of the common people everywhere, was hard enough, and there was little consideration shown for their comfort or amusement, for the limitation of their hours of labor, or their protection against the oppression of their employers, against that most iniquitous form of sweating that even to-day is the disgrace of civilization. The England of Elizabeth was "Merrie England," but it was a merriment more on the surface than in the hearts of the beast of burden — the common people — who bore England on its back. Elizabethan statutes made it legal for men to work on Sunday; more than that, "if, for any scrupulosity or grudge of conscience, men should superstitiously abstain from working on those days, that then they should grievously offend and displease God."[2] Gradually there came to be no distinction between Sunday and the secular days of the week, until with the death of Elizabeth Parliament refused to sit on Sunday, servile labor was

[1] Campbell: *The Puritan in Holland, England, and America*, vol. ii, p. 162.

[2] Campbell: *op. cit.*, vol. ii, p. 161.

abolished on that day, and the so-called "Puritan Sunday," in contradistinction to the "Continental Sunday," was established both in England and the United States.

The Puritans have been accused of taking their pleasures sadly,—which is the same accusation that has been brought by the French[1] against the English and the English against the Americans in our day, — and much fun has been made of the Thursday lecture, the Puritan's one idea of enjoyment, which naturally took a theological form. As a matter of historical accuracy, again, the Thursday lecture was not a Puritan institution, but was borrowed from England. Hume tells of the intention in 1637 "to suppress all the Wednesdays' lectures in London,"and he adds: "It is observable, that the church of Rome and that of London, being both of them lovers of form and ceremony and order, are more friends to prayer than preaching; while the puritanical sectaries, who find that the latter method of address, being directed to a numerous audience present and visible, is more inflaming and animating, have always regarded it as the chief part of divine service." He concludes with this philosophical observation, which is as pertinent to-day as it was when written: "Such circumstances, though minute, it may not be improper to transmit to posterity; that those, who are curious of tracing

[1] "Il m'a semblé qu'une sorte de nuage couvrait habituellement leurs traits; ils m'ont paru graves et presque tristes jusque dans leurs plaisirs." — de Tocqueville, vol. iii, p. 274.

the history of the human mind, may remark how far its several singularities coincide in different ages."[1] In other words, the eternal revolution of the wheel.

The Thursday lecture of the Puritan became the Puritan dissipation. Many people went to the lectures because they found it more comfortable to listen to an exhortation than to bend their backs in field or household labor; the young people across the meeting-house could at least see one another. So seriously did the lectures interfere with orderly arrangement that the magistrates made repeated attempts to restrict them.

Admirers of the Puritans have found evidence that they were men of extraordinary logical minds, and to this quality has been ascribed so many of their actions and the results they accomplished. This is again to invest them with attributes little short of the miraculous and to set aside perfectly natural causes. They were not more logical than the rest of their race — Bacons and Lockes are the human veins of gold in a dull mass of quartz — although they were hard-headed and had much common sense; despite their fanaticism in religion, which was their concept of life, there was another side of their character, which appears contradictory and was, in fact, contradictory; but all men worth the study are bilateral. Fanatics they were, and yet in all things affecting civil government and

[1] Hume: *History of England*, p. 549.

the development of society and the state they showed splendid sanity and an equable poise, two most admirable qualities, without which a sustained course leading to definite results is impossible. While they were in many things narrow and obstinate, judging as they asked to be judged, paltering neither with the truth nor the right, firm in their convictions, steadfast in their faith, not so much because it was a duty, which is the most contemptible code of virtue man can adopt, but because it brought its own reward in the satisfaction of well doing, they yielded to outside influences; they were as malleable as the finely tempered steel that bends but will not break; and they were possessed of an extraordinary power of assimilating all that was best in the civilization and institutions of the rest of the world. It made them always mindful of the thing required. Typical of this was the response of a member of the Legislature at the time of the historic "Dark Day," when the Day of Judgment was supposed to be at hand. He opposed adjournment, saying: "Either the Day of Judgment has come, or it has not; if the Day has come, I choose to be found at the post of duty; and if it has not come, there is no reason for an adjournment."[1]

There is one great quality about the reformer that has ever been noted. Whether he is narrow, stern, and harsh as Calvin, or more pleasure-loving and human as Luther, whether he is obsessed with but a

[1] Byington: *The Puritan in England and New England*, p. 120.

single idea or touches life at many points, the reformer — not the mere mouthing demagogue who uses his cunning to advantage himself but the man of strong and deep-rooted convictions, willing to die if necessary in the defense of what he knows to be right—has in him always something of the imagination and imagery of the poet, the vision of the seer, the wisdom of the prophet, the common sense of the statesman; and he sees farther and deeper into the great heart of humanity than even he is consciously aware. Every great reform, those great reforms that have swept society from its old moorings and driven it with irresistible force into new channels, has had small beginnings and has gained momentum because its end lay far beyond the horizon of the mind of the reformer when he began his self-imposed task. He has grown on what he created, and a part at least of his own personality, his own courage and self-denial and righteousness he has put in the hearts and minds of his followers.

In making Sunday a day devoted to religious observance and prohibiting secular employment, the Puritan simply struck a blow in defense of the common people and anticipated by three hundred years a great economic truth. It was long after the factory system had been established in England at the close of the Napoleonic wars that English statesmen and legislators had the knowledge forced upon them that men and women engaged in manual labor, like the machines to which they were yoked, could not be driven beyond their capacity, and that when they were overtaxed they broke down under the strain. So densely ignorant were men of economic laws that at first they believed that human life had no economic value, and while machinery represented capital, and therefore must be conserved, humanity was the inexhaustible supply of raw material always pressing on the market and always to be purchased at a trifling cost, and, like all raw material, of no value until it had been converted into the finished product. Men and women were fed to machines as human lives were laid in the arms of Moloch. When it was discovered that labor was not raw material but an asset, that the vigor of its workers measured the commercial strength of the state, only then was the workman accorded some of the consideration shown to the machine; then began that great mass of statutes whose purpose it is to protect men and women against the rapacity and ignorance of their employers; to make employment less hazardous; to keep children of tender years out of the factory and the mine, and to give them a brief respite before they are chained to their never-ending drudgery.

The Puritan Sunday was threefold in purpose. First: It was economic, as I have already pointed out, because it brought to rest for one day in seven all the machinery of society, human as well as material. It was as sound in theory and principle then as it is to-day. The necessity for this cessation from toil having been recognized, it could only be enforced by the concrete expression of the community voiced in legislation. Second: It was political, because it was the assertion of the rights of the people to control at least a part of their time and to assert their independence. Puritanism sowed the seed of democracy. Third: It was religious, because it was ordained that "six days thou shalt labour, and do all thy work: but the seventh day is the sabbath of the Lord thy God: in it thou shalt not do any work, thou, nor thy son, nor thy daughter, nor thy manservant, nor thy maidservant, nor thine ox, nor thine ass, nor any of thy cattle, nor the stranger that is within thy gates; that thy manservant and thy maidservant may rest as well as thou."[1]

Much as the Puritan might discuss the interpretation of his constitution, he did not dare to arrogate to himself the right to discuss its fundamental provisions nor to disregard them. His attitude was perfectly consistent.[2] There was no distinction to be made between the major and minor clauses of his code. The command not to commit adultery was no higher than the injunction to keep holy the Lord's day. He read in his Bible that while the children of Israel were in the wilderness they

[1] Deuteronomy v, 13, 14.

[2] "Cartwright, who had a chief hand in reducing puritanism to a system, held that the magistrate was bound to adhere to the judicial laws of Moses and might not punish nor pardon otherwise than they prescribed, and him the Massachusetts people followed." — Hutchinson, vol. ii, p. 463.

found a man who gathered sticks on the sabbath day, who was brought before Moses to be judged, who sought the counsel of the Lord and was told that the man must be stoned to death, "and he died, as the Lord commanded Moses."[1]

The religious side of the Puritan Sunday we can of course easily comprehend, and because the formal religious observance was on the surface to be seen by the dullest intellect, while the political and economic effects were more subtle and lay buried deep in the brains of a few men of far vision, Sunday as a day of austere religious ceremony has alone been remembered. I have said that Sunday was a day of keen enjoyment to those men who found pleasure in intellectual discussion, and Sunday was the day on which a moving preacher gave to his audience enough material to fill their minds and hearts for the following six days. Fiske has pointed out that "it was absolutely essential that every one should be taught from early childhood how to read and understand the Bible. So much instruction as this was assumed to be a sacred duty which the community owed to every child born within its jurisdiction."[2] Just as to-day American boys and girls are expected to acquire at least a rudimentary knowledge of the American Constitution, so in those days the children of the Puritans were taught the code of their state.

[1] Numbers xv, 32–36.

[2] Fiske: *The Beginnings of New England*, p. 151.

As men advance in years and understanding their point of view shifts with the ever shifting attitude of society; but children have always been the same, because they are born without prejudice and without restraint, and it is only as hereditary influences develop and education makes itself felt that they cease to act by natural impulse and become conventionalized. We have abundant evidence that the children of the Puritans no more relished the preaching of their ministers or the enforced attention they were compelled to give to long and tedious sermons that were over their heads, that either set their little heads nodding in sheer weariness or held their eyes wide open in terror as they listened to the threats of eternal damnation, than children of to-day really enjoy the hours spent at school or the routine of Sunday clothes and Sunday church, where they fidget and grow hot and long for their release. Puritan children were either normal, healthy children with all the undisciplined spirits of the virile young animal, or else fear and a vivid imagination that they were too young to control made them intensely morbid and introspective; they would have become neurotic had they lived in a more genial clime; in an older and more luxurious civilization passion would have been aroused by an appeal to the senses. Nothing is more pathetic than to read of the mental tortures through which some of these little children passed, and the few words set down in diaries and letters, incidentally and almost casually, reveal the overwrought state in which so many of these unhappy boys and girls lived.

Betty, the young daughter of an eloquent preacher, once heard her father deliver a sermon that greatly stirred his congregation, so much so "that they all cried out," and this is the effect the discourse had on her: —

"A little while after dinner she burst out into an amazing cry, which caused all the family to cry too. Her mother asked her the reason; she gave none. At last she said she was afraid she would go to Hell; her sins were not pardoned. She was first wounded by my reading a sermon of Mr. Norton's, text, ye shall seek me and shall not find me. And those words in the sermon, ye shall seek me and die in your sins ran in her mind and terrified her greatly . . . told me she was afraid she should go to Hell, was like Spira, not elected."[1]

A boy wrote in his diary: "Of the manifold sins of which then I was guilty of none so sticks upon me as that being very young I was whittling on the Sabbath day; and for fear of being seen I did it behind the door. A great reproach of God." This youth died at nineteen.[2]

But we get glimpses of the other side of childhood, the irrepressible spirit of fun and pleasure, that broke the law of the family for the mere pleas-

[1] Fisher: *Men, Women, and Manners in Colonial Times*, vol. i, p. 141.

[2] Fisher, *op. cit.*, p. 142.

ure of defiance and because youth must have its fling. As early as 1657 it was found necessary to pass this law in Boston: —

"Forasmuch as sundry complaints are made that several persons have received hurt by boys and young men playing at football in the streets, these therefore are to enjoin that none be found at that game in any of the streets, lanes or enclosures of this town under the penalty of twenty shillings for every such offence."[1] Really that law does not differ much, except in the severity of its penalty, from the municipal ordinances and regulations of to-day, and it shows that the Puritan boy could at times make himself just as much of a nuisance to his elders as the twentieth-century youngster.

The stern control the Puritan had over himself is typically illustrated in two matter-of-fact entries in Samuel Sewall's diary, Sewall "the Puritan Pepys": —

"October 29, 1698. Thomas Savage junr, shop-keeper, and Sarah Threeneedles were brought face to face in a very great Audience: She vehemently accused him, and he asserted his innocency with vehement Asseverations. She said he had ruin'd her; if he would have promis'd her any thing, it had not come to this. Said she forgave him, Judgment of God hung over him if did not repent.

"Fifth-day, Novr 17th. Very fair serene wether; Mr. Cotton Mather preaches at the South-Meeting-

[1] Earle: *Customs and Fashions in Old New England*, p. 20.

house; Sarah Threeneedles is an auditor; is a very vast Assembly, and the street full of such as could not get in; 51. Psalm 2d verse sung, 9–15 verses. Mr. Willard read the whole, and I set the tune. After Lecture Sarah Threeneedles is executed. Mr. Woodbridge went to the place of execution and pray'd with her there." [1]

Not a word as to the unfortunate Sarah Threeneedles; not a superfluous adjective. What in the hands of Hawthorne became a classic, is to Sewall a bare record of fact.

While the Puritan fathers carefully regulated marriage — because marriage was an economic necessity and both spinsterhood and bachelorhood were frowned upon, as the unmarried of suitable age were a drag upon the proper development of the colony—even Puritanism could not crush out the romance of love. An English traveler gives this glimpse of Boston in 1663: —

"On the south there is a small but pleasant Common, where the Gallants, a little before sunset, walk with their Marmalet-Madams till the nine o'clock bell rings them home to their respective habitations." [2] This picture of gallants and marmalet-madams trysting in the soft twilight and losing themselves in the mazes of an undiscovered country rather upsets the preconceived idea of Puritan austerity and their horror of even an approach to

[1] Sewall: *Diary*, Massachusetts Historical Society, vol. v, p. 486.

[2] Earle: *op. cit.*, p. 40.

sentiment. Sacred ground that small but pleasant common to Priscilla and her sisters, who, Puritans though they were, had all of woman's infinite capacity for love and passion.

Just as the Puritans discovered a great economic truth that only received the world's indorsement three centuries later, so a great social law was revealed to them, the importance of which philosophers did not grasp until the nineteenth century was waning. Until the dominant force of Puritanism made itself felt and changed the whole social system of England, education was a thing distinctly the prerogative of the classes 'and denied the masses. There was reason for this. It was not advisable that the people should know too much, that they should be able to read and think for themselves. The strength of feudalism, and later the divine right of kings and the autocracy of sceptre and mitre, was buttressed in the ignorance of the great mass to whom majesty temporal and spiritual could not be questioned because men were denied the capacity of voicing what they dumbly felt.

The Puritan struck a blow at ignorance and in doing so fought for liberty. So long as the people were unlettered, so long would they believe in superstition and meekly submit to political despotism. The surest way to raise the social level was to raise the general level of intelligence and to teach men the habit of thinking for themselves. The Puritans were the originators of the "campaign of education." Curious indeed that what the Puritans did in their meeting-houses and at their hearthstones the modern state has simply done more elaborately with the complicated machinery of board schools and compulsory school attendance, factory laws and other statutes that prohibit the employment of children unless they can give evidence of having received at least the rudiments of education; that when a democracy must convert men from the heresies of false economic beliefs it adopts the methods of the Puritan theocracy. It is axiomatic that the civilization of a state is in inverse ratio to the illiteracy of its people.

Because the Puritans saw the necessity of overthrowing superstitions and encouraging resistance to political despotism it is not to be assumed that they emancipated themselves from superstition or despotism. The candid historian has little to choose between Popish and Protestant superstition; theocratic despotism was as harsh as monarchical. That has ever been the case; and if the Puritans had simply exchanged one fetich for another, things alike would simply have been called by different names and the world would have advanced not one step. But in their passion for knowledge the founders of the Puritan state put into the hands of the people a weapon that was to prove their undoing and should destroy theocracy and set up in its place a broader, a more tolerant, a more humanizing code.

The more educated men became, the more

clearly they saw that a theocratic state, theoretically ideal, was practically impossible; and the force of circumstances and the broadening of intellect and the humanizing effect that education has on the whole concept of life compelled them to question the right of man to regulate all human affairs by the teaching of the Bible. In the very nature of things it was inevitable. Modern society has been able to accept the spiritual teachings of the Bible, but has dissociated it from the temporal. That the Puritan, at first, could not do, for the essence of the Puritan character was consistency, and consistency when pushed to the extreme leads to narrowness, stubbornness, rigidity. It hardens character, and with that hardening is lost a certain amount of intellectual pliability, the power to see both sides of a controversial question, or to admit that there may be some merit in your adversary's morals or manners. The Puritan stands on the page of history as an extremely narrow and self-centred man, but it was his consistency, his steadfast adherence to the code that he had created for himself, that made him so, and not because he was racially different from the men who were not of his faith.

It was demanded of these early settlers that they should be orthodox, that they should accept the Word as it was delivered to them, and neither question its authority nor seek to give it an interpretation that might be more comfortable. But a people must either accept orthodoxy and remain under the thrall of its superstition, or with their intellectual growth, in their ardent desire to solve the great mystery of the universal scheme, first have their doubts aroused, and then begin to question, and then finally boldly deny, or at least challenge their opponents to bring proof in support of the faith that is in them. The very methods adopted by the Puritan fathers to inculcate obedience and to maintain the supremacy of the theocratic state were the methods that were most conducive to quicken intellectual agnosticism, and whatever divergent views we may entertain of the Puritan, there can be no question as to the force of his intellect and his power as a controversialist. The perpetual discussion of the Biblical constitution, the polemical warfare carried on through the printing-press, the one great thing which occupied men's thoughts almost to the exclusion of everything else, that unconsciously colored their lives and moulded their conduct as soil and sunshine give to a flower its fragrance and delicate texture, were, as Fiske says, no mean school of intellectual training. In addition there was the basic Puritan theory that ignorance lay at the root of all civil and religious despotism and kept men in a state of moral and intellectual slavery. In putting this theory into practical effect we see again that the Puritans were less logical than some of their admirers have assumed. Logically they should have realized the danger of education, and had they retained knowledge in the hands of the Puritan hierarchy the Puritan theocracy would have lived longer. "In this energetic diffusion of knowledge they were unwittingly preparing the complete and irreparable destruction of the theocratic ideal of society which they had sought to realize by crossing the ocean and settling in New England. This universal education and this perpetual discussion of theological questions were no more compatible with rigid adherence to the Calvinistic system than with submission to the absolute rule of Rome. The inevitable result was the liberal and enlightened Protestanism which is characteristic of the best American society at the present day, and which is continually growing more liberal as it grows enlightened." [1]

But a long period elapsed before this era of "liberal and enlightened Protestantism" was reached, and in that interval Puritan theocracy was marked by all the bigotry, superstition, and cruelty that in that day were inseparable from religion and which to-day seem to reflect upon the Puritan character. While the Puritan did not rise above the spirit of his age, he did not sink below it.

The Puritans began by denying citizenship to those who were not members of the church, which was quite natural from their standpoint, but soon opposition arose to a religious test. Thomas Hooker, a Cambridge graduate and an ordained

[1] Fiske: *The Beginnings of New England*, p. 151.

clergyman of the Church of England, may not inappropriately be called the father of American democracy. "Government rests on the free consent of the governed" and "government of the people, by the people, for the people," are simply paraphrases of his declaration that "the foundation of authority is laid in the free consent of the people," which with the further declaration, "they who have the power to appoint officers and magistrates, have the right to set the bounds and limitations of the power and place of those who are called," are the foundation on which, a century and a half later, the American Constitution was reared. Hooker, a rebel among rebels, led a band to Connecticut, where he founded a colony and a written constitution was adopted,[1] which, like the American Constitution, prescribes no religious test. This movement had great influence on the older colony of Massachusetts, which modified the religious qualification for the right of suffrage, and eventually abolished it.

But before that golden day dawned bigotry was long to remain enthroned.

Historians have delighted to heap obloquy upon the Puritans for their persecution of the Quakers, just as they gleefully relate the whipping of Obadiah Holmes, the Baptist, who had the temerity to go to Lynn to give a dying brother consolation, as evidence of Puritan intolerance.

[1] See p. 340.

That persecution requires no apology from the impartial historian, for men are to be judged not by the moral statutes of the present, but their actions are to be weighed in the scales of the time in which they lived and the then existing state of morals. It is as great an anachronism to apply the twentieth-century test of morals to the seventeenth as it would be absurd to blame the Puritans for being content with the discomforts of the pine torch instead of using the electric light. That they would have used the electric light if it had been known to them we may feel sure, and we may with equal certainty convince ourselves that their moral attitude would have been that of to-day had the morality of the twentieth century been invented in the seventeenth. That time had not yet come.

The Puritans persecuted the Quakers and drove forth Roger Williams, who had already been driven out of England by Laud, for the very simple reason that all society was founded on persecution, and he who differed from the majority and was courageous enough or foolish enough to challenge the established order, whether in church or state, was to be tortured or put to death. In that tremendous conflict which made Europe for centuries one vast house of mourning in the name of religion, its champions sincerely and honestly believed with all the intensity of besotted ignorance that their faith was alone the true faith, and that those who would not accept conversion and who remained stubborn in their obstinacy after the persuasion of the torture chamber were better dead. Between Philip II of Spain and Luther and Calvin and Paul IV there is nothing in common except the common belief in the punishment of the heretic. "Each side," as Lea so forcibly puts it, "was equally sure that it alone possessed the true faith, which was to be vindicated with fire and sword. If the canon law required sovereigns to put heretics to death, Luther, in 1528, subscribed to a declaration of the Wittenberg theologians prescribing the same fate for those whom they classed as such. If Paul IV, in 1555, declared that all who denied the Trinity should be pitilessly burned, he but followed the example that Calvin had set two years before. If France had her feast of Saint Bartholomew, Germany had led the way in the slaughter of the Anabaptists. If Spain had her inquisition, England, in 1550, under the reforming Edward VI, created a similar organization with Cranmer at its head." In all that long struggle for what has with unconscious and grim irony been called freedom of conscience, men only asked for freedom to enslave the consciences of others, inspired often by what they believed to be the highest and purest motives, but blind to their own tyranny. Because of our inability to absorb the spirit of a bygone age, we are too apt to regard the persecution of Protestant and Catholic and the savage crimes committed in the name of religion as proof that cruelty was practiced for the sole delight that man perverted derived from witnessing suffering, and that the agony of the victims of the rack and the thumbscrew was music to brutal and bestial natures; just as the North American Indian often tortured his white captives for the mere pleasure of gloating over their pain. In this we do fanatics and zealots an injustice. There were of course many violent and passionate men who took as keen delight in inflicting torture as the average man, humanized and softened by contact with his fellow-men and the refining influences that come from an orderly and well-regulated system of society, now takes in relieving suffering and endeavoring to prevent it; but the great majority who maimed and slew for the glory of religion believed in their mission, and were sustained by the thought that they were carrying on the work for which they were anointed.

Had the Puritans of New England treated the Quakers otherwise than in the way they did, we might well believe in the theory of "miracle" set up by their over-zealous but injudicious defenders and find proof that they were touched by the divine spark; but the fact that the Puritans went about their congenial work of hanging and flogging and imprisoning is evidence enough to the impartial investigator that the Englishman in Massachusetts was no different from the Englishman in London or Lincolnshire. Quakers were put to death on Boston Common for the same reason that the fires had been lighted under the bodies of Protestants in Smithfield Market. Salvation was free, it was offered with outstretched hands to whoever would embrace it, but it must be salvation of the approved brand. Whoever was presumptuous enough to crave a different brand of salvation from that which the ruling powers regarded as their own monopoly was a traitor to God and man. And God was always invoked to justify every vile impulse. What abominable hypocrisy it seems to praise God for an epidemic of smallpox which swept away the Indians, but to the conscience of the seventeenth century it was a mark of divine favor. In 1633 the Aberginians near Charlestown were sorely stricken, and thus piously writes a Puritan who saw in everything the hand of God:—

"By which awful and admirable dispensation it pleased God to make room for his people of the English nation; who, after this, in the immediate years following, came from England by many hundreds every year to us, who, without this remarkable and terrible stroke of God upon the natives, would with much more difficulty have found room, and at far greater charge have obtained and purchased land."

Excuses have been found for the Puritan persecution of the Quakers. We have been told that they offended the sober taste of the Puritans by their extravagance and indecency in dress; that their manners and speech were offensive; that they made sport of religion and sought to overthrow civil institutions; that women shocked public morality by appearing in public places clothed in the garments of original sin. Stern as the Puritans were in their morality, it was no shock to their moral nature to look upon women naked in the hands of the executioners. Women bared to the waist had been flogged through the streets, other women had been stripped naked for examination. It was not a day when the offender was treated with consideration or pains were taken not to wound his feelings. The Puritan treatment of the Quakers was brutal in the extreme, unthinkable in this day, but exactly in keeping with the day in which it happened.[1]

In 1656 Anne Austin and Mary Fisher came to Boston from the Barbadoes, and Richard Bellingham, the deputy governor, arrested them and kept them in prison for five weeks until a ship was ready to return them whence they came. Soon after their departure, the stern and fanatical Endicott returned home. He found fault with Bellingham's conduct as too gentle; "if he had been there he would have had the hussies flogged. Five years afterwards Mary Fisher went to Adrianople and

[1] I have not considered it necessary to cite specific instances of Quaker persecution or the numerous statutes directed against these pestiferous enemies of the theocratic state, as the general fact is too well known to the student of early American history; but the curious reader who seeks more light on the subject may read with interest Elliott's *New England History*, Sewell's *History of the Quakers*, Hallowell's *Quaker Invasion of Massachusetts*, Bishop's *New England Judged by the Spirit of the Lord*, Besse's *Sufferings of the Quakers*.

tried to convert the Grand Turk, who treated her with grave courtesy and allowed her to prophesy unmolested. This is one of the numerous incidents that on a superficial view of history might be cited in support of the opinion that there has been on the whole more tolerance in the Mussulman than in the Christian world. Rightly interpreted, however, the fact has no such implication. In Massachusetts the preaching of Quaker doctrines might (and did) lead to a revolution; in Turkey it was as harmless as the barking of dogs. Governor Endicott was afraid of Mary Fisher; Mahomet IV was not." [1]

On all fours with the persecution of the Quakers the Puritan treatment of witches and witchcraft, and the happenings that have made Salem world-famous when much more important places are unknown, is a stone always cast by the ignorant defamers of Puritanism. "Writers who dislike Puritanism have rubbed the sad old story into the sore place unmercifully, as if the colonists at Salem ought to have been superior to the ideas of their age." [2] Professor Kittredge, in his "Notes on Witchcraft," [3] holds a brief for the men of Salem and by a plea of confession and avoidance argues that instead of being worse than their kinsmen at home they were really better. Here again it is not necessary to seek excuses. Belief in evil spirits, in the league between the devil and his agents in human

[1] Fiske: *The Beginnings of New England*, p. 183.

[2] Lang: *Salem Vindicated*, London *Morning Post*, October 18, 1907.

[3] *American Antiquarian Society*, new series, vol. xviii, p. 148.

form, in necromancy, witchcraft, and black magic existed from the dawn of creation until long after the Puritans set foot on New England soil. It was a belief confined not alone to the ignorant or the superstitious; it was shared by some of the most learned and subtle minds of the day. The Puritan had only to turn to his constitution to read there the punishment to be meted out to witches and those who practiced witchcraft. "Thou shalt not suffer a witch to live," was one of the divine commandments;[1] and again the Puritan read that "there shall not be found among you any one that maketh his son or his daughter to pass through the fire, or that useth divination, or an observer of times, or an enchanter, or a witch."[2] Of Manasseh the Puritan read that "he caused his children to pass through the fire in the valley of the son of Hinnom: also he observed times, and used enchantments, and used witchcraft, and dealt with a familiar spirit, and with wizards: he wrought much evil in the sight of the Lord, to provoke him to anger."[3]

The belief in witchcraft was not confined to any one people or to any particular religion; it was as profoundly a conviction among the poor and unlettered as it was among the rich and learned. In the reigns of Henry VIII, Edward VI, Elizabeth, and James I statutes against witches were enacted in England; on the continent witches were tortured

[1] Exodus xxii, 18. [2] Deuteronomy xviii, 10.

[3] 2 Chronicles xxxiii, 6.

and burned. One has only to recall the fate of the Maid of Orleans, who "heard voices" and was supposed to be in communion with the spirits of darkness. Men of such profound minds as Sir Matthew Hale and Sir Thomas Browne and that great legal writer, Blackstone, believed in witchcraft, and so did the gentle John Wesley and Martin Luther. Mather, as might have been expected, was convinced that the devil assumed human form.[1] "Flashy people," he says with scorn, "may burlesque these things, but when hundreds of the most sober people in a country, where they have as much *mother-wit* certainly as the rest of mankind, know them to be *true*, nothing but the absurd and froward spirit of *Sadducism* can question them."[2] We have no exact statistics, but probably not more than a dozen people were put to death in New England on the charge of witchcraft (some writers, however, estimate the number as high as thirty), while Fisher,[3] in his *History of the Christian Church*, says that prior to the witchcraft epidemic in Massachusetts 30,000 persons were put to death in England, 75,000 in France, and 100,000 in Germany. Incredible almost as these figures appear, there is reason to believe they are not exaggerated. Between 1580 and 1680 there are said to have been 3400 executions in Scotland, and in a single year, 1645–

[1] *Magnalia*, vol. i, p. 186 *et seq.*, and vol. ii, p. 388 *et seq.*

[2] *Magnalia*, vol. i, p. 187.

[3] Fisher: *History of the Christian Church*, pp. 479–483.

1646, in one of the eastern counties of England, 200 persons were put to death because they were accused of practicing the black art. It was often a convenient way of disposing of an obnoxious person. It was easy enough to find evidence to support a *prima-facie* case, and the burden of proof was not on the prosecutor, but it was the accused witch who had to bring evidence in the vain hope of being able to prove a negative. Before a packed court and a prejudiced jury the instances of the acquittal of witches are so rare as scarcely to be noted. When a case could be proved by the admission of "spectral evidence," conviction was always certain.

A distinguished American writer, Brooks Adams, has reflected more harshly on Massachusetts than even the most biased foreign critic. Writing of the court created to try the witches, which was presided over by William Stoughton, he says: "Even now it is impossible to read the proceedings of this sanguinary tribunal without a shudder, and it has left a stain upon the judiciary of Massachusetts that can never be effaced";[1] and again he says: "Stoughton was already at work, and certain death awaited all who were dragged before that cruel and bloodthirsty bigot; even when the jury acquitted, the court refused to receive the verdict. The accounts given of the legal proceedings seem monstrous."[2] Later, somewhat grudgingly, it would

[1] Adams: *The Emancipation of Massachusetts*, p. 225.

[2] *Op. cit.*, p. 266.

seem, he finds excuse for these monstrous proceedings, for in a brief note [1] he retracts much that he has previously written and is able to extenuate what Massachusetts did. "In England," he says, "throughout the eighteenth century, counsel were allowed to speak in criminal trials, in cases of treason and misdemeanor only. Nor is the conduct of Massachusetts in regard to witches peculiar. Parallel atrocities might probably be adduced from the history of every European nation, even though the procedure of the courts were more regular than was that of the Commission of Phips. The relation of the priest to the sorcerer is a most interesting phenomenon of social development; but it would require a treatise by itself."

Another count in the indictment brought against the Puritan is the ferocity with which he warred against the Indians and the "Cromwellian thoroughness" with which he used the sword and the torch. It is only necessary to admit the truth, but no excuses are needed. It was a day of stern reprisals, when *lex talionis* was the code observed by men in Old England as well as in New England, in all parts of the world wherever the sword was drawn and the fiery cross was raised. When white men warred against men of their race they found it more convenient to put their captives to death than to make them prisoners, and as a military and economic measure it was often impossible for the

[1] *Op. cit.*, p. 310.

victor to burden himself with a defeated army. In making war against savages extermination was the object sought to be attained, and no consideration of humanity softened the unloosed wrath. To have been merciful would have been regarded as a sign of weakness. The Indians were killed to strike terror in the hearts of other tribes, exactly as sepoys were blown from the muzzles of cannon after the Indian Mutiny. It was punishment swift and horrible, but all punishment, to be effective, must act as a deterrent to the living. It was effective.

CHAPTER XII

THE PURITAN HATRED OF COLOR A MYTH

In continuation of the purpose of previous chapters to clear away the fiction that has grown up about the character of the Puritan and present him as he really was, because, as I have already pointed out, of the importance of a proper interpretation of the Puritan if the character of the present-day American is to be correctly understood, it becomes necessary briefly to consider the Puritan in his home.

Fiction has given us the sombre-clad man and woman, to whom color was hateful, enjoyment of recreation an abomination in the sight of the Lord, and discomfort and voluntary hardship evidence of a saintly nature, who by his transplanting to America lost his sense of innocent pleasure and became a different being from what he had been in England. A careful reading of the chronicles of those days fails to reveal any evidence of this transformation. That the Puritan both in England and America was austere and looked with disgust upon the licentiousness that prevailed both in the church and society we know and has already been referred to, but the Puritan by his passage across the Atlantic did not become a man of gloom or frown upon the things that constituted the pleasures of those days. He did not deliberately mortify the flesh. We can find no testimony that he wore a hair shirt or found delight in self-inflicted pain. Austere he was, and yet he loved his wife and was affectionate to his children, although his affection did not find expression in exuberant demonstration. This is interesting in contrast with the modern American, who has little restraint, and whose emotions are vivid and quickly reached. It is another of those cumulative proofs to the student of American character that the American is not a hybrid Englishman but is the product of a new race, a race that has been produced by the forces of nature and the social and political institutions which he has created to satisfy the demands of his own nature instead of accepting those that belonged to another race in different environments.

Those famous Blue Laws of Connecticut, which all the world long believed in, never existed except in the luxuriant imagination of Rev. Samuel Peters, who had been driven out of America during the Revolution and took this ingenious means of gratifying his revenge. Women were not forbidden to kiss their children on the Sabbath; they were not prohibited from making "minced pies"; it was fiction and not truth that "no one should play on any instrument of music except the drum, trumpet, or jew's-harp."[1] A somewhat malevolent person this

[1] Peters: *A General History of Connecticut*, p. 71. *Cf.* Palfrey, vol. ii, p. 32, n.; p. 375; Trumbull: *Blue Laws, True and False.*

clergyman, who was denied the pleasure of knowing how much mischief he caused.

The modern idea of the Puritan is that he was the barbarian of his times, rude in his manner of living and uncultured. But this we know to be incorrect. The Puritanism of the first forty years of the seventeenth century, Palfrey says, was not tainted with degrading or ungraceful associations of any sort. "The rank, the wealth, the chivalry, the genius, the learning, the accomplishments, the social refinements and elegance of the time were largely represented in its ranks. Not to speak of Scotland, where soon Puritanism had few opponents in the class of the high-born and the educated, the severity of Elizabeth scarcely restrained, in her latter days, its predominance among the most exalted orders of her subjects. The Earls of Leicester, Bedford, Huntington, and Warwick, Sir Nicholas Bacon, his greater son, Walsingham, Burleigh, Mildmay, Sadler, Knollys, were specimens of a host of eminent men more or less friendly to or tolerant of it. Throughout the reign of James the First it controlled the House of Commons, composed chiefly of the landed gentry of the kingdom; and, if it had less sway among the peers, this was partly because the number of lay nobles did not largely exceed that of the Bishops, who were mostly creatures of the Crown. The aggregate property of the Puritan House of Commons of 1692 was computed to be three times as great as that of the Lords, according to Hume. The statesmen of the first period of that Parliament which by and by dethroned Charles the First had been bred in the luxury of the landed aristocracy of the realm; while of the nobility, Manchester, Essex, Warwick, Brooke, Fairfax, and others, and of the gentry a long roll of men of the scarcely inferior position of Hampden and Waller, commanded and officered its armies and fleets. A Puritan was the first Protestant founder of a college at an English university.

"It may be easily believed that none of the guests whom the Earl of Leicester placed at his table by the side of his nephew, Sir Philip Sidney, were clowns. But the supposition of any necessary connection between Puritanism and what is harsh and rude in taste and manners will not stand the test of even an observation of the character of the men who figured in its ranks, when the lines came to be most distinctly drawn. The Parliamentary general, Devereux, Earl of Essex, was no strait-laced gospeler, but a man formed with every grace of person, mind, and culture to be the ornament of a splendid court, the model knight, the idol, as long as he was the comrade, of the royal soldiery, the Bayard of the time. The position of Manchester and Fairfax, of Hollis, Fiennes, and Pierrepont, was by birthright in the most polished circles of English society. In the memoirs of the young regicide, Colonel Hutchinson, recorded by his beautiful and high-souled wife, we may look at the interior of a Puritan household, and see its graces, divine and human, as they shone with a naturally blended lustre in the most strenuous and most afflicted times. The renown of English learning owes something to the sect which enrolled the names of Seldon, Lightfoot, Gale, and Owen. Its seriousness and depth of thought had lent their inspiration to the delicate muse of Spenser. Judging between their colleague preachers, Traver and Hooker, the critical Templars awarded the palm of scholarly eloquence to the Puritan. When the Puritan lawyer Whitelock was ambassador to Queen Christina, he kept a magnificent state, which was the admiration of her court, perplexed as they were by his persistent Puritanical testimony against the practice of drinking healths. For his Latin secretary, the Puritan Protector employed a man at once equal to the foremost of mankind in genius and learning, and skilled in all manly exercises, proficient in the lighter accomplishments beyond any other Englishman of his day, and caressed in his youth, in France and Italy, for eminence in the studies of their fastidious scholars and artists. The king's camp and court at Oxford had not a better swordsman or amateur musician than John Milton, and his portraits exhibit him with locks as flowing as Prince Rupert's. In such trifles as the fashion of apparel, the usage of the best modern society vindicates, in characteristic particulars, the Roundhead judgment and the taste of the century before the last. The English gentleman now, as the Puritan gentleman then, dresses plainly in 'sad' colors, and puts his lace and embroidery on his servants."[1]

The Puritan was terrifically in earnest; he became self-centred, and was more influenced by that which he had within him than he was by the sense of exterior impression, but just a little more of that gracious spark of humanity and he would have given birth to a race of poets instead of a race of business men. And some were. There was Milton, the great poet of the Puritans and one of the greatest names in English literature; and the prose writings of the leaders of Puritan thought are full of poetic expression and the flash of imagination. The clearest insight into a man's character is to be gained from his letters to his wife, for the intimacy, the unrestraint of conventional expression, the revelation of aspirations, the word of affection, that mean so much to two persons in perfect sympathy, reveal the natural man, the man as he was and not as his biographer would make him. The reader who doubts the human quality in the Puritan may study with profit, and with even greater pleasure, the letters of John Winthrop to his wife.

They are admirable letters, full of sentiment and graceful allusion, with constant reference to the goodness of God and much practical advice to his son. But what particularly appeals to me, because it so conspicuously disproves the popular belief

[1] Palfrey: *History of New England*, vol. i, pp. 278–282.

that natural affection was crushed out of the Puritan, are the lover-like expressions used by this man who had long passed his first youth. "It grieves me," he writes, "that I have not liberty to make better expression of my love to thee, who art more dear to me than all earthly things." He closes a letter, as many a modern lover has written to his beloved, "so I kisse my sweet wife, and thinke longe till I see thee." Puritan though he was, there was enough of the pagan in him to know the universal language of love; for in a postscript written on February 14, 1629, he says, "thou must be my valentine, for none hath challenged me." His common salutation to his wife was "mine own sweet Self," or "mine own dear Heart"; and there are letters beginning with such extravagance of affection as "Mine owne, mine onely, my best Beloved," and "My Love, my Joy, my Faithful One."[1]

To understand the family and home life of the Puritan, the biography of Colonel Hutchinson, one of the regicides, who "could dance admirably well" and "had a great love of music," as his widow records, may be read with satisfaction.

"We are wont to think of our Puritan forbears," an American writer says, "indeed we are determined to think of them, garbed in sombre-colored garments, in a life devoid of color, warmth, or fragrance. But sad color was not dismal and dull save in name; it was brown in tone, and brown is

[1] Winthrop: *Life and Letters of John Winthrop.*

warm, and being a primitive color is, like many primitive things, cheerful. Old England was garbed in hearty honest russet, even in the days of our colonization. Read the list of the garments of any master of the manor, of the English yeoman, of our own sturdy English emigrants from manor and farm in Suffolk and Essex. What did they wear across seas? What did they wear in the New World? What they wore in England."[1]

They wore doublets and breeches of brown leather (*brown*, not gray), buff coats, russet hose. These people had an eye for color and did not despise it. We read of "Wastecoats of greene cotton bound about with red tape," of waistcoats dyed red with stammel, and of the colonists writing to England for "stammel dyes." In England, in 1586, Philip Stubbes published "an Anatomie of Abuses." He was the typical Puritan of imagination—austere, severe, a hater of the follies and wickedness of his times. He thundered against extravagance in dress, but it was the extravagance of those persons who dressed beyond their means, and not the condemnation of the rich who could properly gratify their tastes. Just as to-day our social reformers preach a crusade against the men who go into debt to maintain their pretensions, so Stubbes censured "Excesse in apparell" where it was not justified. "I would not be so understood," he quaintly writes,

[1] Earle: *Two Centuries of Costume in America*, vol. i, p. 4; *cf.* Palfrey: *History of New England*, ii, p. 63 *et seq.*

"as though my speeches extended to any either noble honourable or worshipful; for I am farre from once thinking that any kind of sumptuous or Gorgeous Attire is not to be worn of them; as I suppose them rather Ornaments in them than otherwise. And therefore when I speak of excess of Apparel my meaning is of the inferiour sorte only who for the most parte do farre surpasse either noble honourable or worshipful, ruffling in silks, Velvets, Satins, Damaske, Taffeties, Gold, Silver and what not; these bee the Abuses I speake of, these bee the Evils that I lament, and these bee the persons my words doe concern."

In the day of the Puritan, and long before he came to America, and long after America had ceased to be Puritan and become American, dress betokened rank. It had a significance then which it has long since lost. Social station and official position were marked by the clothes that men wore. It was contrary to the spirit of the age and class distinction that master and servant should sartorially find the same common expression, for if the master were not distinguished from the servant by the richness of his apparel, it might well be that a stranger should address the servant thinking he was holding speech with the master, and that would be to make the master ridiculous and destroy discipline. The Puritan was in essence a Democrat, but democracy did not mean to him the destruction of class distinction that tended to the destruction of society.

Early in the history of the Massachusetts Colony sumptuary laws were enacted, which were in keeping with the general concept of the Puritan theory of government that the lives and morals and manners of the people were not subject to the whim of the individual, but were to be regulated by the combined wisdom and experience of society. As it was in religion so it was in dress. The Puritans welcomed no creed save their own and took stern measures to repress schismatics, as we have seen in their persecution of the Quakers. They would tolerate no defiance of authority in a matter that appears to us so unimportant as dress, but which then had a significance that can be understood only by properly balancing it in its relation with life as a whole. And these struggling colonists were constantly being watched and nagged by their proprietors and guardians in England, who naturally delighted in the opportunity of being super-virtuous at the expense of their protégés, for nothing produces a greater glow of contentment in even the most lofty nature than vicarious virtues that cost nothing and cause no personal inconvenience. Governor Winthrop was reminded from London in 1636 that "many of your plantacions discover too much pride," and it was grievous sin in the eyes of the virtuous in London that some of the colonists wrote for "cut work coifes" to be sent to them.

Puritan or Parisian, seventeenth or twentieth centuries, has the feminine world ever ceased to think of the latest fashion or to long to look attractive?

Sumptuary laws were passed, and the magistrates of Massachusetts were evidently of the belief of Stubbes that there must be a sharp dividing line between the "noble and the worshipful" and they that "be base by byrth, meane by estate and servyle by calling." In 1651 the Massachusetts General Court expressed its "utter detestation that men and women of mean condition, and calling, should take vppon them the garbe of gentlemen by wearing of gold or silver lace, or buttons or poynts at their knees, or walke in great boots, or women of the same ranke wear silke or tiffany hoods or scarfs." It will be seen that there was no "utter detestation" of men and women wearing the clothes that were proper to their station in life; it was only against the lower orders aping the fashions of their betters that censure was directed. In Newbury, two years after the passage of this law, two women were "presented" for wearing silk hoods and scarfs, but they were discharged on proof that their husbands were worth £200 each. A few years later in Northampton, thirty-eight women were presented for wearing silk because they were below the degree permitted for that feminine luxury. Sixteen-year-old Hannah Lyman, a rebel at heart if there ever was one, was presented for "wearing silk in a flaunting manner, in an offensive way and garb, not only before but when she stood presented."[1] One would like to have a picture of Hannah, who, knowing the power of silk on the obtuse masculine intellect, boldly flaunted her flounces before that grave and dignified bench as if defying man ever to make woman change her fashions because of the law's decree.

Many curious mistakes have been made in the name of philology, and nothing is more interesting than to note how through the perversion of words a meaning entirely different to that which they originally possessed has been given to them. In the chronicles of the early Puritans the term "sad color" as applied to dress is frequently used, from which the modern writer has naturally but erroneously gathered the impression that "sad color" meant sombre hues, the colors that we should to-day wear to express spiritual dejection; in other words, black or dark shades. Now to the Puritans the term connoted an entirely different meaning. No further evidence is needed than a letter written by Winthrop to his wife in which he tells her that he has ordered for her a "grave gown," "not black, but sad colour." "Sad colors" in those days were the quiet tints, the same shades that the well-dressed woman of to-day, who does not want to be conspicuous, selects for her walking suit; the quiet colors as opposed to the more brilliant hues, but not

[1] Earle: *Home Life in Colonial Days*, pp. 283-284.

necessarily gray or "a dingy grayish brown — nor even a dark brown." We read distinctly in an English list of dyes of the year 1638 of these tints in these words: "Sadd-colours the following; liver colour, De Boys, tawney, russet, purple, French green, ginger-lyne, deere colour, orange colour." [1] De Boys, tawney, russet, ginger-lyne, and deere colour were various shades of brown, and brown is not now regarded as an emblem of mourning or sorrow; and there were also among the "sad colors" liver gray, which was gray with a tinge of purple; purple, green, and orange; surely variety enough to suit all tastes and complexions, and to prove that the Puritans did not restrict themselves to the use of only one shade. In those days men and women disposed of their clothing by will. A Dorchester woman who died in 1688 enumerated among other articles "best red kersey petticoate," "sad grey kersey wascote," "a blew apron," "red serge petticoat," "green searge wascotte," "green linsey woolsey petticoate," "a greene under coat," "my murry wascote," "six yards of redd cloth," "my coate and my blew wascote," "my green apron," a combination of hues diverse enough to destroy the fiction that these people loved monotony and hated color.

It would not have been surprising if the Puritan had dressed in one shade, and that dark, for the Puritan was a pioneer, and the pioneer, controlled

[1] Earle: *op. cit.*, p. 27.

by utilitarian motives and not swayed by religious or other impulses, has always selected the garb that would be most serviceable and would withstand the hardest usage and show the fewest marks of wear. The pioneers of a later day, the men who settled the West, the men of a still later day who followed the overland trail, used leather and homespun, not because they disliked color or other fabrics, but because these were most suited for their purpose. Modern military experience has taught that attractive as scarlet may be in times of peaceful parade, on active service the monotone of khaki, less pleasing to the eye, serves a much more useful purpose. The war offices of the world have simply learned the lesson that the pioneer of more than a century ago acquired by intuition and experience.

The Puritans were comfortably clothed and housed, comfortably, that is, for their time and surroundings and always remembering they were settlers in a new country, where everything to support life had to be raised by their own hands or was brought across the seas in slow-moving vessels that came at irregular intervals. As Massachusetts became systematically colonized by the London proprietors the emigrants were outfitted in no scrimping fashion. The following is an inventory of the "apparrell for 100 men," furnished to each member of Higginson's company in 1628:—

"4 peares of shoes, 4 peares of stockins, 1 peare

Norwich gaiters, 4 shirts, 2 suits dublets and hose of leather lyn'd with oyld skin leather, ye hose & doublett with hooks & eyes, 1 suit of Norden dussens or Hampshire kersies lynd the hose with skins, doublets with lynen of gilford or gedlyman kerseys, 4 bands, 2 handkerchiefs, 1 wastecoat of greene cotton bound about with red tape, 1 leather girdle, 1 Monmouth cap, 1 black hatt lyned in the brows with lether, 5 Red knitt capps mill'd, about 5d apiece, 2 peares of gloves, 1 Mandillion [mantle or great coat] lyned with cotton, 1 peare of breeches and waistcoat." [1] A larger wardrobe this than many of the descendants of these pioneers both in Old and New England now possess; and green waistcoats bound with red tape and red knit caps certainly betoken no dislike for color or a preference for "Puritan gray."

While the dress of the common people among the Puritans was simple and in keeping with their life and their surroundings, it is a mistake to suppose that men and women of station did not indulge their love of finery. That saintly and well-beloved man, Elder Brewster, boasted among his other worldly possessions a blue cloth coat, a violet-colored cloth coat, and a green waistcoat. Governor Winthrop delighted in gold lace. So eager were the women to be in fashion that the pseudo-humble follower of Saint Crispin, the Simple Cobler of Aggawam, who seems to have concerned himself

[1] Ames: *The May-Flower and Her Log*, p. 212.

more with women's souls than men's soles, vented his scorn on the "nugiperous gentledames" of the Colony who were so frivolous as to ask "what dresse the Queen is in this week," and who instead of listening to pious exhortations must needs fill their minds with the "very newest fashion of the Court"; and he poured forth all the vials of his wrath on the "woman who lives but to ape the newest court fashion" by pronouncing her "the very gizzard of a trifle, the product of a quarter of a cypher — the epitome of nothing, fitter to be kickt, if she were of a kickable substance, than either honour'd or humour'd."[1] Only a few years after the establishment of the Colony it was found necessary to enact ordinances prohibiting the wearing of short sleeves by women so as to reveal their arms; nor must women appear with "naked breasts and arms; or as it were pinioned with superstitious ribbons on hair and apparel," that is, women of mean estate. The rich have always been a law unto themselves, even in Puritan America. Pretty women might display their natural charms without fear of the law, and apparently in the sight of the favor of the Lord. We have numerous portraits of ladies in velvets and satins and laces, with bared necks and sleeves ending at the elbow. One author calls attention to the fact that a French portrait of Madame Maintenon shows precisely the same "whisk" [lace collar] as is represented in the por-

[1] *The Simple Cobler of Aggawam*, p. 20.

trait of a young, pretty, and extravagant Plymouth woman of the name of Padishal.

Sumptuary laws, it may not be amiss to point out, were not an English invention discovered in America or a peculiar institution of the Puritans, but were part of the economic and class legislation of England that the Puritans brought with them as they brought other social customs. It is partly inconscient cant and partly ignorance that make so many writers and social reformers bewail the "good old times" and deplore class distinctions and long for a return to that Arcadian age when all men were equal and there was no dividing line between rich and poor, the high and the low. Yet in the good old times, which being dead must only be mentioned in terms of eulogy, class distinctions were greater than they are to-day and social divisions were more sharply defined. To-day the beggar may wear silk if his trade is lucrative enough, and the millionaire may wear fustian if his taste runs in that direction, and society treats both with cynical indifference as the law is occupied with things more important than the regulation of dress. With all their humility and intense love of democracy the Puritans never subscribed to the doctrine of the equality of birth or intellect, but always recognized the difference existing between men as the result of birth and education and natural abilities.

Social lines were distinctly marked in the seventeenth century. Winthrop, in his state papers, writing as governor, talked of "the common people." The "common people" were whipped and set in the stocks when they misbehaved themselves; the gentry were fined and admonished.[1]

"Mayflower furniture" has become a standing joke among collectors since Americans set up genealogical trees and proved their descent from the passenger list of the Mayflower by the possession of heirlooms. If all the furniture and other belongings now proudly exhibited as the heritage of colonial ancestry had been brought over in the hold of that historic ship, she must have had the capacity of a modern transatlantic cargo vessel, and the four-posters and the highboys, the warming-pans and the candlesticks, must have overflowed from hold to cabin, and from cabin to deck, greatly to the inconvenience of the Pilgrims. Mayflower furniture, properly pedigreed, made in the vicinity of New York and some other large cities, is a lucrative trade, and by the employment of the proper agent one can find "genuine" colonial furniture as easily as your Belgian guide will produce bullets dug up that morning on the field of Waterloo.

Yet while the Colonists lived in log houses with thatched roofs, their houses sheltered them from the extremes of both heat and cold, and without

[1] Adams: *Three Episodes of Massachusetts History*, vol. i, p. 335.

"43. No man shall be beaten with above forty stripes, nor shall any true gentleman, nor any man equal to a gentleman, be punished with whipping, unless his crime be very shameful, and his course of life vicious and profligate." —*Body of Liberties*, 1641, iii. *Massachusetts Hist. Coll.*, vol. viii, p. 224.

being luxurious, as we should consider luxury in these days, they were comfortable and served their purpose admirably. Less than a quarter of a century had passed since the first migration when one of their chroniclers wrote: "The Lord hath been pleased to turn all the wigwams, huts, and hovels the English dwelt in at first coming, into orderly, fair, well built houses, well furnished, many of them, together with orchards filled with goodly fruit trees, and gardens with variety of flowers."[1] Not a picture this of squalid poverty; and another writer says that the settlers were better housed and better fed than they had been accustomed to in England.

Johnson tells of the houses "well furnished," which they were not in the modern sense, although there were furniture and household equipments enough for necessity and comfort, as comfort was understood in that day. It is probable that very little furniture, that is chairs or tables or bedsteads, was brought over on the first voyage of the Mayflower, and I am inclined to this opinion because while there is frequent mention of the cargo in authentic records, no reference is made to furniture; but I admit this is not conclusive, as furniture may simply have been regarded as household belongings and therefore not important enough to be separately listed. But later furniture was undoubtedly sent over from England, and it is undisputed

[1] Johnson: *The Wonder Working Providence of Sion's Saviour*, p. 174.

that many of the well-to-do colonists brought with them some of those pieces of mahogany that Americans now prize so dearly. Forks in that day were practically unknown and silver was to be found only on the tables of the rich, but there were spoons and dishes of pewter, candlesticks of brass and iron, coarse sheets and blankets, and with greater social requirements came the luxury of tablecloths.

At first there was often great scarcity of food, as is natural among a new people in a strange land unfamiliar with the soil and climatic conditions and ill provided with proper implements of husbandry. In 1622 Bradford, in that history of which Senator Hoar has said "there is nothing like it in human annals since the story of Bethlehem,"[1] wrote "famine begane now to pinch them sore,"[2] but they were saved from starvation by the unexpected arrival of a ship, whose captain was able to spare them a small supply of provisions, so scant, however, that "it arose to but a quarter of a pound of bread a day to each person; and ye Govr caused it to be daily given them, otherwise had it been in their own custody, they would have eate it & then starved. But thus, with what els they could get, they made pretie shift till corne was ripe."[3] On more than one occasion they were driven to "pretie shifts" to fend off starvation, there were times when starva-

[1] Address before the Massachusetts Legislature, May 26, 1897.

[2] Bradford: *History of Plimouth Plantation*, p. 150.

[3] Bradford, *op. cit.*, p. 151.

tion and disease made sad inroads into their ranks, but in a comparatively few years after their landing the question of food no longer troubled them. They came to no sterile land. America is peculiarly a land of Nature's bounty, where the earth and the waters yield to man their riches. A year before the time when Bradford wrote of the pinch of famine, he notes the great store they took of "codd, & bass & other fish," and as winter approached "began to come in store of foule." "Beside water foule, ther was great store of wild Turkies, of which they took many, besides venison &c. Besids they had aboute a peck of meale a week to a person, or now since harvest, Indean corne to yt proportion. Which made many afterwards write so largely of their plenty hear to their friends in England, which were not fained, but true reports."[1]

I would not be understood as implying that life was soft and easy for these people, that they were surrounded with great luxury and comfort, or that they were required to put forth little exertion to support themselves. Life was hard and a constant struggle, they were in perpetual danger from their enemies, they were very often at first, as we have seen, menaced by starvation, while disease and sickness must yield to empirical methods or claim them. But it was no hopeless or despairing struggle in which they engaged, it was no barren or fever-stricken land which they planted. Even in that

[1] Bradford, *op. cit.*, p. 127.

early day it was a land of hope and promise, demanding incessant toil and the qualities of industry and fortitude that so conspicuously distinguished these settlers, but holding the reward of rich return for labor intelligently directed and inspired by the determination to succeed.

In the air of traditional gloom that surrounds the Puritan we see him sourly condemning all innocent amusements and acting as a killjoy, rather than fostering those normal pleasures of the people that were supposed to mark the light-hearted joyousness of the masses of Merry England. But the sports of the English people were not so innocent as they appear now, filtered through the pages of writers, colored by their surroundings; and in an age when life was held less sacred and passion was unrestrained by convention, brutality was mated with pleasure. It is an idyllic picture we have of the Maypole set up on the village green, innocent young girls dancing about it garlanded with flowers, the men with rough good humor finding pleasure in cracking each other over the heads with quarter staves or bending their sinews in wrestling bouts. This is the stage-setting familiar to every student of English literature who plaintively but sincerely regrets that the good old times with their simple amusements have passed away; but few know that before the Maypole was set up rural England imitated the practices of Rome and spent a night of saturnalia in the woods. The Puritans frowned, not on the innocent pleasures of the Maypole, but on the immorality that had been sanctioned by custom to be part of its observances. For the same reason, the worrying to death by dogs of a chained bull or bear was as repugnant to men of a finer nature as the slaughter of rats by a terrier is to the great majority of decent men to-day. But the gentle Puritan might still take part in a sporting event. Bull-baiting and cockfighting he banned, but the wolf, who was his natural enemy, might be harried and hunted, and wolf-baiting was as popular in New England as bull-baiting was in Old England.

Many of the customs of Old England the Puritans brought with them, but some of them were wisely left behind, and the saturnalian observance of the first of May was not to their liking. When Morton set up his Maypole at Merry Mount, "drinking and dancing aboute it many days together, inviting the Indean women, for their consorts, dancing and frisking together, (like so many fairies, or furies rather,) and worse practices. As if they had anew revived & celebrated the feasts of ye Roman Goddes Flora, or ye beastly practices of ye madd Bacchinalians," as Bradford tells us, the Puritans were naturally shocked, and saw the necessity, for moral no less than social reasons, for the maintenance of discipline as well as to prevent the corruption of the Indians, of promptly suppressing such improper and dangerous proceedings. The Maypole was cut down and Governor Endicott "rebuked them for their profannes, and admonished them to look ther should be better walking." The Puritans frowned on the theatre, because the drama of that age was an appeal to lust and passion; it was profane and gross; it emphasized the worst side of man and woman; the vice of the English people was gambling, and gaming was sternly prohibited; dancing was also under the ban because it was associated in the Puritan mind with "worse practices."

But in their own way the Puritans found means of amusement. Many writers have attempted to demonstrate that in every observance of every relation of life the Puritan gave to it a religious symbolism, and in support of that they point to an institution peculiarly American, Thanksgiving. Now here again we see how institutions lose their original meaning, precisely as certain words are given a modern interpretation quite foreign to their significance a century or so ago. The *raison d'être* for the modern Thanksgiving is to give praise for Divine blessings, and many persons in obedience to the suggestion of the President and Governors go to church, but the majority regard the day as a secular holiday and treat it as a pause in their daily toil instead of to be set apart for the searching of hearts. And in this they simply follow the example set by the Pilgrims (again there is that confusion of associating events with the Puritan that belonged to the Pilgrims) when they celebrated their first Thanksgiving. Mourt in his *Relation* shows that it was a holiday and not a holy day, and there is not the slightest hint that it was given a religious observance. "Our harvest being gotten in," the chronicler writes, "our Governor sent foure men on fowling, that we might after a more special manner rejoice together, after we had gathered the fruits of our labors. They foure in one day killed as much fowle, as, with a little help beside, served the Company almost a weeke, at which time, amongst other Recreations, we exercised our Arms, many of the Indians coming amongst us, and amongst the rest, their greatest King, Massasoyt, with some ninety men, whom for three days we entertained and feasted, and they went out and killed five Deere, which they brought to the Plantation, and bestowed on our Governor, and vpon the Captaine, and others."[1] Entertainment and feasting for three days and the exercise of arms, which the modern writer would express as a military parade, do not convey the impression of a day of gloom, which began with church services and ended with the whole community painfully reading the Bible as a matter of duty and longing for the day to close and bring with it relief from this oppressive method of thanking the Lord for His manifold blessings. The periodical fast days and feast days, sanctified by the ancient reverence of the

[1] *Mourt's Relation*, p. 133.

Church, were scrupulously disregarded and discountenanced in New England. But, for special occasions, fasts and thanksgivings were frequently observed by the whole community, or by single churches; and after a time, in the place of Good Friday and of Christmas, a Fast Day was regularly kept at the season of annual planting, and a feast day (Thanksgiving) at the time of the ingathering of the harvest.[1]

The hard-faced, atrabilious, earnest-eyed race, stiff from long wrestling with the Lord in Prayer, and who had taught Satan to dread the new Puritan hug [2] is a familiar figure, but Puritan humor is less often remembered. To pun may be the lowest form of humor and indicative of only a rudimentary perception of wit, but it at least shows that there is an appreciation of the lighter side of life. The writings of the Puritan reveal this tendency, and a vein of dry, sarcastic, ironic humor is to be found in their sermons and religious discourses. It was humor not without its sting, but it evidenced that they had a lively sense of the ridiculous and were not averse to malevolent pleasantry. Yankee wit has become proverbial, and it survives in the literature that is typical of Massachusetts, in the writings of Lowell and Holmes; in a lesser degree it may be found in the works of Emerson and Hawthorne, and it occasionally flashes out in Whittier.

[1] Palfrey: *History of New England*, vol. ii, p. 44; *cf.* W. DeLoss Love, Jr.: *The Fast and Thanksgiving Days of New England.*

[2] Lowell: *Biglow Papers.*

Was the Puritan really as austere as he has been represented, or does he merely appear so when seen through the softened light of to-day? In comparison with the men of his own time he was an uncomfortable person with a fixed idea, and all men of fixed ideas are uncomfortable to the great mass, which never rises above mediocrity because of its constitutional inability to concentrate; because it scatters what few thoughts it has and dissipates its energies instead of bringing all its force to bear on the particular work in hand. Ability is pertinacity.

In England, after the Restoration, there was a very natural tendency not only to reverse everything that Puritanism had accomplished politically, but socially to seek revenge for the rigid morality that Puritanism had imposed; to do everything that Puritanism frowned on was to show the contempt in which Puritanism was held. It was this reaction that, to a large extent, was responsible for the vice and profligacy of the court and the low moral tone of politics for the next hundred and fifty years succeeding the death of the Protector. In America the same causes operated. With the downfall of the theocratic state, with the beginning of the end of colonial isolation and the bringing of the colonies into a quasi-political entity which sowed the seminal principle of political union, with the great impetus given to expansion, there was a rebound from the weight which Puritanism had laid on men and a temptation to scoff at the things which had been held sacred. It is a singular fact that most of the American historians have been anti-Puritan, and even those historical writers who are descended from the Puritans have been influenced by the prevailing popular opinion and, as if to show their superiority to their ancestors and make parade of their "liberality," either sneer at those qualities of the Puritan that made them a race apart or else seek to extenuate the virtues of an age that are vices when seen through the eyes of a more advanced and refined civilization.

CHAPTER XIII

THE FOUNDATION ON WHICH THE AMERICAN CHARACTER RESTS

THIS is a convenient point to recapitulate briefly what has been said in the last six chapters. My aim has been to show the solid foundation on which the American character has been slowly built. These things are to be remembered:—

First. That it was the Puritan and not the Pilgrim who founded American institutions.

Second. That Pilgrim and Puritan are not synonymous terms, and that Pilgrim and Puritan had little if anything in common.

Third. That while the Pilgrim was a separatist from the Church of England and conceded the right of every man to worship God in his own way, the Puritan was a Church of England man and tolerated no other form of worship.

Fourth. That the Puritan was in all things an Englishman. He brought with him to America English institutions, English morals, the English mental attitude. He was an Englishman in America as he had always been an Englishman in England.

Fifth. That the Bible was the Constitution of the

Puritan state. It was a civil no less than a religious and a moral code.

Sixth. That Puritanism, beginning as a religious movement, soon became political, and was the force that made the English people assert their rights against the oppression of the Crown and those set in authority over them, both spiritual and temporal. It made the Puritan always ready to resist constituted authority when his conscience demanded it. It sowed the seeds of democracy. It was not only religious and political, but it was also economic. It was, summing up everything in one word, one of the greatest *Social* movements the world has ever known.

Seventh. That the Puritan, while austere and fanatical and much given to morbid introspection, was neither without natural human affections, nor a sense of humor, nor averse to rational amusement.

Eighth. That the Puritan lived neither in squalor nor in abject poverty. For his day and generation he was well found; in many respects better clothed and fed and housed than the mass of the English people living in England.

Ninth. That the English Puritan who emigrated to America, by the force of circumstances, by his environment and climatic influences, by his social, moral and political code, diverged from the parent stock, and in less than a century after his migration produced a new race.

And *tenth,* and finally. The Puritan was a human Englishman and not a miraculous or a mythical creation.

With these facts established it becomes easier to understand how it came about that in the fullness of time there was to be born a new race in America.

CHAPTER XIV

TOBACCO AND SLAVERY

We turn now to the South and retrace our steps a few years. The psychology of the men who first settled Virginia does not require the detailed study given to the Puritans. Social conditions in Massachusetts were different from Virginia, which more nearly reproduced those of England on a smaller scale. The theocracy which was set up in Massachusetts found no lodgment in Virginia. Each community followed its natural impulse, and each developed along certain lines that were to mark the distinction between the North and South. The character of Massachusetts was laid in its theocratic system, that of Virginia in its system of slavery and the production of tobacco; and the effect of those influences, tobacco and slavery, we are now to see. The American character was formed no less by Virginia than it was by Massachusetts, and each contributed its own share to that composite and complex nature.

In 1607, thirteen years before the little band of Pilgrims found meagre shelter on the inhospitable coast of Massachusetts, a company of Englishmen laid the foundation for a Greater England at Jamestown in Virginia. "I shall yet live to see Virginia an English nation," Raleigh with inspired vision wrote to Sir Robert Cecil shortly before the accession of James I, and the prophecy was fulfilled. It was the Puritan who was the heart of the new civilization, who brought to the New World a new concept of life and who gave birth to a new system of political philosophy, but it was the Virginian who gave to the heart its life's blood and supplied an element that saved a theocracy from subordinating the liberties of a people to the narrow and iron bound rule of the church. Had the original design of the first settlers of Massachusetts succeeded, had this New England across the sea been merely the old morality amidst new surroundings, had the church grasped the power which for long centuries it fought to retain and made America church-governed and priest-ridden, the story which has been written in the last three centuries would have a different meaning.

It has been the fashion to talk of Puritan New England and Cavalier Virginia, and inexact historians and careless writers have created the misleading impression that the men who first settled Virginia were drawn from a higher social scale than the Puritans, and that morally and intellectually they were their superiors. The legend of the South is no less fantastic than that of the North. Whatever the vices or the faults of these founders of a nation they were first of all men, and the majority of them, those who survived and from whose loins the nation sprung, were strong, courageous men who would have laughed at attempts of dilettante admirers to effeminize them.

That the Virginians at the beginning were "aristocrats," to distinguish them from the "plain people" who planted Massachusetts, is as mythical as the common belief that Puritanism stamped out all natural affection and sunk its believers in perpetual gloom. Between the Englishman who in the early days of the seventeenth century went to Virginia and the Englishman who later followed him to Massachusetts there is little difference, and that difference is in favor of the men who established themselves in the north. More than a half of these first planters of Virginia "were poor gentlemen who were unaccustomed to manual labor and despised it; many were small tradesmen or servants; some are described as jewelers, gold refiners, and a perfumer"; not the stuff out of which empires are fashioned, and yet they were the beginnings of Virginia. The Puritan of the early days was animated by a very high and noble purpose, mistaken as we now see his views and aspirations often were, but every man who clings steadfastly to an ideal is the better for it. The Virginian was under no such influence. Religious persecution, sublime devotion to a higher cause, a passionate craving for the spiritual, did not drive him forth. He went to Virginia as an adventurer, with the spirit of the gambler and the speculator in him, to find there the fortune which had eluded him at home. And in the early days many of them went there because they had no option, because they were criminals and paupers; they were transported by the Government, as in later days English criminals were sent to Botany Bay.

An Englishman whose book on Slavery appeared shortly after the outbreak of the Civil War and was much quoted at the time, has with diligent dullness packed a surprising amount of misinformation into a couple of pages. "Massachusetts and the other New England States," he tells us, "were colonized principally from the *élite* of the middle and lower classes — by people who, being accustomed to labour with their hands, would feel less need of slaves; and who, moreover, owing to their political views, having little to hope for in the way of assistance from the country they had quitted, would have little choice but to trust to their own personal exertions. On the other hand, the early emigration to Virginia, Maryland, and the Carolinas was for the most part composed of the sons of gentry, whose ideas and habits but ill fitted them for the struggle with nature in the wilderness. Such emigrants had little disposition to engage personally in the work of clearance and production, nor were they under the same necessity for this as their brethren in the north; for, being composed in great part of cavaliers and loyalists, they were, for many years after the first establishment of the settlements, sustained and petted by the home government; being furnished not merely with capital in the shape of constant supplies of provisions and clothing, but with laborers in the shape of convicts, indented servants, and slaves. In this way the colonists of the Virginia group were relieved of the necessity of personal toil, and in this way, it is said, slavery, which found little footing in the North, and never took firm root there, became established in the Southern States." [1]

As a matter of fact, Virginia instead of being petted was exploited for British profit, as was customary in a day when a colony was simply regarded as valuable according to the revenue it put into the pockets of its proprietors. "We find one governor recommending that an act of Parliament should be passed forbidding the Virginians to make their own clothes. If the British merchants complained of one of the colony's laws it was promptly suspended." Charles I "petted" his royal colony by trying to obtain a monopoly of its tobacco crop. Nor does the careful historian forget that Navigation Act passed in the interest of English merchants and shipowners and aimed at the growing competition of Virginia and the other American colonies, which led to the first defiance of English authority when Nathaniel Bacon indicted Sir William Berkeley for abusing his Majesty's prerogative.

From such statements as this and those of other writers it has come to be commonly believed that while there was a fashionable, highly cultivated and

[1] Cairnes: *The Slave Power*, pp. 34–35.

amusement-loving society in Virginia, in New England society was rough and uncultured and dull; that the gay young blades who made things lively went to Virginia, and the good young men of sanctimonious mien were sent to New England to add to the general gloom. The golden age of the colonies was from the end of the seventeenth century to the middle of the next, and it was during that time that Virginia became a land of large estates, around which cluster so many historical memories and romantic associations. George Washington came into possession of Mount Vernon and its 2500 acres in 1755; across the river at Belvoir was the Fairfax estate; it was from the "White House" in New Kent County that Washington took the young and comely widow of Daniel Parke Custis and made her his wife. To mention any of those estates is to recall the history of the colonial era and to see again these pleasure-loving Englishmen, but who were men of affairs as well as of pleasure. The life of the Virginian was lived in the country, that of the New Englander in the city or settlement, and allowing for the difference between rural and urban life, men of the same class found their pleasures in much the same way. If sprigs of nobility went to Virginia and brought with them the fashions and manners of the court, New England did not suffer because of the absence of mentors. Around the governors of the various New England provinces, we are told, there was in each capital "a little circle of card-playing, horse-racing, fox-hunting court attendants, who naturally wore the best dress in the province; English younger sons sent to America to sober down, where they proceeded to liven America up. The constant correspondence of the governor and his officials with England kept this circle fully informed upon all the changes in dress; and many of these letters, both private and official, have been preserved. From them we gain an excellent notion of the importance of good dress, and the prevalence of good dress in the colonies, and of good living in every respect — furniture, carriages, wine, food. There were proportionately more carriages in Boston than in Lincoln. Many had coaches."[1]

In Boston the influence of the royal governor and his staff established a miniature court, which closely imitated English dress and manners, and rivalled English luxury. An English traveller, Bennett, wrote of Boston in 1740, "Both the ladies and gentlemen dress and appear as gay in common as courtiers in England on a coronation or birthday." Whitefield complained bitterly of the "foolish virgins of New England covered all over with the pride of life"; of the jewels, patches, and gay apparel commonly worn.[2]

But in Virginia, at the beginning, it was different. If the colony were to live, it was necessary to have

[1] Earle: *Two Centuries of Costume in America*, vol. ii, p. 339.

[2] Earle: *op. cit.*

labor, and Virginia at that time offering no great inducement to the thrifty or capable Englishman to begin a new life, recourse was had to involuntary servitude. Sir Thomas Dale, one of the early governors, a man of force and character, thus bitterly writes to the Earl of Salisbury on August 17, 1611:—

"Nor can I conceive how sutch people as we are inforced to bring over hither by peradventure, and gathering them up in sutch riotous, lasie and infected places can intertaine themselves with other thoughts or put on other behaviour than what accompanies sutch disordered persons, so prophane, so riotous, so full of Mutenie and treasonable Intendments, as I am well to witness in a parcell of 300 which I brought with me, of which well may I say not many give testimonie besides their names that they are Christians, besides of sutch diseased and crased bodies as the Sea hither and this Clime but a little searching them, render them so unhable, fainte, and desperate of recoverie as of 300 not three score may be called forth or imploied upon any labour or service."[1]

A year before, the "Council of Virginea" in London had found it necessary to exercise more care in the selection of immigrants, and in "a publication touching the Plantation there" it gave public notice "that former experience hath too dearly taught, how much and manie waies it

[1] Brown: *The Genesis of the United States*, vol. i, p. 506.

hurteth to suffer Parents to disburden themselves of lascivious sonnes, masters of bad servants and wives of ill husbands, and so clogge the business with such an idle crue, as did thrust themselves in the last voiage, that will rather starve for hunger, than lay their hands to labor."[1]

But even before Dale, that romantic figure John Smith, who was none too fastidious in his tastes, complained of the quality of the material out of which he was to fashion an English nation. Germans and Poles were sent over to make pitch, tar, soap, ashes, and glass, when the colony could not yet raise provisions enough for its support. "When you send again," Smith was obliged to reply, "I entreat you rather send but thirty carpenters, husbandmen, fishermen, than a thousand of such as we have."[2]

The only drawback to the prosperity of the colony, Doyle tells us, was the abject character of the settlers. But so insistent was the demand for labor that Dale recommended that England follow the example of Spain and "banish hither all offenders condemned to die out of common gaols." As late as 1670 a Virginian statute prohibited the further importation of criminals because of "the great number of felons and other desperate villains sent hither from the several prisons of England," showing that long after the Cavalier migration the practice of disposing of undesirables by shipping them

[1] Brown: *op. cit.*, vol. i, p. 355.

[2] Bancroft: *History of the United States of America*, vol. i, p. 95.

to Virginia continued. "There has been a natural tendency among Americans," an American historian observes, "to insist that the offenses of which the transported malefactors had been convicted were chiefly political," [1] and some American writers have made what they consider a strong case in being able to cite that after the battle of Worcester 1610 prisoners were sent to Virginia; and two years later a license was granted to one Richard Nethersole to transport a hundred Irish Tories to Virginia; but these exceptions are rare, and the number of political prisoners of whom we have knowledge is small compared with the large number of criminals and malefactors; and it is a matter of record that the death sentence was often commuted to banishment to Virginia.[2] There was also another class from which the colony was recruited, men who were not criminals but whose lot was unbearable, or ne'er-do-wells who welcomed any change for the better. These men, and later women of the same class, sold themselves into a form of limited slavery by becoming "indentured servants." For the price of transportation and subsistence they bound themselves to work for masters for a term of years, and at the expiration of their service they were released from bondage and had to shift for themselves. "Cheap labour is supplied by white servants, bound to their

[1] Avery: *A History of the United States and its People*, vol. ii, p. 58.

[2] After the restoration, in 1662, thirty-four members of the Privy Council were constituted a Council for Foreign Plantations, who were instructed to consider the supply of servile labor to the colonies.

masters by indentures for some such term as six or seven years; they are to some extent a shiftless and degraded set of creatures from the slums and jails of English seaport towns, but many of them are of a better sort."[1]

Much has been written about these indentured servants, a few of whom entered into bondage of their own volition; while others, paupers and criminals, were sold into limited slavery without their consent. Some of them at the end of their period of service became men of substance and founded families and fortunes, but they were the exception. But although these serfs became free, they did not become independent; there were causes, as we shall see later, that made them dependent on their former masters.

Prejudice and ignorance have gone to the other extreme, and attempts have been made to prove that the founders of what for convenience may be called the aristocracy of Virginia and the South were these paupers and criminals, and Defoe and other seventeenth century English writers sedulously cultivate that impression. While the Southerner as a rule is very proud of his Cavalier descent and glories in it as much as the Northerner does in being able to trace his blood through the veins of the men who founded Massachusetts, there have been Southern writers who hold the Cavaliers in light esteem, just as there have been men of Puri-

[1] Fiske: *Old Virginia and Her Neighbours*, vol. i, p. 217.

tan stock who were the severest critics of Puritanism. The remark of Robert Toombs in 1860, "We are the gentlemen of this country," was characteristic of the passion of the time and the contempt the South had for the North; but a well-known Virginian writer, Huge Blair Grigsby, had no high regard for the Cavalier, whom he describes as "essentially a slave, a compound slave, a slave to the king and a slave to the Church. I look with contempt on the miserable figment which seeks to trace the distinguishing points of the Virginian character to the influence of those butterflies of the British aristocracy." Mr. Grigsby was not happy in his simile. Pleasure loving these Cavaliers were, men who loved the light and sun and color, but that stout old Cavalier Governor with a temper "peevish and brittle," Sir William Berkeley, was no butterfly, and Strafford and Laud beat their wings with some purpose.

Instead of arbitrarily and empirically attributing the difference between Massachusetts and Virginia to the temperamental difference that marks Roundhead and Cavalier, it would be more correct to ascribe it to physical and economic conditions. The Massachusetts man grew corn. The Virginian planted tobacco. It was the difference between life in a village and life on a feudal estate. The world's greatest luxury, which has become one of the world's greatest necessities, worked a social and political revolution that was to have lasting and far-reaching consequences. "A true history of tobacco would be the history of English and American liberty," Moncure Conway aptly remarks, but it would be more than that, it would be the history of the times from Jamestown to the civil war. When in 1612 John Rolfe, that "honest and discreet young Englishman," began the systematic cultivation of Virginia tobacco little could he foresee that as the unconscious instrument of fate he had become the American Cadmus, and that his tiny Indian weed should bring forth a crop of armed men who would build a greater and more enduring Thebes.

Virginia is a land of rivers, "a kind of sylvan Venice," as Fiske poetically describes it. The men of Massachusetts had to hew their way through the unbroken forest, and before their settlements could expand they must clear the wilderness and engage in the laborious task of road-making, and the path of English civilization is marked by good roads, a legacy inherited from Roman ancestors. The Virginian found his roads already built in the navigable rivers, which gave him cheap and convenient transportation for his products to the seaboard and thence to his great market in England; but this very facility of transport destroyed the sense of community and made less necessary the small and compact settlements, where every one must do his share in the common work. The London Company that planted Virginia gave to the world the first striking illustration of the fallacy of communism. The early settlers were members of an industrial army, whose labor was for the community, and who shared equally in what it produced, but that was no incentive to work, and, as usual, the idle fattened off the industrious. Dale, displaying that rare common sense that ever marked him, changed the system and gave to every man the proper incentive by being able to profit from his own endeavors. Instead of being a communist the colonist became a small land proprietor, and the change had marked effect. Idleness and wretchedness gave way to industry and reasonable plenty, and the later settler knew none of the horrors of famine that had made the early days of the colony such a grim story.

When the first Englishmen came to Virginia they found the Indians cultivating tobacco on a small scale. It was John Rolfe, the first Englishman in the New World to marry a "foreigner" by taking to wife Pocahontas, the daughter of Powhatan, who began to experiment with tobacco, and a few years later its cultivation, "by far the most momentous fact in the history of Virginia in the seventeenth century,"[1] had become firmly established. Very quickly the Virginians saw they had in tobacco a commodity which could always find its market, and from this time on it changed the whole course of events. It not only modified social conditions,

[1] Bruce: *Economic History of Virginia*, vol. ii, p. 566.

but it produced a new economic *r'gime.* A clear and positive inducement was now offered for emigration such as had not existed since the first dreams of gold and silver were dispelled. After the first disillusionment it became difficult to persuade men of hard sense to go to Virginia, and we have seen what a wretched set of people were drawn together by the Company's communistic schemes. But those who came to acquire wealth by raising tobacco were of a better sort, men of businesslike ideas, who knew what they wanted and how to devote themselves to the task of getting it. With the establishment of tobacco culture there began a steady improvement in the character and fortunes of the colonists, and the demand for their staple in Europe soon became so great as forever to end the possibility of perishing from want. Henceforth whatever a Virginian needed he could buy with tobacco.[1]

To raise tobacco profitably it must be grown on a large scale, and the little garden patch of the first cultivators soon gave way to the plantation of many acres; and properly to care for the growing plants, to harvest the crop, to cure and prepare the weed for market, required a large increase of agricultural labor. Conditions in England were peculiarly propitious to stimulate emigration, just as two centuries later they were the exciting cause to turn that human stream from Ireland to the land of hope and

[1] Fiske: *Old Virginia and Her Neighbours,* vol. i, p. 170.

promise. The sixteenth and seventeenth centuries witnessed the splendid growth of England's greatness and rang with the deeds of her great captains and adventurers who laid the foundation for her commercial supremacy and that vast over-sea empire, but the condition of the mass of the peasantry—and there existed at that time a peasantry in the true sense of the word—was deplorable. In reviewing an age when sociological investigation was unknown and the science of statistics had not yet been discovered, we are hampered by the absence of exact knowledge, but there is enough information obtainable to show that much discontent existed, and the constantly increasing poverty and degradation of the peasantry occupied the serious attention of thinking men. There had been an enormous rise in prices, but no corresponding increase in wages. The farmer was in every way better off and living in more comfort and luxury than he had before known, but the class on whose labor the farmer depended for his prosperity, the agricultural laborer, was sinking lower and lower.

It was natural that this state of affairs should swell the ranks of the vagrants and the criminals, that to the idle and the worthless as well as the industrious and worthy the opportunity of beginning a new life under more favorable circumstances should be regarded with sullen resignation or keen enthusiasm. The emigrant has always been drawn from the two extremes of the moral and temperamental scale; he has either been devil-loving or God-fearing; the failure, the unstable man, who having tried everything has made a success of nothing because he has neither industry nor application, and who turns to emigration as he has played with everything else; the resolute, courageous man, practical but imaginative, who sees the future and has the pluck to grapple with it; the weak, who is alone responsible for his own misfortune; the strong, who having succeeded is self-reliant enough to know that with larger opportunity there will come to him a greater measure of success.

Times were ripe for recruiting Virginia from the slums of London and the rural villages of England, and an inducement was offered by the London proprietors to their grantees to engage in this traffic. The men who subscribed to the company, its financiers and original promoters, were given vast tracts of land and became really feudal lords; others of smaller means could obtain a grant by paying their own passage, and for every "servant" they brought with them a further allotment of land was made. A rare combination of circumstances made the scheme dovetail to a nicety. In tobacco lay the wealth of the Virginian, to raise tobacco he must have a large plantation, to take care of his plantation he must have a large body of laborers; the larger the number of laborers the greater the number of his acres, and England was the breeding-ground to supply his manual labor.

It may be convenient to bear in mind a few dates. It was in 1612 that John Rolfe began the cultivation of tobacco, and in 1616 his example had been generally followed, and tobacco became the life of the colony. Charles I was sentenced in 1649, forty-two years after the first settlers landed in Jamestown, and the great Cavalier exodus from England did not begin until the rigors of the Commonwealth drove these broken followers of a lost cause into exile. When they came they found no handful of shivering, ill-housed adventurers, gaunt with famine and dying from disease, as Lord Delaware had found forty years earlier. They came to no "starving time." These Cavaliers, driven forth from England by political persecution as the Puritans had been driven forth by religious persecution more than a quarter of a century before, came to a land that smiled on them and invited them to remain, a land that welcomed them with the caressing softness of a woman's wiles; a land where the skies were bright and the air balmy, where there were streams to be fished and game to be hunted, where there was good cheer in abundance. It was a prosperous and, for that time, large community to which they came. There were no signs of poverty or distress. The wooden houses were roomy and well aired, "and the settlers already point to them with some degree of pride as more comfortable than the houses of laboring men in England." This was in 1624, and the succeeding quarter of a century had still further improved their material conditions. They found there, also, many Puritans, most of whom had come from the bleak north, but many had emigrated from England. It detracts nothing from the greatness of the Cavaliers and their descendants, those really great men who did so much to make the greatness of America and to give birth to a nation, to the memory of Washington and the fame of Madison and Monroe, Lee and Jefferson and Jackson, the descendants of Cavaliers, to state the facts of history.

In a previous chapter I have dwelt at some length on the effect of climatic conditions and physical environment on race development, and it is a subject of such vast importance and so little has its significance been understood and appreciated, that I feel compelled again to refer to it, because of the bearing it has on the study of the American people as we trace their origin through Virginia and Massachusetts. The American to-day does not understand why the men of his own race living in the East are different from those of the West, although he recognizes and admits this difference, but with a hasty generalization, conveniently and quickly to dispose of a too complex problem that has no immediate bearing on the things of the hour, attributes it to the fact that the West is "new" and the East is "old." But age, that is a relative term only. Far deeper than mere years in forming character and habits of thought are those towering mountains, those arid plains, those long, burning summers, those winters of Arctic-like severity, that feeling of boundless space and unlimited opportunity, that is the inheritance of every Westerner. One must be of the West to know and share this feeling. The Westerner may live in a city, a great city that is a part of the complex scheme of civilization, a city whose sudden extinction would for so long as it takes men to recover from their astonishment disarrange the complex scheme, and yet it is not the city that makes him what he is, but it is the unconscious influence of environment. The city is to him what the port is to the sailor; but it is the ocean that the sailor loves, not the port; it is the battle with, and the mastery over the ocean that make the sailor what he is; it is the struggle and the victory, the risk and the toil, the constant vigilance, the hope, the despair, the final triumph; the self-reliance wrought out of danger, the majesty and scorn and treachery of the implacable foe that have bred a race of conquerors. And all that the sea is to the sailor to an adventurous people is a great and only partially developed country, where mountains must be tunnelled, and rivers spanned, and plains brought under cultivation; where space, illimitable space, makes men breathe deep, where mountains and plains speak of the infinite and are a perpetual challenge to the daring to conquer or to be crushed.

The Appalachian Mountains, which stretch from

New England to the South, are in New England only from fifty to eighty miles from the coast, while in the south they are two hundred and fifty miles from the ocean. Physical conditions, therefore, made the Englishman who settled in Massachusetts cling close to the coast and did not affect his territorial ideas. The Englishman who went to Virginia had a much larger area in which to work, and soon acquired that desire for expansion which later became a part of the early American character. In New England, which had long lain under a heavy glacial deposit, much and arduous work was required before the land could be broken with the plough; in Virginia the land "produceth, with very great increase, whatsoever is committed into the Bowells of it," writes an enthusiastic anonymous pamphleteer, in 1649,[1] and he regrets that those industrious New Englanders had not planted themselves in Virginia, for in New England so sterile was the soil that "except a herring be put into the hole that you set the corn or maize in, it will not come up"; while in Virginia is "a fat rich soile everywhere watered with many fine springs, small rivulets, and wholesome waters." It was a very delightful land to which these people had been led. The winters were keen, but the summers were long and warm, which invited the free, outdoor life so dear to the heart of the Englishman, who thinks in brick and mortar, but loves nature. The great

[1] "A Perfect Description of Virginia," Force, vol. ii, p. 8.

woods, the long stretches of greensward, the rivers teeming with life, the abundance of game, the fertility of the soil, made a strong appeal to him, and induced him soon to expand beyond the limits of the original settlement, and inclination had a powerful stimulus in necessity.

The cultivation of tobacco requires a virgin soil. As soon as the land was cleared it was planted in tobacco, and as artificial fertilization was then unknown and the scientific rotation of crops had not been learned, in from three to eight years the land was exhausted and worthless for tobacco planting. When the plantations could no longer be worked with profit they were abandoned, the forest was again invaded and the frontier of the settlement still further pushed into the wilderness. In 1685, "although the population of Virginia did not exceed the number of inhabitants in the single parish of Stepney, London, nevertheless they had acquired ownership in plantations that spread over the same area as England itself."[1] Under this state of affairs there naturally grew up a class of great landed proprietors. Conditions, it would seem, should have created a class of *mètayer* tenants, or peasant proprietors, from whom would have sprung the yeomanry of America as their forbears had been the yeomanry of England. The causes that arrested this social condition are obscure, and there is little in contemporary writings or in the researches of

[1] Semple: *American History and its Geographic Conditions*, p. 44.

later investigators to throw much light on the subject. It is possible that in the early days of the colony there was no intermediate class between the landowners, the proprietors or the representatives of the proprietors of the London Company, and the sweepings of the jail and the slums, the indentured servants or the victims of the kidnappers who in effect had been sold into slavery. Between the servants of the company and their masters there existed a wide gulf not lightly to be bridged in a day when class distinctions were so firmly established, and there was nothing in the political or social organization of the colony that would bring men together or make them forget class in the perils of a common danger. "In none of the other colonies were class distinctions so clearly marked and so thoroughly believed in. After the negroes came the indented servants and poor whites, with a distinct position from which few of them arose; then the middle class of small proprietors, who were distinct but constantly rising into the class of the great landlords who were the rulers of the province, the creators of opinion, and always the most typical and representative men of Virginia. There was a constant effort to maintain position or to acquire it."[1]

In New England the life was that of a community bound together by every consideration of necessity and always fearing a relentless and treacherous foe,

[1] Fisher: *Men, Women, and Manners in Colonial Times*, vol. i, p. 70.

but in Virginia this ever-present menace of an Indian massacre did not exist. Many of the indentured servants eventually worked out their period of bondage and as free men, "redemptioners," as they then were, ought to have become peasantry to feed the yeomanry, as the yeomanry has always fed and revitalized the aristocracy. But when that time came it was too late, for Virginia was then a colony of great landed proprietors, and there was no place for the yeoman with his small holdings. Doyle's conclusion, I think, is correct that "just as in earlier English history the free socage tenant often surrendered that position and voluntarily took a dependent place in the feudal chain, so we may believe that in Virginia the small holder would find his position untenable, and seek security and society where it alone could be had, on the plantation of his richer neighbor." [1] With the continued increase in the growth and wealth of the colony and an insistent demand for cheap agricultural labor, which placed no premium on intelligence but was only valued according to its strength and docility, the opportunity to create a white peasantry had been lost and slavery, later to become the greatest social and political issue in America, was an economic fact.

The year 1619 is memorable to the student of American development. It forged the shackles of American slavery and broke the first link that

[1] Doyle: *English Colonies in America*, vol. i, p. 188.

bound these feeble colonists to the mother country. It sowed slavery and reaped freedom. It deprived men of their liberty and made them creatures at the whim of their masters, and it taught men that to be masters of themselves they must be their own rulers. Had the Puritan been able to stand outside himself and see life as from a high mountain, he might well have believed that he was witnessing in the flesh that eternal conflict between the forces of good and evil which was a fundamental article of his creed.

In that year, on the thirteenth of July, the first assembly of Burgesses met in Jamestown, the first experiment of constitutional government in the New World. Heretofore Virginia had been "little better than a penal settlement, ruled by martial law," now it was given some of the rights of self-government; rights which Englishmen have never surrendered once they have been granted or won. These Virginians, but Englishmen first, were not to prove recreant to their traditions. And in this same year slavery was introduced into Virginia, when a Dutch vessel dropped anchor in the James and its master sold his cargo of twenty blacks. From that time there were always enslaved negroes in Virginia, but it was not until the last quarter of the seventeenth century that there was a heavy accession of the slave population. In 1670 the colony comprised, according to Governor Berkeley's estimate, 40,000 people, of whom 32,000 were free whites, 6000 were indentured white servants, and 2000 were negroes. In that year a statute of Virginia enacted that "all servants, not being Christians, imported into this country by shipping shall be slaves," and as there were some pious masters who attempted to convert their slaves, it was later enacted that "conversion to the Christian faith doth not make free." For an owner to kill his slave "from extremity of correction," was not a felony, "since it cannot be presumed that prepensed malice, which alone makes murther felony, should induce any man to destroy his own estate." In 1700 there were probably 6000 negroes and 60,000 whites, but it was not until after the Asiento article of the Treaty of Utrecht of 1713 gave to England a monopoly of the African slave trade that the kidnapping of black men became a recognized and respectable business; and so profitable had the trade become and so great was the demand for servile labor, that in 1750 there were believed to be 250,000 negro slaves in Virginia, and an equal number of whites.

It is not necessary at this time to deal further with the subject of slavery or the political, social and moral effect of the institution and the psychological influence which it exercised, as in the logical development of the theme we shall see how powerful that influence became and how momentous its consequences.

CHAPTER XV

VIRGINIA AN ARISTOCRATIC OLIGARCHY

We have already shown that the men who first settled Virginia were not substantially different from those who exiled themselves to Massachusetts, and Virginia, like the northern colony, built a social system on the feeble foundation laid by men who were deficient in those qualities that are necessary for nation building. The strength of Massachusetts was the Puritan, not the Pilgrim. The character of Virginia was made by the Cavalier, not by the men who followed John Smith, but here the parallel ends. The Pilgrims, too gentle and unresisting to oppose the force of stronger wills, were merged in the Puritans, to the advantage of the latter. The Pilgrim strain in the Puritan blood was a refining and softening influence that did not destroy the Puritan qualities, but brought a ray of sunshine into the darkened recesses of minds abnormally self-centred. In Virginia it was otherwise. The descendants of the first settlers did not cease to exist after the coming of the Cavaliers, they were not absorbed by a stronger or coarser mentality, they did not intermarry, but both lived side by side, and each influenced the other to the injury of both. As the Cavaliers rose they pressed down the class below them and more sharply emphasized the distinction of class. In any state of civilization where there is a wide gulf between classes the consequences are always detrimental. The possession of power, the knowledge that the people may be exploited with impunity and cannot successfully resist, makes the upper and ruling class selfish, arrogant and unrestrained; but there is also developed a high level of social refinement; there is as much luxury as is compatible with the means to gratify it, and among a few an extraordinary mental culture that amazes the world by its boldness and philosophic insight. The lower class becomes resigned to its subordinate position; it is deprived of the great incentive, ambition; and the mass constantly sinks lower.

Virginia strikingly exhibits the working of this social law. It developed a race of arrogant, quick-tempered aristocrats, and a large number of men extraordinarily endowed mentally, whose philosophic grasp is still the admiration of the world; and simultaneously it gave birth to "the mean whites," a degraded, shiftless, mentally deficient class, whose maleficent influence made the South for many generations far behind the North in culture and civilization and lowered the general level of intelligence. A single drop of poison corrupts the whole blood. Against the corrupting influence of "the mean whites" all the genius and wisdom of philosophers and humanitarians and statesmen were powerless. The men who have made some parts of the South "a dark and bloody ground," where to this day the only law known is the law of the rifle and the knife, where dense ignorance prevails and superstition holds sway, are the legacy of this colonial era and its social system.

Just as the dominant and lasting impression was made on New England when the religious persecution of Charles I drove the Puritans to build new temples in the wilderness of the New World, so the character of Virginia was laid when the political persecution of the successor to Charles I drove the Cavaliers to find an asylum on the banks of the rivers and streams of Virginia. The great Puritan hegira covered about thirteen years. The Cavalier migration to Virginia began seven years after Charles's power for evil had ceased to exist, and lasted eleven years. There is here a remarkable correspondence of time and cause, and the coincidence is still further emphasized by the almost identical increase in the population of the two colonies. The heavy hand of the Church forced 20,000 Puritans into exile. Cromwell's root and branch policy swelled the white population of Virginia from 15,000 in 1649 to 38,000 in 1670.

Nothing has become more firmly fixed in the minds of perhaps a majority of Americans than the belief that the Cavaliers were nearly all men of title and long descent, and the Puritans or Roundheads were drawn from the people or lower classes.

Many great noblemen and landed squires without title, it is true, supported Charles I and were thus enrolled in the Cavalier party, but in the parliamentary ranks are to be found the names of the holders of some of the most historical peerages in the kingdom; and the great leader in the cause of parliamentary government, John Hampden, whose refusal to pay ship money lit the torch that flamed into rebellion, was entitled to the designation of "gentleman"; and so were Pym and Vane and Cromwell and many others, all men of gentle blood. The distinction between Cavalier and Roundhead was no more a difference in respect to lineage or social rank than the analogous distinction between Tory and Whig; no more distinction than to-day Liberal or Conservative in England or Republican or Democrat in the United States connotes wealth or station. There are great territorial magnates who can trace their descent back to the mists of antiquity who train with the Conservative party just as men of equal birth and rank and wealth are Liberals; in America, it is impossible to tell a man's wealth or intellectual attainments or social status by his political affiliations. It is important to correct a historical fable that has become accepted as a historical truth.

American writers have made much use of the term "English aristocracy," with the implication that in England there exists a caste or class of special privilege apart from the people, who are necessarily excluded from it. In that sense of the term there is no aristocracy in England, and never has been. Macaulay points out the peculiar "relation in which the nobility stood here to the commonalty. There was a strong aristocracy; but it was of all hereditary aristocracies the least insolent and exclusive. It had none of the invidious character of a caste. It was constantly receiving members from the people, and constantly sending down members to mingle with the people. Any gentleman might become a peer, the younger son of a peer was but a gentleman. Grandsons of peers yielded precedence to newly made knights." The dignity of knighthood, he tells us, was not beyond the reach of any man who was worthy of it; it was no disgrace for the daughter of a duke, a royal duke even, to espouse a commoner; "pedigrees as long, and scutcheons as old, were to be found out of the House of Lords as in it." The constitution of the House of Commons promoted the intermixture of classes. Side by side with the goldsmiths, the drapers and the grocers who represented the commercial towns, were men who in any other country would have been called noblemen. The heirs of great peers who sat in the House of Commons as representatives of the people, and not because of their prospective enjoyment of a title, "naturally became as zealous for its privileges as any of the humble burgesses with whom they were mingled. Thus our democracy was, from an early period, the most aristocratic, and our aristocracy the most democratic in the world; a peculiarity which has lasted down to the present day, and which has produced many important moral and political effects."[1]

It has been a subject of much speculation what peculiar influence made it possible for the men of the South to join the men of the North in resisting common oppression, inasmuch as they were drawn from different classes and their outlook of life was so unlike. But there is no mystery about it. They were men of the same stock, with the same ideas and the same ideals. They reached the same ends through different ways. Religious persecution made the Puritan no more resolute for liberty than political persecution made the Cavalier. Both had been defiant in England: the one had proved it by refusing submission to things spiritual, the other had risen in opposition to the temporal power, and they brought the same spirit of defiance with them across the sea. When Charles I threatened to chastise the rebellious colony of Massachusetts, those born rebels, with no thought of surrender, threw up a fort and mounted their pop-guns to defy the might of England. When Cromwell sent an expedition to make Virginia understand that he was master, those haughty Virginians drew up a treaty of peace that reads more like the terms dictated by a sovereign nation than a weak colony. They were always the same, those quiet Puritans and those

[1] Macaulay: *History of England*, vol. i, pp. 19–20.

laughter-loving Virginians; it is only the historian who has made them different.

To us it is of less importance whether Virginia was founded by Cavalier or Roundhead, it is the consequences that compel our study. It was the accident of the tobacco plant and climate that made it possible for an aristocracy to thrive in Virginia, and an aristocracy it was in every sense of the word. It absorbed into its order all political and social power. It was an oligarchy as well as an aristocracy. It held with firm grip military as well as civil authority. To it the Church was subservient. It did not receive members from the people, nor was it "constantly sending down members to mingle with the people." Its power, its arrogance and its pride made it a more haughty and exclusive aristocracy than any then existing in Europe. And all this — interesting enough though it is to the student of social institutions — would be of little moment if we were not able to trace back to this aristocracy certain American characteristics and institutions that have become part of the American race and American civilization. The American is a blend of the Puritan and the Cavalier, to accept an inexact terminology so rich in contrast; a mixture of Massachusetts and Virginia; a product of the corn that ripened slowly under northern skies and the tobacco that sprung into life in the soil of the south. The influence of Massachusetts is there, but so also is that of Virginia; and great as the influence of Massachusetts, that of Virginia is no less. It was tobacco that made Virginia so different from Massachusetts; it was Virginia that made the American so different from what he would have been had another Massachusetts taken root in the South.

When the Cavaliers came to Virginia they found a thriving community in the enjoyment of a profitable monopoly. Many of the newcomers had been badly crippled in estate by devotion to a cause that was fated to be lost — curious the eternal weaving of the same pattern in the great fabric of history; two hundred years later the descendants of these same Cavaliers championed a cause, and again they lost and suffered — but many of them were still sufficiently endowed to be able to resume life under circumstances very similar to those they had known in England. For them there was only one thing to do, and that was to plant tobacco and enjoy its profits. They acquired large grants of land, they worked their plantations with white servants and slaves; the great house reproduced as nearly as possible the castle or the manor house of England; its master looked after his lands and servants and slaves as in the old days he had directed the harvesting of his crops and taken a paternal interest in the welfare of his tenantry. In England property passed from father to the first-born son and was entailed. Being Englishmen and having property to devise, they established the custom of primogeniture and the law of entail.

There was no such law in Massachusetts, and the accident of birth counted for little in favor of one son over another. In grafting an "aristocratic" custom on the new civilization of Virginia proof has been found of the aristocracy of Virginia contrasted with the democracy of Massachusetts, which is further strengthened by the difference between the political system of the two colonies. But economic rather than social causes developed those distinctions. Tobacco could not be profitably cultivated except on a large scale, and to divide up an estate among many children would be to benefit none and impoverish all. The English law and custom, despite its manifest injustice and often injurious results, worked reasonably well, and the Englishmen saw no reason to make a change. In Massachusetts conditions were different. There were no large estates to be protected from loss by division; wealth was commercial rather than landed. A system that seemed to be peculiarly adapted to the needs of Virginia would have been out of place in Massachusetts.

Considerations equally cogent resulted in local institutions dissimilar in the two colonies. In Massachusetts the people lived in small congregations or communities clustered around the meeting-house, each intended to be a petty, self-governing republic and reproducing in a way the Roman city state; whose people could rally for support and mutual defense; where the sense of fellowship was very strong, and where inclination and self-interest fostered the spirit of close companionship. In a community thus organized the natural system of government was the mass meeting, where all the males took part in the proceedings and shared in the advantages and responsibilities of citizenship. This logically developed into that peculiarly New England institution the town meeting, the local parliament, where its affairs are discussed in public and every person may have a voice in his own government.

The town meeting was impossible in Virginia, because in place of the settlement and town of Massachusetts there were those plantations of many thousand acres, which were so widely separated "that no man could have seen his neighbor without looking through a telescope, or to be heard by him without firing off a gun." There was no sense of community, of touching elbows with one's neighbors, of being dependent upon them and creating the spirit of helpful and free assistance, which develops one type of local civilization. The Virginian was developed by his isolation. The English system of the parish and the vestry was transported to Virginia, and the vestrymen, at first elected by the parish, were soon given power to fill vacancies, which made the vestry a close corporation and centred local authority in a few hands. It was foreign to the English spirit of genuine representative government, and gave great dissatisfaction, and could not last.

It has been said with equal inexactness that Massachusetts was Nonconformist and Virginia Church of England, and that the religion of the two colonies was a factor as important in differentiating them as the social status of the founders of the two colonies, but this like all generalizations, is true only so far as it goes. In 1638, which was eleven years before the beginning of the great Cavalier exodus, there were believed to be a thousand Puritans in Virginia, or seven per cent of the total population, but the time was soon to come when Virginia should almost equal Massachusetts in theological bigotry. In 1642 Sir William Berkeley came to Virginia as its governor, and to him Puritanism was a heresy that merited only sharp treatment. The year after his arrival the Assembly passed an act "for the preservation of the purity of doctrine and unity of the Church," which enacted "that all ministers whatsoever, who shall reside in the colony, are to be conformed to the orders and constitution of the Church of England, and not otherwise to be admitted to teach or preach publicly or privately, and that the Governor and Council do take care that all nonconformists, upon notice of them, shall be compelled to depart the colony with all convenience."

In 1662, under a codification of the statutes of the colony, conformity was required and a tax was laid for the support of the Established Church; Quakers were persecuted even as they were in

Massachusetts. If no Quakers were hanged in Virginia as they were in New England, Jefferson says, "it was not owing to the moderation of the Church, or spirit of the legislature, as may be inferred from the law itself; but to historical circumstances which have not been handed down to us." [1] Puritans were required to take the oath of obedience and supremacy; a penalty of two thousand pounds of tobacco was imposed upon "schismatical persons" who refused to baptize their children.

The Puritan's passionate love for education, which was part of his creed, finds no response in Virginia, and Berkeley's oft quoted *Dei gratiâ*, "I thank God, there are no free schools nor printing; for learning has brought disobedience and heresy and sects into the world and printing has divulged them, and libels against the best government. God save us from both," has been cited to prove that the narrow Puritan was in truth more liberal than the so-called liberal Virginian. But Berkeley's attitude was logical and is easily understood. In New England servile labor was almost unknown, while in Virginia it was growing larger every year and the Virginians believed that servants and slaves were necessary for the prosperity of the colony; and the fewer free schools the less the output of the printing-press, to that extent the less danger that servants would be encouraged to become masters or slaves would aspire to their freedom.

[1] Jefferson: *Notes on Virginia*, p. 233.

We must remember, however, that the governing class of Virginia was not deficient in culture or a knowledge of the classics. After the Restoration the corresponding class in England had distinctly retrograded, and the character of the squirearchy may be read in the pages of the prose Homer of human nature, as Byron termed Fielding; but the Virginians had become stronger and intellectually better men. Every great Virginian family had its tutor, usually an Episcopal clergyman, who directed the education of the sons of the house, and when they outgrew their master they were sent to New or Old England to complete their studies.

There was no town life in Virginia, and its absence was felt to be a serious menace to the prosperity and future growth of the colony, and its rulers attempted to correct this weakness. With the exception of Williamsburg, the seat of government, there was even as late as the beginning of the eighteenth century "hardly so much as a village in Virginia." By the middle of the century Williamsburg could boast only two hundred wooden houses, and its streets were unpaved. Richmond, founded in 1737, had a population of less than four thousand in 1790. Norfolk, a port of very considerable pretensions, which did a large trade with the other southern colonies and the West Indies, had in 1776 only six thousand inhabitants, while Philadelphia numbered thirty-five thousand and New York twenty-five thousand, though the population of the two Northern states did not equal that of Virginia. To create towns, various expedients were resorted to. By statute, tobacco grown in certain counties had to be sent to Jamestown to be stored there for shipment. But the planter refused to add to the cost of his crop by submitting to arbitrary and hampering ordinances. Every planter had his wharf, which was to him what the siding is to the great manufacturer to-day. It was foolish to break bulk when a vessel could be loaded at his door and sent direct to its destination. "When Thomas Jefferson entered William and Mary College in 1670, a lad of seventeen years, he had never seen so many as a dozen houses grouped together."

Despite their extensive coast line, the Virginians were not a sea-faring people and had no love for the sea, like the men of the North or the Carolinas to the south of them. They owned no shipping except small coasting vessels. Although engaged in trade, they were not merchants and had no genius for manufacturing. Everything they needed they imported, nearly every man for himself, and paid for it in the great staple of the colony, tobacco.

The Tobacco Aristocracy of Virginia, which flourished for two centuries, roughly from the middle of the seventeeth century until it fell under the shock of battle at about the same period of the nineteenth, was one of the most remarkable phases of social development the world has known. Perhaps its nearest parallel was Rome when the patricians were in their glory, whose wealth was in land, and who, surrounded by their slaves and dependents, lived, for their age, much the same life that these Virginians did. In the society of Rome of that day, as in the social system of Virginia of the era of which we are treating, pride of class was its distinguishing feature, and this sharp distinction in social conditions was emphasized by the institution of slavery, which discredited manual labor and destroyed industry. "For in a warm climate no man will labor for himself who can make another labor for him. This is so true that of the proprietors of slaves a very small proportion, indeed, are ever seen to labor."[1]

The chasm between master and servants was so deep that it was impossible almost for the latter to hope to rise into the class above him. Black slavery, in that period of the world's history when the dominance of centuries had made the white race regard itself as superior to all others, was more destructive, morally and economically, than any other form of slavery that has ever existed since the strong enslaved the weak. In the time of Greece and Rome, after that in those long years when slavery was accepted as a matter of course, there was always a possibility that the slave, by extraordinary ability or unusual circumstance, might rise, and with his freedom find his place among men. There was no such hope for the son of

[1] Jefferson: *Notes on Virginia*, p. 241.

a black mother. The taint of color set him outside the pale, it was always a stigma and condemned him to a life of servility. For him Pandora's box was sealed.

The history of civilization is the history of slavery and its final overthrow, and it was overthrown not alone because it was repugnant to the moral sense of an enlightened civilization — for morals are merely convention and change with the varying needs of society — but because it was an economic untruth and cost more than it produced. Its destruction in the United States, after having existed for more than two hundred years, was precipitated by causes that at the time seemed to be far removed from economic and were purely moral and political, and yet we shall see later how much economic causes had to do with ending slavery. It was bound to come. The war accelerated it and hastened the march of events, but slavery could not have endured because it was an economic fallacy.

We have accepted the doctrine of the survival of the fittest, but in accepting the result we too often overlook the intermediary stages and their consequences. It is true that the fit alone survive, that the plant or bird or animal or race that can adapt itself to circumstances and the conditions of its environment can alone live and propagate its species, but that is a long process of slow and gradual transformation in structure and function, in the case of the plant or the animal; in structure and mental equipment in the case of man. Before that end is reached the unfit have left their impress upon their race and surroundings, they have transmitted their characteristics to their descendants, they have affected the civilization of their time, they have planted evils which can only be extirpated by that gradual progress by which the unfit, marked for extinction, are merged in the fit, who are foreordained to live. A race dies because it cannot reproduce itself, because it propagates the seed of its own destruction, but there is no catastrophic climax. There is no period on which we can put our finger and say, "here the unfit ceased to exist and the fit came on the scene." Side by side the fit and the unfit lived, the unfit exercising their destructive influence until the time when evolution had accomplished its predestined task.

The men who survived and made Virginia were a virile and intellectually powerful race, but the men who disappeared during the course of the struggle influenced many generations, and that "white trash" of the South to which I have already referred, those idle, dissolute, shiftless creatures who looked with contempt on the negro and for whom the negro had even greater contempt, no less powerfully affected Southern civilization, and through it the entire country, than the men who were in every sense leaders and raised up to establish a nation. Extraordinary as this assertion may appear, we shall see later that it is sustained by the facts.

It was a very remarkable civilization that was built on tobacco. It produced great wealth, it gave birth to great intelligence and independence; it was the acid to correct the alkali of New England. To Virginia the American people owe as much as to Massachusetts, but their sense of obligation must take another form. It was the difference between Cromwell and Marlborough, and it would be another English history if neither, or perhaps only one, had lived. It was a civilization reared not on a necessity, not on something without which the world could not live, but on a luxury. That in itself is remarkable. It could exist only so long as it was fed by the lifeblood of negro slavery, which in the eyes of the world was a crime long before the world was no longer content to close its eyes and dull its ears to that which offended its finer impulses. And finally, this pure luxury was the most wasteful of all crops. From the earth it took everything, but it gave nothing. It was the agricultural Minotaur that devastated a virgin soil.

Yet with all this Virginia grew and prospered and raised a great race of great men, who like other races of great men were devoid of the commercial sense and with the indifference of the spendthrift lived on capital. With the exhaustion of the soil, with the competition of other countries that practiced a more scientific culture of tobacco, the Virginians found themselves at the end of their resources, for their principal was gone and there were no means to replace it. But while it lasted, while money was made quickly and those virgin lands yielded their fullness, it was a day of great plenty and a free, generous life that developed the minds and bodies of men and dwarfed them spiritually. It left a legacy that future generations have still to pay.

Here is a picture of the Golden Era of the plantation age by a writer whose sympathies are frankly Southern. It is not historically accurate, and the author's sense of proportion is distorted, but it conveys a fair impression of the plantation life when Virginia enjoyed a monopoly of tobacco:—

"There was a blacksmith shop, woodburners to keep the house supplied with charcoal, brickmakers, masons, carpenters, a mill which ground flour for sale as well as for the family's use, coopers to make barrels for it, and a schooner to carry all products to market. Besides these there were a shoemaker, and weavers who in the year 1758 produced eight hundred and fifteen yards of linen, three hundred and sixty five yards of woolen, one hundred and forty yards of linsey, and forty yards of cotton goods. There was an important fishery on the shore, and large herds of cattle, horses, and sheep, not to mention the great waving fields of grain, for Washington planted little or no tobacco.

"It was a large enterprise, somewhat resembling,

in the ability required, our modern manufacturing industries, but more varied. In fact, in colonial times the Southern plantations were the great business undertakings of the country, and more broadening in their effect on character than the petty trades and small farming that were followed in the North.

"The man who successfully ruled this property and its retainers and at the same time led the life of a sportsman and a gentleman, mingled with military service on the frontier in the French and Indian wars, was receiving an education which cannot be given in modern times by any university, city, or community in the United States. No amount of book learning, no college curriculum imitated from plodding, mystical Germans, no cramming or examinations, and no system of gymnastic exercises can be even a substitute for that Virginian life which inspired with vigor, freshness, and creative power the great men who formed the Union and the Constitution."[1]

Another American writer gives us a somewhat different picture of the Tobacco Aristocracy. The isolation of these semi-feudal plantations created "two great classes, a class of vast landowners, haughty, hospitable, indolent, passionate, given to field sports and politics, and a class of impoverished white plebeians and black serfs." As was inevitable in a dominion where lands and laborers

[1] Fisher: *Men, Women, and Manners in Colonial Times*, vol. i, pp. 83–85.

were the chief constituents of wealth, where slaves, black and white, were counted by the thousand, and into which the Cavaliers had brought the English system of primogeniture and entail, a favored class held all military, judicial, legislative, and executive power. This aristocracy had not hitherto acted as a political party, but the English restoration was a Virginian revolution. It took the power from the people, who did not regain it for more than half a century.[1]

But this takes us somewhat ahead of the time with which we are dealing. Before the Golden Age the colony had to pass through the usual vicissitudes of political turmoil and become schooled in that political training which made it possible for the new American political philosophy to be accepted.

Had England deliberately set to work to train up these expatriated sons of hers so as to make them rebel against the home government and its attempts to keep them in perpetual tutelage, she could not have gone about it with greater skill or adopted methods more certain to be successful. It was a day when the people were more fully conscious than ever before of the immense power that resided in them. The seed of democracy had been planted, although it must take another century and more before its fruits were visible, but in the meantime the souls and minds of men were stirred in a way new to them and vague longings possessed

[1] Avery: *A History of the United States*, vol. ii, p. 187.

them. When in 1619 the first House of Burgesses was created in Virginia, an eminent historian quaintly speaks of it as having "broken out," and a later and equally eminent historian comments on this expression, "as if there were an incurable virus of liberty in the English blood, as it were something that must come out as inevitably as original sin."[1] It was that "incurable virus" that, like the sap in the tree rising in springtime, was now infusing the blood of Englishmen.

The struggle between King and Parliament was an effort on the part of Charles arbitrarily to control the purse. His successor, James II, no less arbitrary and with an even greater dislike of the interference of Parliament, still had wisdom enough to reaffirm the principle that Cromwell's commissioners had recognized and George III was to ignore, that taxation implied representation. Thus twice in a little more than three decades had these Englishmen in Virginia won without bloodshed and almost without effort what at home had been gained only at the point of the sword. When Lord Howard of Effingham was sent to Virginia as Governor his instructions from the King authorized him that in all matters relating to taxation he was to "recommend" measures to the Assembly. It was the recognition that the sole power to impose taxes was inherent in the Assembly as the representatives of the people.

[1] Fiske: *Old Virginia and Her Neighbours*, vol. i, p. 240.

But before that Cromwell had acknowledged the right of the Virginians to tax themselves. Following the execution of Charles the Assembly passed an act declaring that commissions of the Crown were still valid and refused to recognize the authority of the Commonwealth. Two ships were sent from England to bring the rebellious colonials to terms, who yielded without striking a blow. The incident is not important except for the recognition by the Parliamentary Commissioners "that Virginia shall be free from all taxes, customes and impositions whatsoever, and none to be imposed on them without the consent of the Grand Assembly, And soe that neither ffortes nor castles bee erected or garrisoned without their consent."[1] In many ways the Virginians had been taught the wisdom of loudly demanding what they wanted, and in case of refusal to offer a bold front; and they knew very well that so long as they controlled their own taxation they had little to fear from royal governors.

The life led by the Virginians made them tremendously self reliant and showed them what an artificial creation society is. In their own England customs had become stereotyped, there was machinery of government and law of whose workings they knew little, but which they accepted as a matter of course; it had become as mechanical and as much a matter of routine as the rising of the sun or the succession of days through the calendar of

[1] Hening's *Statutes*, vol. i, p. 364.

the month. In Virginia society was stripped of its coverings. What had before seemed mysterious, nebulous, too complicated to be grasped by little minds, was found to be on near approach extraordinarily simple and easily comprehended. There was no remote system of poor law rising in some distant fountain head and filtering its way to the object of its relief. If one man starved, all starved. There were, at first, no judges and courts and terrifying machinery of justice, that was the more terrifying because it was so impersonal. Justice was quick and direct. There were no involved processes of trade by which a dozen barriers must be broken down before consumer and producer are brought together. Commerce was direct barter. All the dead fustian with which civilization delights to clothe itself, and which is inseparable from civilization, was swept away and men stood face to face. Had these Englishmen not been the product of a civilization highly developed, they would have acted from instinct and in their ignorance believed that their own was the only practical way. But they had the advantage of comparison, and were able to see that to lay the foundation for their own social order was a task not so difficult.

They were, however, left largely to shift for themselves. It is true they were given assistance from England and except for that help they would have perished in the early days, but it was chiefly on their own reliance they depended. When they realized how well they were able to take care of themselves, they quickly resented the efforts of the home government to treat them politically as children and constantly to remind them of their dependence. They were feeling their own strength and were conscious of what they had done.

Everything tended to stimulate resistance. The mental attitude of the Englishman of the seventeenth and eighteenth centuries, in one respect at least, was not unlike that of the Englishman of the nineteenth century in his insular contempt for foreigners and the tactlessness he displayed in dealing with his children who had become colonists. He seems to have forgotten that the men who were building a new empire across the Atlantic were men of his own blood, often men of his own family; and "colonist" was almost a term of reproach, if not of disdain. It was characteristic of this attitude that when Dr. Blair went to England to try to obtain money to establish a college in Virginia and approached Sir Edward Seymour for a grant from the treasury, he met with a curt refusal. "You must not forget," Blair mildly told him, "that people in Virginia have souls to save as well as people in England." "Souls," Seymour echoed in derision, "damn your souls! Grow tobacco!" And the character of the governors that administered the colony was a direct invitation to defy authority. Many of them were men of ability who had the interests of the colony at heart, but more of them were men of little capacity, court favorites who were pitchforked into office as an easy means of finding them a profitable job, and to whom Virginia meant nothing except a place of exile and the means of replenishing a depleted purse. A little more tact in dealing with a proud and self-reliant people, a little more sympathy with their aims and aspirations, a little better understanding of their character, and the friction of the first hundred and fifty years would have been avoided and the great drama of 1776 need not have been staged. They were a people easily led but difficult to drive. And few Englishmen, from Argall to George III, ever understood that simple truth.

In Virginia as in Massachusetts, from the time when the colonists first obtained a measure of self-government until they threw off their allegiance to the mother country, there was constant agitation to check the encroachment of the governors, which sometimes existed only in the imagination of the colonists; and to increase the measure of popular liberty, or to oppose legislation that was enacted solely in the interest of British merchants and destroyed or hampered colonial commerce and enterprise. Usually this discontent voiced itself in discussion and protest, to which we may trace the extraordinary power of political oratory which distinguishes the American, and it was an excellent school of political training; but from time to time there was open and armed resistance to royal authority, which should have been a warning to men less blinded by their own conceit. Every American schoolboy is familiar with Nathaniel Bacon's attempt to overthrow Sir William Berkeley's rule and his indictment of that stout old Cavalier, which foreshadowed by a hundred years the indictment of George III, there being in both instruments a curious similarity of language and thought, which proves conclusively, I think, that long before the American nation was born the seed had been sown in the spirit of resistance and opposition and a determination to submit to no form of government that did not first consider the rights and welfare of the people.[1] But Virginia was not alone in having to put down rebellion in the early history of the colonies. In Maryland, in Massachusetts, in New York, there was resistance to authority;

[1] Bacon's *Indictment of Sir William Berkeley*, the original of which is in the British State Paper Office, contains many counts, of which the following are the most important and characteristic:—

"For having upon specious pretence of public works raised unjust taxes upon the commonalty for the advancement of private favourites and other sinister ends, but no visible effects in any measure adequate.

"For not having, during the long time of his government, in any measure advanced this hopeful colony either by fortifications, towns, or trade.

"For having abused and rendered contemptible the majesty of justice, of advancing to places of judicature scandalous and ignorant favourites.

"For having wronged his Majesty's prerogative and interest by assuming the monopoly of the beaver trade.

"For having in that unjust gain bartered and sold his Majesty's country and the lives of his loyal subjects to the barbarous heathen.

"For having protected, favoured, and emboldened the Indians against his Majesty's most loyal subjects, never contriving, requiring or appointing any due or proper means of satisfaction for their many invasions, murders, and robberies committed upon us."

there was always the latent spirit of rebellion swift to flame into open defiance.

A strong race, similar to a man of strong character, is never content, but always finds present conditions capable of improvement and endeavors to better them. A race that is satisfied is like the man whose ambition is gratified, and then quickly follow stagnation and decay. It is this wholesome discontent, this unrest, this longing for something finer, this ever striving for excellence, this criticism, that make the man stronger and better and the race more resolute and capable of accomplishing great things. That these Englishmen were to found a great and vigorous race was indicated by their never being quite satisfied, even when life ran easily and smoothly for them, and they never sank into that destructive state of smug complacency which is the beginning of the end of all progress; the corollary of a fatuous optimism that accepts whatever is as the best of all possible things in the best of all possible worlds. Their descendants, strong men sprung from a strong stock, have the same spirit. The American of to-day is properly dissatisfied, always wanting something better, always trying to reform, ever seeking to improve himself and his conditions, which is the long struggle that leads to perfection.

Tolerance, a courteous yielding of individual opinion to that of an adversary and a recognition that although men may differ there is some merit in the argument of an opponent, was not a virtue of the seventeenth century; but religious intolerance has always been much harsher than political, unless the latter, under the guise of a civil polity, involved the supremacy of the Church. Virginia was not free from the prevailing harshness of the age, but it was a more tolerant community than Massachusetts, and by contrast it seemed to be more liberal, as if its morals were looser and the state of society generally more lax. And yet in that early day, about the time that Puritanism was seeking a foothold in Massachusetts, Virginia enacted a code of blue laws that should have compelled the admiration of the most rigid Puritan. Drunkenness was a crime to be severely punished. Men must dress according to their station in life, and every married man had a direct interest in preventing the undue extravagance of his wife, as they were assessed "according to his own and his wife's apparel." Maidens who flirted and men who engaged themselves to more than one woman at the same time were liable to be whipped or fined. The crime of bringing the governor into contempt or ridicule was punished by the pillory, and to disparage a minister was to risk the censure of the governor and council. "Profane swearing" could be indulged in only at the risk of a shilling an oath. To make a journey upon the Sabbath, "except in case of emergent necessitie," was punishable by a fine of one hundred pounds of tobacco. The code sanctioned by the London Company was Draconian in its severity. Blasphemy, denying "the known articles of the Christian faith," speaking against the King, or vilifying the London Company, were crimes punishable with death.

But these laws were not considered unduly harsh for their day, and they did not sorely oppress the colonists. Men were whipped and fined and pilloried and a few were hanged, but Virginia had slight cause to complain of tyrants who punished for the mere delight of inflicting suffering and gratifying a love for cruelty. It was this moderation that left Virginia almost indifferent to the great struggle in England and made no unclosable breach between the Virginians and the New Englanders. In Virginia there were no wrongs to be avenged, no bitter memories of persecution, no fortunes wrecked or estates confiscated because Commonwealth had succeeded King and King had replaced Protector. Individual preference of course the colonists had, but they accepted the change almost with unconcern. It is true that in 1661 the Virginia Assembly passed an act making the thirteenth of January, the anniversary of the execution of Charles I, a day to be solemnized with fasting and prayer, "that our sorrows may expiate our crime, and our tears wash away our guilt," but that was partly sentiment and affection for the memory of the "murdered" sovereign, and partly expediency. The successor of Charles was firmly seated on the throne, Puritanism was another lost cause, politically speaking, and the colonists knew the advantage of having the favor of the King and the Court. But whether King reigned or Protector governed was of less consequence to these fiery colonists than the enjoyment of their rights that had so early "broken out" in the history of the colony. They were quick enough to resist encroachment, they were prompt in defying the Company or the Court when their liberties were threatened, but English politics never raised up among the colonists two formidable parties always waiting to fly at each other's throats. In England the hope was cherished that the King's party would be built up in Virginia and that when the time was ripe Virginia could be relied on to contribute men and money for the restoration of the monarchy. But it was empty hope. There was party neither of the Crown nor of Parliament, and the Virginians cared more to save the colony from spoliation and bloodshed than they did to become involved in English politics.

The whole course of American history, even in the colonial era, when American history was being written, although no one was wise enough to read it, shows that the Englishman in America cast off some of the political traditions that had governed him in England and adopted new principles that were the necessity of his new environment and his new conditions. And, curiously enough, broadly and fundamentally, from these principles there has been no deviation. The cardinal principle of American polity from the time of Washington to the present day has been no "entangling alliances," and in keeping aloof from the struggle of Roundhead and Cavalier, and in refusing to be made a pawn in the great game of English politics, the Virginians unconsciously adopted a policy that later was to have the sanction of the American people and become incorporated into the unwritten constitution. We shall see how an unbroken thread runs through the complicated arabesque of American history, and how it appears and reappears at every stage of American development and with what fidelity it has been adhered to.

After the Virginians brought the wilderness under subjection and the peril of Indian massacre was no longer to be feared, it was natural that they should settle down to the enjoyment of the good fortune that was theirs. In all the accounts of contemporary Virginia we are impressed by the spirit of content, by the emphasis laid on pleasant surroundings and the life of ease and pleasure, which is in such marked contrast to life in the northern colonies, where hearts were still being searched in the vain endeavor to solve the unfathomable mystery of sin and suffering. The Virginian was no metaphysician or hair-splitting theologian; polemical discussion did not appeal to him; whether a soul could dance on the point of a needle was a foolish speculation when the hounds were straining to raise the fox, and the skies were blue and cloudless, and the air was balmy and perfume laden, and after the chase there was tobacco and toddy to bring enjoyment and defy sour-faced preachers.

This contentment resulted in another significant mental change. From mere adventurers and transients the Virginian had been transformed into a people with a country. The spirit of patriotism, which makes nations, was springing into life. The discovery that Virginia was not a land of fabled wealth and mythological miracle, that the ground was not encumbered with gold and rivers did not run contrary to the laws of Nature, was a great blow to the first settlers, who in many things were as simple as children and as easily imposed upon by fairy tales. But back of their ingenuousness was the substratum of English solidity and obstinacy. The gold existed only in imagination, but the wealth was there to be won by effort. Virginia was no longer a place of exile, but a country in which men were to live and prosper; a country not only to be endured but to be liked, for the Virginians soon came to have an affection for this wondrous land that was so rich and rewarded them so lavishly. They were not only content to remain, but few had any desire to leave.[1] "The romantic era of colonization, with its wild hopes and ambitions, is over." It was no longer necessary to hold out alluring but impossible

[1] "Leah and Rachel; or The Two Fruitful Sisters, Virginia and Maryland," Force, vol. iii, p. 12.

promises. God need not be propitiated by the sanctimonious lie of the conversion of the heathen, nor greed excited by illusory tales of gold. Even the importance of Virginia to England as a commercial and military outpost was less dwelt upon. Virginia was appreciated for herself, and the once stony-hearted stepmother had become a sweetheart to be wooed and a wife to be cherished.

And climate worked its end. "The cloudless skies and genial air had changed the heavy, sombre Englishman into the spirited, keen, vivacious beings who produced the Jeffersons, Madisons, Randolphs and Lees." They were a united people, those Virginians, and believed in themselves. Perhaps this — this intense confidence in themselves — was the great reason why they achieved and became great.

CHAPTER XVI

THE FIRST CATHOLIC COLONY

It has been well said by Bancroft that "the United States were severally colonized by men, in origin, religious faith, and purposes, as varied as their climes"; and by another American writer that "in travelling from Massachusetts to the Carolinas one passed through communities of such distinct individuality that they were almost like different nations. Each had been founded for a reason and purpose of its own, each had a set of opinions and laws peculiar to itself, and it was not uncommon to find the laws and opinions of one a contradiction to those of another"; and we have only to turn to the early history of Maryland to recognize the truth of these observations. Thrust like a wedge between the older colony of Virginia and the younger of Massachusetts Bay, the one in everything so unlike the other, Maryland, in that early day, was the connecting link between North and South; southern, because of its geographical position and climate and soil; northern, because by one of those whims of fate it practiced tolerance and gave asylum to the intolerance of Puritanism and the narrowness no less of those Virginia "butterflies" who, lightly as they regarded theological dispute, had all the stubbornness of ignorance in defending the faith.

Maryland interests us as being the first and only American colony established to afford a refuge to Roman Catholics. To escape persecution, to be permitted to lead their lives in their own way unhindered by civil or ecclesiastical law, the Puritans went to Massachusetts. It was with the same purpose that George Calvert, the first Lord Baltimore, led his company of adventurers first to Newfoundland and then to Virginia, which would have none of him because of his religion; and later found shelter in Maryland. We are interested in Maryland, in tracing American development, because of the influence exercised on the American character by the religious faith of its first settlers, which made Maryland so different from both Massachusetts and Virginia. "The darkened and gloomy mind of the Puritan" gave to the American the strength and moral purpose that made Ethan Allen demand the surrender of Fort Ticonderoga " in the name of the Great Jehovah and the Continental Congress"; the Virginian gave him imagination and the love of reckless adventure that drove the frontier ever forward and spread a handful of men to fill a vast continent; the Marylander sowed the seeds of a church with its discipline and traditions that were the needed counterpoise. A plant is nurtured no more by its sun than by its snow. Virginia and Massachusetts and Maryland — take away any one of those elements and you subtract from American psychology.

With the political history of Maryland we need not concern ourselves, deeply interesting as it is to the historical student because of the extraordinary powers it vested in its proprietor. Baltimore died a month after he had received his grant, and the work of colonization was carried on by his son Cecilius, a remarkable man in an age of remarkable men, to whom may be accorded the honor of having been one of the first English colonial administrators worthy of the name; who during the forty years that he governed the province had its welfare always at heart and displayed much wisdom, tact and liberality.

Among other things, Baltimore's charter conferred upon him the patronage and advowsons of all churches, "together with license and faculty of erecting and founding churches, chapels and places of worship," and "of causing the same to be dedicated and consecrated according to the ecclesiastical laws of our kingdom of England."[1] Doyle, whose painstaking research and sound judgment have made his work so invaluable to students of colonial history, finds in Baltimore's acceptance of this clause in the charter that "it quite dispels the idea that he intended his colony as a special refuge for his own sect, a stronghold for persecuted Romanism"; and other writers, American as well as Eng-

[1] Scharf: *History of Maryland*, vol. i, p. 54.

lish, have asserted that Baltimore could not establish Catholicism in his province as he was pledged to maintain the established Church of England. But it was a casuistical age, and kingly consciences were not overburdened with scruples when favorites were to be rewarded. The first Lord Baltimore was well known to be a Catholic and so was his son, and in granting the charter to them Charles had inserted no prohibition against freedom of religion. A Protestant king ruling a Protestant people would find it necessary to insist in the terms of the charter that Protestantism should be the religion of the colony, but having nominated the bond he need not be over-particular as to its observance. At any rate, in November, 1663, Baltimore equipped two ships, the Ark and the Dove, for Maryland, which carried twenty gentlemen adventurers and some three hundred servants and two Catholic priests; the first time we find mention made of Catholic priests in an English colonizing expedition to America. What proportion of Baltimore's gentlemen adventurers and servants were Protestants has never been authentically stated, but in his first advertisement for settlers he significantly announced that he would accept people of all religious faiths, and with that wisdom that always distinguished him, forbade "all unreasonable disputes on points of religion tending to disturbance of the public peace and quiet and to the opening of faction in religion." On arriving at their destination one of the priests records that "on the day of the Annunciation of the most Holy Virgin Mary in the year 1634 we celebrated the mass for the first time, on this island. This had never been done before in this part of the world. After we had completed the sacrifice, we took upon our shoulders a great cross, which we had hewn out of a tree, and advancing in order to the appointed place, with the assistance of the Governor and his associates and the other Catholics, we erected a trophy to Christ the Savior, humbly reciting, on our bended knees, the Litanies of the Sacred Cross, with great emotion."[1]

To speak of religious freedom in the seventeenth century is to link antipodal forces. There was no religious liberty in the modern sense. The Puritan was no more narrow than the Catholic, and neither was exceeded in liberality by the Episcopalian, but all were anxious to have their own creed established by law and certified to as the only certain way by which salvation could be found. Sons of the Church might occasionally disgrace their mother, but the worst churchman, whether Puritan, Episcopalian, or Catholic, was better than the best heretic; for the good heretic was a perversion of nature on which the Church had never laid eyes. "For howsoever bitterly Catholic and Protestant divines have hated and persecuted each other, they have united like true brethren in their hatred and their persecution of heretics; for such was their inexorable destiny."

[1] Scharf: *op. cit.*, vol. i, p. 75.

The religious liberty that distinguished Baltimore's Maryland palatinate, which has been belittled by some American writers as having existed in imagination rather than in fact, was wide enough to give the colony a character different from the older ones. It is probable that had an avowed Catholic king sat on the throne of England, and had the majority of Englishmen been spiritual subjects of the Pope, Cecil Calvert would have been no more liberal in his views or religion than the Puritans; but circumstances compelled another course. Much as the Catholics might have desired to establish their religion to the exclusion of all others, much as they may have hated or sorrowed over the heretic and have regretted that he was doomed to everlasting damnation, it was impossible to exclude Protestantism from the palatinate, where it had been enjoined by the charter. What they could do was to recognize liberty of worship, and they could not sanction Catholicism and exclude Puritanism, which would not only have been inconsistent but inexpedient and impolitic. Cecil Calvert may not have been in advance of his age and at heart no more liberal than Laud, he may have regretted that he could not complete his machinery of government by the establishment of the inquisition and the star chamber, but the fact remains that Maryland, in the seventeenth century, was the only place on the American continent under English rule in which religious sects were unmolested.

It is not easy at the present day, Lea says, for those accustomed to universal toleration to realize the importance attached by statesmen in the past to unity of belief, or the popular abhorrence of any deviation from the standard of dogma. These convictions were part of the mental and moral fibre of the community and were the outcome of the assiduous teachings of the church for centuries, until it was classed with the primal truths that it was the highest duty of the sovereign to crush out dissidence at whatever cost, and that hatred of the heretic was enjoined on every Christian by both divine and human law. The heretic was a venomous reptile, spreading contagion with his breath, and the safety of the land required his extermination as a source of pestilence.[1]

At a time when Catholics and Episcopalians were disfranchised in Massachusetts and Quakers were scourged at the cart tail until their bodies ran with blood, and Roger Williams was driven forth, and John Cotton boldly proclaimed that "the Church never took hurt from the punishment of heretics"; when Virginia compelled nonconformists to depart the colony and prevented "popish recusants" from holding office, and Quakers were persecuted as felons, Maryland neither flogged nor maimed, and instead of driving out heretics opened her arms to them.

In 1649 the Assembly passed "An Act concerning Religion," the first American toleration act

[1] Lea: *History of the Inquisition of Spain*, vol. ii, p. 1.

that shows the liberality of the lord proprietor and his legislature. Any person "who denominated any other person a heretic, schismatick, idolator, puritan, presbyterean, independent, popish priest, jesuit, jesuited papist, lutheran, calvinist, anabaptist, brownist, antinomian, barrowist, roundhead, separatist, or other name or term in a reproachful manner, relating to matter or religion," was subject to a fine of ten shillings, one half to the lord proprietor and the other to the person "of whom such reproachful words are or shall be uttered or spoken"; and in case of not being able to satisfy the fine, "the person so offending shall be publicly whipt and shall suffer imprisonment without bayle or mainprise, until he, she, or they respectively shall satisfy the party offended or grieved by such reproachful language, by asking him or her respectively forgiveness publicly for such his offence before the magistrate or chief officer or officers of the towne or place where such offence shall be given." A further section recognized that the "inforcing of the conscience in matters of religion hath frequently fallen out to bee of dangerous consequences in those commonwealths," therefore, "for the more quiet and peaceable government of this province, and the better to preserve mutual love and unity amongst the inhabitants here," it was provided that no person "professing to believe in Jesus Christ shall henceforth be any waies troubled, molested, or discountenanced, for or in respect to his or her religion, nor in the exercise thereof . . . nor in any way compelled to the belief or exercise of any other religion against his or her consent."

All through the colonial period Catholics were looked upon with suspicion, which long afterwards colored the New England view, but was less noticeable in the South, possibly because of the early influence of Maryland. We have only to examine the various commissions and charters to see that Catholics were always discriminated against. In the commission for New Hampshire of 1680 liberty of conscience was granted to all Protestants, but not to other sects. In the Massachusetts charter of 1691 William III allowed liberty of conscience "in the worship of God to all Christians (except papists)." Rhode Island, defaming the memory of Roger Williams, enacted a statute depriving Catholics of the franchise; Oglethorpe's charter for Georgia permitted "free exercise of religion" to all persons "except papists." Even in Pennsylvania, the most liberal of all colonies, the Catholics were compelled to walk with great circumspection and permitted to make little public announcement of their faith. Penn, in 1708, rebukes his secretary of the colony for having suffered "public mass in a scandalous manner," and the Philadelphians opposed the erection of a Catholic chapel because it was "in too public a place."

If Baltimore had done nothing else than make it

possible for Catholics to be placed on an equality with other Englishmen and to bring under the protection of the organized machinery of government the Catholic Church among English-speaking colonists, he would have won his place in history. His motives, I repeat, may have been selfish and unworthy, he may have been as illiberal as his contemporaries, policy may have cloaked his hopes, and under the guise of tolerance he may have patiently waited for the day when the Church was to become supreme and the temporal power bow to the spiritual. With hidden motives we have nothing to do. He was as much a pioneer and did as great a work in his own way as John Smith did in the South or Bradford in the North. I have always regretted that Cecil Calvert was no diarist and had none of the love of introspection that so marked the Puritans, who had a perfect passion for self-analysis and the vivisection of their emotions. It would be supremely interesting if we knew what was in the back of this man's head, whether he was simply, as his life and public acts would seem to indicate, a person of moderation, shrewdness and generous instincts, or whether he was a cunning visionary who toiled patiently to accomplish an end that was never realized. It is a fascinating speculation, but profitless, as it leads nowhere.

The circumstances that gave a Catholic proprietor a Protestant charter, that made him realize that he was always under suspicion and was narrowly watched by his enemies in England, who, controlled by bigotry no less than covetousness, were alert to find an opportunity to oust him so as to profit by his misfortune, made the Maryland Catholics more moderate and tolerant than their age, and those qualities have always characterized the Church in America. There has never been any clash of authority between the Catholic hierarchy in the United States and the temporal power; no American Catholic has served Church and State with a divided allegiance; the Catholic Church, while teaching its own creed, has ever taught the higher creed of obedience to the State and respect for civil authority. Catholicism in America has not destroyed or weakened the fibre of American Republicanism; from a small beginning the Church has grown and become a mighty instrument in the development of American character, but it has been accomplished without the direct participation of the Church in politics. In other countries the Catholic Church found it necessary, or at least believed it to be advisable, to become an active political factor and to endeavor to influence the action of parties, but it has never done so in America. Baltimore's first settlers were moderates, and their descendants were equally moderate. Ultramontanism was unknown, and it was only later, after the Revolution, in the first decade of the nineteenth century, that the heavy immigration of Irish Catholics, to be later strengthened by the immigration from other Catholic countries of Europe, profoundly affected and modified the character of American Catholicism, aroused the last vestige of Puritan intolerance, and led to Know-Nothingism and the abortive attempt to inject religion into politics by the creation of the A. P. A.[1]

But in Baltimore's day Catholics and Protestants lived on neighborly terms. At one time the domi-

[1] The American Protective Association, or A. P. A. as it was generally called, was founded in 1887 as a secret political association, nominally to embrace "all who will be true Americans, irrespective of race, color, creed, original nationality, or previous conditions of life," but actually to curb the power of the Catholic Church in America. In its high-sounding declaration of principles the animus of the association is revealed in holding "that support of any ecclesiastical power of non-American character which claims higher sovereignty than that of the United States, is irreconcilable with American citizenship"; and in its protest "against the employment of the subjects of any un-American ecclesiastical power as officers or teachers of our public schools." Bowers, who founded the Association, explained its purpose in these words: "The chief idea we had in view in the constitution was this: that we had no right under the Constitution of this country to oppose any religious body on account of its dogmatic views, faith, etc., but we did believe we had a right to oppose it when it became a great political factor. We believed then and we believe now that every man in this country has a right to worship God according to the dictates of his conscience, but we did not believe that the Constitution intended to convey the right to any set of men to control and manipulate the political affairs of this country to the aggrandizement of any ecclesiastical power." — Malcolm Townsend: *Handbook of United States Political History*, pp. 152–153.

The A. P. A. rapidly gained a large membership and for a brief time was a terrifying bogey to timorous politicians, but it never exerted any political power and soon collapsed, an exotic that could find no nourishment in the soil of America, which nurtures every liberal idea, no matter how preposterous, but breeds no bigotry.

The Know-Nothing Party, formed in 1852, was avowedly opposed to Romanism and in favor of the election to public office of none but native-born Americans. It existed for four years, and during that time exerted considerable political influence.

nant religion, later Catholics were sorely persecuted; the Church of England, that afterwards was to be more powerful than any other creed, was, in the first years, surpassed in wealth and the number of its communicants by noncomformism, and as late as 1677 there were only three Anglican clergymen in the colony, and the few churches were without endowment and had to rely on the uncertain generosity of their congregations for the support of their ministers. In the House of Burgesses a few years before three quarters of the members were Puritans. They had come from Massachusetts as well as Virginia, and were in numbers sufficient to establish a community of their own at Ann Arundel.[1] Maryland, it is true, was a Catholic colony, but the influence of the Puritans was strong, and it was this coexistence of sects and creeds that differentiated Maryland from Virginia and Massachusetts and brought a new element to form the American character.

The men who first planted Maryland were made of better stuff than the neighboring Virginians, and in this as in so many other things Baltimore showed his sound sense and his wide vision, and probably he was able to profit by the experience of the Virginia Company. The scum of the jails and the slums was not gathered up to be thrown down in Maryland, and inducements were offered to sound energetic men to start a new life. But Mary-

[1] Bozman: *History of Maryland*, vol. ii, p. 393.

land, to speak quite frankly, similar to all the other English possessions of that day, was regarded as a convenient place for the disposal of criminals, and to it convicts were sent in large numbers. "The number of convicts imported into Maryland before the revolution of 1776," Scharf tell us, "must have amounted to at least twenty thousand. From the year 1750 to 1770 not less than four to five hundred were annually brought into the province."[1] This estimate is confirmed by other writers. The colonists bitterly resented that Maryland should be made a penal colony, and protests proving vain, acts were passed by the legislature prohibiting the importation of criminals, but these acts were declared void by the Crown. The legislature then resorted to the expedient of taxing criminals, under the clause of the charter which gave the colony the power to levy duties on imported merchandise, on the ground that as convicts were sold for service on their arrival in the colony, they were merchandise and not men, and subject to duty. But this construction of the charter the Crown overruled, and the practice of exporting criminals to Maryland as well as to other American colonies continued until the Revolution broke the power of England to make the New World a dumping-ground for its criminals and paupers. It is only proper to add, that while many of the criminals were felons, many were unfortunate rather than vicious; many had committed no greater

[1] Scharf: *op. cit.*, vol. i, p. 371.

offense than to fail in business; some were political prisoners who had plotted against the Crown or had been taken with arms in their hands. They were a mixed lot, not all bad, but few of them better than indifferent.

Climatically very similar to Virginia, and like Virginia with convenient water transportation making the laborious work of road-building unnecessary, the culture of tobacco was carried on in Maryland and was a source of great wealth, which required the use of African slaves and white indented servants. In Maryland as in Virginia, everywhere, in fact, where slavery became an institution, it put a stigma upon free labor and caused the free white man to lose his self-respect by being compelled to do work that was regarded as fit only for bondsmen belonging to an inferior race, or criminals who were made to labor in the fields as a punishment. With the growth of the colonies Maryland became a wheat-raising as well as a tobacco-growing province, and some of the largest landowners found it more profitable to turn their tobacco lands into wheat. Virginia always clung to tobacco and slavery; Maryland, as her wheat-fields multiplied and the export of flour became a profitable trade and Baltimore a port of first importance, was less dependent upon servile labor for her prosperity, which in time modified political views. Virginia after wavering threw in her lot with the other slaveholding states and joined the Confederacy; Maryland remained loyal to the Union that she had helped to create.

Baltimore laid the foundation of his local government in the manorial system of England, and every grant of 2,000 acres or more was created a manor with court baron and court leet, the master of the manor exercising feudal rights, and around him grew up a tenantry. The cultivation of tobacco had the same political and social effects in Maryland as in Virginia; the proprietor found it more profitable to cultivate the Indian weed himself on a large scale than to split up his holding among tenants and be paid in kind, "and the feudal society of the manor" was transformed into "the patriarchal society of the plantation." As in Virginia so in Maryland, tobacco "afforded an instance of how much a staple may not only regulate a people's conduct and habits, but become part of their thoughts and even enter into their dreams." From the lord proprietor down every one was paid in tobacco, tobacco meant wealth, wealth was reckoned in hogsheads of tobacco. All law, all society revolved around this little brown plant; society was organized to protect it and to make it more valuable; like gold it was the yardstick of value because to it the mints were always open. "Its purity was more fiercely defended than the chastity of woman, and the forger of an inspector's note was to be whipped and pilloried. Debts in tobacco were protected over debts in coin, and judgment, bonds and mortages might be both given and paid in tobacco." The mint for the free and unlimited conversion of tobacco into money was found in the official warehouse of the province, where tobacco was stored and inspected and a receipt given by a sworn inspector, which could always be negotiated for a bill of exchange on London.

Both the feudal and patriarchal states of society created a class of large landowners, who lived a free, hospitable and generous life, which later became reckless and impoverished their descendants; but in the Golden Age of Tobacco it was very delightful and fascinating; the men were developing the wealth of the colony and taking an active share in its political affairs, and were being strengthened to fit themselves for the part they were to play in that great political drama which was to make the last quarter of the eighteenth century so memorable; the women with all their dainty prettiness bred strong men. Scharf paints none too flattering a picture of the men whose history he has chronicled and of the state he proudly claims as his own. "The Maryland colonists," he says, "were not a well educated people, and it must be confessed that they thought more of horse-racing and cockfighting than they did of books." After Baltimore and his first settlers came the generations who had too much forest to cut down to be able to spare much time for the schoolmaster. The people of means with a desire for education went to England to acquire it, "but the greater part of the young Marylanders were more like Harry Warrington than like his brother George. Fox-hunting in the morning, and cards and dancing at night, left them little time for books."[1] Towards the end of the eighteenth century, in 1770, Scharf notes that there was socially a distinct aristocratic class in Maryland, a class comparatively large, most of whose members were wealthy and some of whom were well educated. As in Virginia, their fortunes rested on lands and slaves. They communicated with one another, but did not associate with the other classes. The province, taking more after Virginia in that respect than Massachusetts, had no general system of schools and no large class of tractarians and disputants whose arguments affected the people as a whole. It was no part of a "gentleman's" requirements of that time to be over particular about his syntax or spelling, and gentlemen could find better and more amusing things to do than to write pamphlets or discuss public affairs through the newspapers, of which there were only two in Maryland in 1775 and the same number in Virginia, while in Massachusetts there were seven; but it is to be remembered that the press exercised far less influence than it does to-day, and it was in the Assembly and the town and other meetings that the real work of government was carried on and public opinion formed.

[1] Scharf: *op. cit.*, vol. ii, p. 18.

The social life of the colony centred in Annapolis, which was a very gay and fashionable little city, where there was much wealth and extravagance, and people were as keen to be amused as high society is to-day in London or Newport or New York. One writer says that no city of the same size in England could boast so many handsome and fashionable women. They danced and went to the theatre and horse races, for the Marylanders have always been passionately fond of horse-racing; the men wagered their money on horses and cards and cockfights, and every one from the highest to the lowest regarded cockfighting as the greatest of all sports; and Puritans, who denounced the theatre as the devil's own device, saw no sin in watching two birds tear each other to pieces.

I pass over the quarrels between Virginia and Maryland, Leah and Rachel, the Two Fruitful Sisters, as a seventeenth century pamphleteer calls them, as merely an incident in the life of a nation and having no lasting influence on the development of character; nor need much more time be given to considering the manifestation of that new spirit that made the Englishman in America always a rebel and always quick to resist the encroachment of his governors. We have seen how these hot-tempered Virginians held on to the purse-strings and clung to the control of taxation as the great safeguard of their liberties, and how Nathaniel Bacon led an armed force against Sir William Berkeley.

Bacon's example was followed in the palatinate. Cecilius died in 1675 and was succeeded by his son Charles, an arbitrary and narrow-minded man, who had none of his father's tact and breadth of vision or that genius for colonial administration that makes the founder of Maryland so respected. Discontent, which had long been smouldering, broke into open fire when Bacon raised the standard of revolt, and a paper was circulated alleging the grievances of the Maryland colonists. Davis and Pate, men of substance, gathered an armed force to intimidate the governor and compel him to grant the concessions they demanded, but the collapse of Bacon's rebellion in Virginia put a speedy end to sedition in Maryland. Davis and Pate were hanged, the people deprived of their leaders had no heart for resistance, and there was no further attempt to overthrow the authority of the lord proprietor. Briefly to be considered as part of the political education of the English colonists in America, which logically led up to their separation from the mother country and resulted in the birth of a new nation, was the development of parliamentary government, which in England manifested itself in the assertion of the rights of the Commons against the assumed prerogatives of the King, and was intensified by being transplanted to a new soil. After the Restoration Englishmen in England were at times careless about the usurped power of the Crown, although they never surrendered the principle of the power of the people to govern, but in America they watched with jealousy every attempt on the part of the proprietors or royal governors to extend their authority at the expense of the popular assembly, and were ever ready to resist it.

There existed in England at that time, and even before the first Englishman set foot on the New World, two schools of political thought, as there have from the day when men first realized that the greatest enemy of progress is that peculiar mental condition which regards with aversion whatever is new or is different from what has long been known. In a word, the forces of progress have always had to contend with the forces of reaction. The political teachings of More and Hobbes and Locke, the entrancing vista of physical research opened up by Bacon and Newton, the religious speculations of Jeremy Taylor and Tillotson and Butler, had with dynamic force driven Englishmen forward on the road to individualism and given them a new conception of the relation between man and the state. They were further fortified by the spirit of adventure and daring that filled them as with new wine and stirred the imagination and taught them the great lesson of self-reliance and determination. These were the Englishmen who were no longer content to believe in the inerrancy of the doctrine of the divine right of kings, and who, while accepting royalty and a class system as a natural social arrangement, still claimed the right to be masters of themselves. The Englishmen who settled America were in the very nature of things individualists. If they developed political methods and political ideals different from the mother country, as some writers contend, it was the result of circumstances and conditions that influenced them mentally as they influenced them physically. Everything tended to the development of individualism, which is one of the marked characteristics of the modern American.

I note here briefly, to be referred to more at length later, that there was another cause to develop this marked sense of political idealism in the Englishman in America. The Englishman in England was never insular, in the larger political sense, but was always continental and international; he was part of the great dynastic and military forces that were never still, whose shock was felt in every hamlet throughout the land. The Englishman in America, in those days, was politically isolated. The Englishman at home was often confused and distracted by many things; war, rebellion, reasons of state made him repeatedly submit to evils that he knew of but which were his sacrifice to patriotism. The Englishman in America had no such demands made upon him. There were no cross currents to vex him and make his course uncertain. He need devote his energies to two things, and two things only: to improve his material condition and to develop the political system which he had founded; and as he was removed from the politics of Europe, so his own politics become to him not only the most important that he knew, but they were the only road that led to fame. In England men could win distinction in the military service, in the church, at the bar, as well as in politics; but in America, in early colonial days, the one reward for ability was political. We overlook one of the fundamental causes that produced the American character if we do not grasp the salient difference between the Englishman at home and the Englishman in America, and fail to give proper weight to the influence of political isolation.

The parliament of Maryland consisted of an upper house or council, whose members were appointed by the lord proprietor and were largely kinsmen or men on whom he could rely to execute his wishes, and the House of Burgesses, whose members were elected; in a word, a miniature reproduction of the Lords and Commons of England. Baltimore intended to deprive the lower house of the power to initiate legislation, and give it merely the form of authority without the substance, by graciously permitting it to comment on acts laid before it by the proprietor or his representative, the governor. To Englishmen, who were full of the spirit of self-government, such an invitation to a Barmecide feast was to be spurned as an insult. They would be no mere slaves to clank their chains in submission at the command of a master. They were freemen with rights and privileges, which were theirs as much in America as in England. Baltimore, tactful and liberal, yielded and gave to the Assembly the right to initiate legislation, but he retained the veto power, which by his own construction permitted him to repeal an act even after it had gone into force. It was one of the great grievances of the colonists, the proprietor's veto power, which they always resented. For many years there were stormy times between the upper and lower houses. The Council insisted that the right to tax was not inherent in the House of Burgesses, the latter asserted that it possessed the functions of the Commons of England and controlled the purse. In all those years nothing very vital happened, but character was being formed, men were learning the great art of self-government, and were preparing themselves to assert their political freedom.

But more important than the petty quarrels between neighboring colonies or incipient rebellion was the persecution of the Catholics. It is one of the delightful ironies of history — and history is so largely a record of sardonic humor — that Maryland, founded by a Catholic, offering asylum to Catholics, and setting an example of tolerance to all sects, should, in a little more than half a century after the first cross was erected at St. Mary's, proscribe and persecute Roman Catholics.

I have pointed out in a previous chapter that the

difference between Protestants and Catholics was political rather than religious, and that English Protestants looked upon English Catholics as enemies of the state and traitors to the cause of civil liberty. It was the Catholics, Protestants believed, who were continually plotting with foreign Catholic sovereigns to overthrow the established order in England and bring it under Catholic dominion and politically enslave the nation. It was not alone the form of worship that was so repellant to English Protestants, it was something more than that, which struck at the Englishman's whole concept of political and civil life. He was free, and to him freedom and Catholicism were incompatible. He had fought to preserve that freedom, and he believed that he should lose his precious heritage if England acknowledged the spiritual supremacy of the Supreme Pontiff.

When James II fled and William of Orange was called to the throne of England, panic seized the Protestants of America, who feared that America was to be made the battle-ground of religions, and that in the coming struggle between the deposed Stuart, backed by the troops of the French Papist, and the Protestant Prince of Orange the Catholics in America would side with their coreligionists in England and celebrate religious freedom in the new world by another Huguenot massacre. It was a senseless panic that possessed these hard-headed, clear-thinking Englishmen, but to them the danger seemed very real. The Protestants in Maryland waited to see what would happen, whether Baltimore would acknowledge William or remain loyal to the deposed King, and the council was eagerly watching for the first sign of official action. Baltimore had promptly dispatched a messenger with instructions to the Council to proclaim William and Mary, but the messenger died on the way and there was a long delay before a second messenger could arrive with his instructions. Meanwhile an "association in arms" had been formed "for the defence of the Protestant Religion, and for asserting the right of King William and Queen Mary to the Province of Maryland and all the English Dominions," and seven hundred men in arms under the leadership of John Goode marched on St. Mary's, the provincial capital. The Council fled without offering resistance, King William brought action to annul Baltimore's charter, and in 1691 sent out Sir Lionel Copley as royal governor of Maryland. In this way Baltimore lost his province, and the palatinate of Maryland no longer existed.

In Virginia the change from Commonwealth to Monarchy had been brought about without bitterness because there were no politico-religious consequences to be feared and liberty was not threatened, but in Maryland the accession of William and Mary gave the Protestants the opportunity they had long sought. They had accepted without enthusiasm a Catholic proprietor, and had always been jealous of the dominant part played by Catholics in the government of the colony; they had feared it would become catholicized, which would put an end to their hard-won civil and political liberties. So long as Baltimore kept his own religious views in the background they gave him loyal support, but they were ever watchful.

And now the time had come when the Protestants could strike down their enemy, and they struck swiftly and brutally. With that charity and liberality that made churchmen at one time regard creed as more important than the moral observance of the teachings of religion, the Protestants proceeded to show how they despised God when he was not worshipped according to their own narrow little formula. Taxes were levied for the support of the Church of England, persons professing the Catholic religion were prohibited from entering the colony, the public celebration of the mass was forbidden. As the Protestant element came to have a firmer grip upon the government, so they persecuted more shamelessly the Catholics. Two Catholic priests, William Hunter and Robert Brooker, were summoned before the Governor and Council, the one for having consecrated a chapel, the other for having said mass in it; and as this was their first offense they were let off with a reprimand, "which his Excellency was pleased to give," in the following gentle language:—

"It is the unhappy temper of you and all your

tribe to grow insolent upon civility and never to know how to use it, and yet of all people you have the least reason for considering that if the necessary laws that are made were let loose, they are sufficient to crush you, and which (if your arrogant principles have not blinded you) you must need to dread.

"You might, methinks, be contented to live quietly as you may, and let the exercise of your superstitious vanities be confined to yourselves without proclaiming them at public times and in public places, unless you expect, by your gaudy shows and serpentine policy, to amuse the multitude and beguile the unthinking, weakest part of them, an act of deceit well known to be among you." Having warned them that there were means to curb their insolence, this mild-spoken governor continued his admonition: "In plain and few words, gentlemen, if you intend to live here, let me hear no more of these things; for if I do, and they are made good against you, be assured I'll chastise you; and lest you should flatter yourselves that the severity of the laws will be a means to move the pity of your judges, I assure you I do not intend to deal with you so. I'll remove the evil by sending you where you may be dealt with as you deserve. Pray take notice that I am an English Protestant gentleman, and can never equivocate." Whereupon the unfortunate priests were dismissed and the sheriff was ordered to lock up the chapel and keep the key.[1]

[1] Scharf: *op. cit.*, vol. i, p. 368.

The Governor, like many another servant of the people, understood the art of popularity by voicing the sentiment of the majority. So pleased was the House of Burgesses with his reprimand that it adopted an address thanking him for having "generously bent to protect her majesty's Protestant subjects here against insolence and growth of Popery, and we feel cheerfully thankful to you for it." In view of the attitude of Governor and legislature it was not surprising that they should go to still further lengths in their zeal to stamp out Catholicism. In 1704, the year after the reprimand, an act was passed imposing a fine of £50 and imprisonment for six months upon any popish bishop, priest or jesuit who "should endeavor to persuade any of his majesty's liege people of this province to embrace and be reconciled to the Church of Rome"; and any person who said mass, or who being a Catholic, should keep school, or take upon himself the education, government or boarding of youth at any place in the province, upon conviction, was to be transported to England to be dealt with there under the statutes for further preventing the growth of popery. And still the work went on. Catholics were disfranchised unless they took the test oath. When Charles Calvert, the fifth Lord Baltimore, was restored to the proprietorship by George I, Calvert having adjured Catholicism and become a Protestant, even more rigorous laws were enacted, which effectually excluded Catholics from all participation in the government. They were required to take the oath of allegiance, abhorrency and abjuration, to which no devout Catholic could subscribe; and while they were excluded from any share in the government they were taxed for its support. But although the Catholics were oppressed and subjected to much petty annoyance and vindictive persecution they were preëminently the picked men of the colony, Fiske points out, an opinion which every historian of Maryland must share. They were the backbone of the colony and gave it a character of its own as the Puritan did in Massachusetts and the Cavaliers in Virginia; and the influence of these early Catholic settlers is seen in the Revolution, in the Civil War, and on the Maryland as we know it to-day. The long religious struggle had sown the seeds of discontent, and curiously enough Maryland was ripe for rebellion before Massachusetts or Virginia. Maryland had felt, as no other colony then had, the injustice of being ruled from across the sea, and while the connection with England was advantageous, it was also oppressive. The time had not yet come for any Englishman seriously to propose to sever the tie, but the folly of rulers had prepared men's minds for it; and when they were faced with the alternative of submitting further to injustice or resisting it in arms, the shock was less violent than it would have been had not the quarrels of churchmen paved the way.

CHAPTER XVII

RICE PRODUCES NEW SOCIAL CONDITIONS

It is in the blood of the Englishman never to be still. Accounted the most phlegmatic of races, the English are consumed with a resistless desire for discovery and adventure. Popularly supposed to have less imagination than the Latin and Celt, and deficient in that quality of poetic and speculative dreaming that is characteristic of the Teuton, nevertheless their imagination has always been profoundly stirred by the mystery of the unknown continent, by the knowledge that seas were to be charted and lands to be mapped; to find out where rivers led or what existed behind a range of mountains has ever been with them a passion. And perhaps more than any other race they have been possessed with an insatiable land hunger. It is this that has made them colonizers and conquerors, that has planted the flag of England deep in the snows of the north and far under the burning skies of the tropics. Love of commerce and love of gain animated them, but these would have been insufficient to make them brave danger and hardship if they had not been possessed of that resistless love of adventure.

That insatiable land hunger was not appeased by transplanting the Englishman from England to America. Love of adventure and the commercial advantages that were to accrue from the planting of the new world were the motives that spurred Raleigh; the desire to expand and to own still more territory made Massachusetts colonize the north and explore the south. The Virginians, with a virgin territory to develop, cast curious and covetous eyes on the *terra incognita* to the south of them; those sturdy Puritans found their energies not satisfied in building up their own colony, but must ever extend their frontiers and carve new settlements out of the wilderness; and "New England enterprise explored the American coast from one end to the other, in search of lucrative trade and new resting places." In the course of their wanderings these men from the north came to the North Carolina coast, and near the mouth of the Cape Fear River settled on land bought from the Indians. But the climate was unsuited to them and the surroundings displeased them, and after a short sojourn they went away; first, however, leaving in writing and affixed to a post for the benefit of posterity their opinion of the country in characteristically blunt New England manner. Here it was found some years later by immigrants from the Barbadoes. But before that a few scattered settlers had drifted in from Virginia, "with here a solitary plantation, and there a little group of farms, and always a restless van of adventurers working their way down the coast and into the interior."[1] This was the beginning of what at that time, 1663, was known as Carolina, but which later was split into the two provinces of North and South Carolina and under those names became states of the Union.

This region, in that day, was a sort of No Man's Land. It was vaguely included in the Virginia grant, it was claimed by the Spaniards as a part of Florida. A hundred years before, in 1562, Jean Ribaut had planted a colony of Huguenots at Port Royal, where he built a fort, and had been treacherously murdered by the Adelantado Menendez, who, in a pious frame of mind, told the French that he was there "to plant the Holy Gospel, that the Indians may be enlightened and come to the knowledge of the Holy Catholic faith of our Lord Jesus Christ, as the Roman Church teaches it." And so when Ribaut fell into his hands after promise of safe conduct, "I," Menendez writes, "caused Juan Ribao with all the rest to be put to the knife, judging this to be necessary for the service of God our Lord and of your Majesty."[2] And for a hundred years the Spanish asserted their claim and nothing was done to dispute it until Charles II granted the territory to eight proprietors, for whom John Locke drew up "the Grand Model," a remarkable and

[1] Lodge: *Short History of the English Colonies*, p. 134.

[2] Parkman: *Pioneers of France in the New World*, pp. 136, 144.

fantastic constitution that was unworkable and was never put into effect.

The territory granted to the Duke of Albemarle and his associates occupied a position of peculiar importance as the frontier of the English colonies in America. It lay between Virginia, then the most advanced southerly British outpost on the American continent, and the Spanish settlements. It was not only the international frontier but it served also, as Fiske points out, "for some time as a kind of backwoods for Virginia"; and he adds that "until recently one of the most important factors in American history has been the existence of a perpetually advancing frontier, where new territory has often to be won by hard fighting against its barbarian occupants, where the life has been at once more romantic and more sordid than on the civilized seaboard, and where democracy has assumed its most distinctly American features." How great this influence of the land beyond has exercised upon the development of the American character and American institutions, we shall see more clearly when we come to study the great migration that swept from the East to the West to populate the plains and build great cities, and the flood that rolled up from the South and fructified that vast region over which the Indian roamed and the buffalo grazed, but for the present we merely mention it as one of the factors in race development; for in almost three centuries of American existence there was never a time that a frontier was not to be conquered, and virgin soil to be broken, and civilization to be planted.

With the early efforts at settlement and the history of Carolina until it was divided into two provinces, there is little need to concern ourselves. To attract settlers to North Carolina a law was passed exempting them from the payment of taxes for one year, all debts contracted outside the province *ipso facto* outlawed, and no person could be sued for five years for any cause of action that might have arisen outside of the colony. North Carolina, or Albemarle, as it was then known, under these beneficent laws attracted the worthless, the improvident and the dishonest, and Virginia, resenting an Alsatia planted at its doors, contemptuously termed the new settlement "Rogue's Harbor." Naturally the worst element in all the colonies found shelter here. The men, we are told, were lazy and made their wives work for them. If the weather was cold, "they lie and snore till the sun had run one third of its course and dispersed all the unwholesome damps," and the low, alluvial land was the breeding ground for malaria. In mild weather "they stand leaning with both their arms upon the cornfield fence, and gravely consider whether they had best go and take a little heat at the hoe, but generally find reasons to put it off until another time." [1]

In 1677, only thirteen years after the first gov-

[1] Byrd MSS., pp. 75–76.

ernor of Albemarle had been appointed by Sir William Berkeley, the governor of Virginia, and one of the eight lords proprietors of the new province, as usual in an English colony in America, trouble broke out between the colonists and their government. That mischievous Navigation Act, which had been the exciting cause of Bacon's rebellion in Virginia, and Bacon at that time had looked to Albemarle to furnish him assistance to defy the power of the Crown, was to drive the Carolinians to open rebellion. A lucrative trade was carried on between the settlers on Albemarle Sound and the New Englanders, and their vessels were constantly crossing the short stretch of blue water to the West Indies, where they exchanged Virginia tobacco and cattle and lumber for rum and molasses and sugar, which could be sold in Europe for a round profit. It was profitable for every one concerned except the lords proprietors, who gained nothing by it, and as the colony existed for the enrichment of the men who owned it, according to the economic philosophy of the day, attempts were made to break up what was regarded as an illicit trade and divert it into its legitimate channels. At the end of the year 1677, a vessel arrived from the North with a cargo of rum and molasses, but as soon as her skipper landed he was arrested by the governor and held in £1,000 bail for a violation of the Navigation Act. Culpeper, a turbulent spirit, incited the mob to resist the governor, who, together with the council, were seized and locked up, and Culpeper proclaimed governor, new justices appointed, and a *de facto* government set up, which existed for two years.

There was constant turmoil for many years. Attempts on the part of governors to establish the Church of England were stoutly resisted by the Dissenters; but Englishmen of all creeds made common cause in attempting to exclude the Huguenots from the franchise. The Indians, a treacherous and vindictive foe, were encouraged by the Spaniards to regard the English as their natural enemies. North Carolina marks the beginning of that important Scotch immigration which has left such a marked impress upon America; and there came also Germans from the Rhine provinces. The older colonies were colonized by Englishmen, and the first work of settlement was done and the government established without the assistance of men alien to their race. The younger colonies gave welcome to Germans and French and Scotch and Irish, and from that time the foreign element has never ceased to flow in a steady stream across the Atlantic.

North Carolina demands very little more attention at our hands. During the proprietary period the people clung to the coast and were behind the other colonies in their civilization. "Of all the thirteen colonies North Carolina was the least commercial, the most provincial, the farthest removed from European influences, and its wild forest life the most unrestrained. Every colony had its frontier, its borderland between civilization and savagery; but North Carolina was composed entirely of frontier. The people were impatient of legal restraints and averse to paying taxes; but their moral and religious standard was not below that of the other colonies. The freedom was the freedom of the Indians, or the wild animal, not that of the criminal and the outlaw. Here truly was life in the primeval forest, at the core of nature's heart. There were no cities, scarcely villages. The people were farmers or woodsmen, they lived apart, scattered through the wilderness; their highways were the rivers and bays, and their homes were connected by narrow trails winding among the trees. Yet the people were happy in their freedom and contented with their lonely isolation."[1] We may question the assertion that their moral and religious standard was not below that of other colonies, and regard the conclusion of another writer as more nearly describing their condition: "North Carolina, the poorest, most backward, and ignorant of all the colonies, was virtually a community of small proprietors living squalidly on the products of their own farms, and occasionally exporting their surplus products, pork, cattle, and tar."[2]

It was characteristic of these turbulent, lawless people that they should not only have taken a

[1] Elson: *History of the United States*, p. 87.

[2] *Cambridge Modern History*, vol. vii, p. 56.

leading part in the Revolution but have anticipated it. On May 31, 1775, more than a year before the adoption of the Declaration of Independence, the people of Mecklenburg County adopted a resolution declaring that British authority had ceased, and officers were chosen to act independently of the Crown and Parliament. An attempt has been made by some writers to prove that the language of the Declaration of Independence adopted at Philadelphia was virtually a paraphrase of the Mecklenburg resolution, but the weight of evidence does not sustain this ingenious theory. The action of these fiery Mecklenburgers is an interesting side light, but without significance. They obtained no support from the rest of North Carolina, and events were neither hastened nor retarded by their defiance of English authority.

South Carolina demands closer study because of the great part it played in all that has gone to produce American development and the influence it has exercised on political and social institutions. About the time that "Rogue's Harbor" was giving haven to its derelicts the proprietors of the Carolinas established a settlement at Cape Fear, a hundred and sixty miles south of Albemarle. We need not again refer to it. The settlement disappeared and became merged into Charleston, from which sprung South Carolina. With the purpose of building up a community that should be self-sustaining, a grant of one hundred and fifty acres was given to every freeman who went out at his own cost, with a like amount for every man servant, and one hundred acres for every woman servant he brought with him, and at the expiration of their terms of service each servant was to be given a hundred acres. Able-bodied men willing to work, but without money, were supplied with food, clothes, and tools. Realizing the sturdy character of the New Englander and noting how he had prospered, the proprietors attempted to induce immigration from the North and reproduce the social conditions existing there rather than those of Virginia and Maryland. Impressed with the economic importance of a colony of towns, they did everything to encourage urban life and check the acquisition of great estates. Some immigrants were attracted from New England, but they left little mark on the province, and recruiting went on actively everywhere, producing a very mixed population in the early days. Englishmen came from England and the Bahamas and the Barbadoes, Dutchmen from New York, Huguenots from France, Scotch and Irish from their own countries, Virginians and North Carolinians drifted in. In nationality they were no less different than they were in temperament and condition, but America has ever been the crucible to fuse the elements of race and amalgamate them into nationality, and what took place in South Carolina at the end of the seventeenth century foreshadowed on a grander scale a more important movement a century later.

The history of the United States is a study of a people always in flux. In the early days there was never a time when they were not "emigrants." They "emigrated" from Massachusetts to the other New England colonies, and then spread to New York; from Virginia they went to the Carolinas and further south; from New England they stretched to the middle West; from the South they bridged the Mississippi. In the first century of their existence there was a reservoir from which to draw the supply to nourish a soil barren of people and only needing men to make it fruitful; later when the drain was too heavy, Europe filled up the reservoir with the stream of its population. Cavaliers and Puritans, Protestants and Catholics, sturdy adventurers and shiftless incompetents, the idle and the industrious, the sober and the dissolute, were the beginnings of North Carolina who came across land and sea, attracted by the promise of gain or the hope of escape from undesirable conditions.

This filling up of North Carolina was typical of those great migratory movements that have always been such a striking and interesting phenomenon of American development. It was the same impulse that turned the tide of immigration to the West at the time of the great gold discoveries, that in the West drove men ever a little nearer to the setting sun, because there was still an undiscovered country; that to-day is the lure of the city to the young man on the farm, and with siren call makes men abandon life in older communities, and begin life anew in mining camps and settlements, whose future is promise and where chances are more equal. The nomadic spirit is in the blood of Americans. As yet they have developed no passionate attachment to the soil or the birthplace of their fathers. To them, to the majority, no sacred associations cling to the roof tree, for to the American home is wherever he makes it, and he feels that the time has not yet come when he can plant his roots deep in the soil, and see a sturdy forest spring from his own seed and grow up around him. There is too much intercommunication between all parts of the United States for any one section to live apart from the other. This freedom of intercourse leads to the daughters marrying and going to the homes of their husbands, five hundred miles, a thousand miles or more away; and the wide scattering of members of a family is regarded as a matter of course. No man will admit failure, it is only the absence of opportunity that prevents his rising, and if opportunity is not at hand it can be found elsewhere. The New York man goes to California and the Californian goes to New York, and they both prosper, which is one of the marvels of a country whose social institutions are unlike those of any other and where conditions are different from those elsewhere.[1]

[1] "We are apt to consider New England as preëminently the region that people go from, and some of these New England states at times have appeared to be scarcely more than breeding-grounds for stalwart men and women to inhabit and build up other parts of the land. Old home week in

Slavery always had a deeper hold and exercised a more baneful influence in South Carolina than in any other colony or state, and to obtain cheap servile labor the South Carolinians enslaved the native Indians. This brought on hostilities between the Indians and the whites that lasted for many years, and the Spaniards of St. Augustine, but two days' sail from the English frontier, watched the growing spread of the English colonists with fear and jealousy. Menendez, who preached Christianity at the point of the knife, had gone, but his methods survived, and in 1680 a Scotch colony that had been planted at Port Royal by Lord Cardross was wiped out of existence. The colonists, who were not of the kind to turn the other cheek and take punishment without retaliating, were anxious to teach the Spaniards a lesson, but they were prevented by the proprietors, who refused to sanction the dangerous doctrine that a colony could make war on a sovereign power without the consent of the home government. Soon they were to have their fill of fighting, and the time was fast approaching "when the battles of the great European powers were fought out on the banks of the Ohio and Lake Erie, and when the war-cry

Kentucky reminds one how true it is that an intense migratory movement has steadily gone on in the middle West for several generations. . . . The first settlers of the West and Southwest, or their children, were ever on the move, pushing onward to new and, if possible, more fertile lands. In later times there has been the same fluidity of population, so that to-day, it is said, Kentucky has 600,000 of her children dwelling outside of her borders. And among them scores of men who have distinguished themselves in public life of sister states." — *Springfield* (Massachusetts) *Republican,* June 14, 1906.

was raised, and the tomahawk wielded amid peaceful American settlements at the bidding of a diplomat in London or Madrid."

It would be wearisome and profitless minutely to trace the constant bickering and quarrels between the colonists and their governors until the rule of the proprietors ceased and the Crown assumed control, and to us they are merely interesting as showing that in South Carolina, as everywhere else in English America, there was displayed that same spirit of independence, that same determination to resist oppression, that same resolution to uphold rights and liberties that the Englishman regarded as his inherently and not vouchsafed to him as an act of grace by proprietor or king. It was in the blood of these Englishmen to be defiant, and by this time we have become so accustomed to their defiance taking the usual form of resistance to the governor, that we should be surprised if South Carolina did not preserve the tradition. It was the customary dispute over taxation, the colonists proposing to raise money to resist Spanish invasion by taxing British imports; and when the governor gave orders to call out the militia to do in Charleston what Cromwell had done in Westminster, the Assembly threw off their allegiance to the proprietors and declared themselves subject only to the authority of the Crown. Johnson, the proprietary governor, was deposed and Moore elected in his place as the king's representative, without shedding blood. When two British men-of-war came into the harbor of Charleston, their captains, yielding to Johnson's request for assistance, sent their crews to quarters and trained their guns on the city, but the rebels had possession of the forts guarding the harbor, and threatened shot for shot. The time had not come for Englishmen to engage in fratricidal strife, there was no firing from the ships, and the proprietary charter was soon afterwards forfeited. This happened in 1719. Fifty-seven years later there was another revolution, but on a larger scale, which was also brought about by differences regarding taxation and in which South Carolina took a prominent part. Another fifty-six years elapse and South Carolina maintains the doctrine of nullification — the right of a state to resist the payment of tariff duties because they are considered unjust and burdensome — and threatens secession; and in another thirty years she puts the threat into execution and leads the procession of the seceding Southern States. The effect of early influences on the character of a people is nowhere more typically exemplified than in the political and social history of South Carolina.

To us, now, these years of friction between the people and the government, like the angry disputes over church matters, seem petty and almost meaningless and unworthy of men who were engaged in that stupendous task of solidly laying the foundation of an imperial empire and giving birth to a nation; whose lives were a constant struggle against savage foes, who had to tame the wilderness and bring barren places under cultivation and build cities; but they were not without results. They made for character, not the finest or highest type, it is true, but a certain strength was necessary at a time when rude strength was essential to future development. These quarrels taught the great truth that constitutions are made for men and not men for constitutions, and that when men have outgrown their constitutions, there is a way to discard that which is no longer useful and still retain the essence and spirit of that which is vital.

In everything that happened in America from the time when the first settlers landed in Jamestown until the warning cry rang out in the stillness of that April night and the belfry's beacon light called a nation into arms, there is nakedly revealed the one great weakness of English rule. No English statesman was able to grasp the obvious truth that the colonies had outgrown their institutions and were simply keeping pace with their development. Proprietors in the beginning, and the Crown and its ministers later, gave to these men a set of rules under the name of charters and constitutions that were supposed to be sufficient and needed neither enlargement nor modification. They made no provision for expansion, they made no allowance for that physical and spiritual growth that was inevitable if the colonies were to live, and could only fail to reveal itself if the colonists remained mere bands of struggling settlers unable to stand on their own feet and always looking to the mother country for support. But they became quickly self-sustaining, and developed that peculiarly self-reliant temper which is a part of the American inheritance; the indifference and carelessness of proprietors and ministers allowed them little by little to claim a still greater control of their own affairs, which stimulated them to demand even more, and finally welded the colonists into a cohesive mass whose aims and purposes were antagonistic to those of their rulers. Such a training can have only one ending. The strain becomes greater year by year, but goes on until the tension becomes too great and the system breaks down.[1]

Virginia was influenced politically and materially — and the material conditions of a country are always reflected in the moral and psychological attitude of its people — by tobacco; South Carolina was influenced in the same way by its two great staples, indigo and rice; the former, however, having only a brief life and giving place to cotton, which has had the widest effect on the lives and character

[1] Since the above was written, the second volume of Channing's *History of the United States* has appeared, and the view so freely expressed by this writer that the revolution of 1776 had long been smouldering is sustained by that eminent American authority. "In recent years," he says, "English writers have united in objurgating George III and the stupid, ignorant politicians who guided England's affairs in the fifteen years before 1775; on their shoulders have been laid the faults which brought about the American revolution; but the causes of that cataclysm lie further back and may be largely found in the settlement of the imperial constitution in the years immediately following William's accession to power." — Vol. ii, p. 219.

of its cultivators. Rice, in a wild state, has always been found in South Carolina, but cultivated rice was introduced into the colony by accident, when a ship from Madagascar brought a bag of rice to Charleston in 1693 and it was planted experimentally. It was found that the swamps of the colony were peculiarly suitable for its propagation, and it was soon cultivated on a large and profitable scale and gave to the South Carolinians the same solid foundation for wealth that tobacco had given to the Virginians, but with far more disastrous physical and moral results. The cultivation of tobacco is not more physically exhausting than any other kind of farming in healthy surroundings, but rice must be grown in swamps and marshy lands under tropical heat, which is fatal to the white man; and the same conditions govern the growing of indigo. In those days rice culture was to other agriculture what the sweated industries of to-day are to manufacturing carried on more scientifically; but the toll in human life that the sweatshop pays does not stand in the way of its existence, and as misery and want drive workers into the sweatshop and society connives at the sacrifice, so force and cunning found labor for the deadly rice-fields. White men were unable to work there, but the negro and Indian could, and were regarded by the proprietor simply as so much machinery, which, having converted a certain amount of raw material into the finished product, is worn out in the operation and must be replaced.

Negroes were imported in such large quantities that every year each man could raise enough indigo or rice more than to repay the cost of his purchase; so that it was cheaper for the South Carolina proprietor to work his slaves to death than to take care of them or to replenish the stock by breeding. "Assuming, then, that human nature in South Carolina was neither better nor worse than in other parts of the civilized world, we need not be surprised when told that the relations between master and slave were noticeably different from what they were in Virginia, Maryland, and North Carolina. The negroes of the southern colony were reputed to be more brutal and unmanageable than those to the northward."[1] In the northern colonies slaves had been softened by contact with civilization and were, as a rule, properly fed and housed and treated without undue harshness; it was as much to the advantage of the slaveholder, whose wealth was in slaves, to keep them in condition so as to get the greatest profit from their labor and their breeding, as it was properly to care for his stock. But in South Carolina no such considerations prevailed, and the slaves were usually brought direct from the savage wilds of Africa to fall under the lash of the overseer in the rice-fields.

The effect of slavery was more demoralizing in South Carolina than in any other colony. In Vir-

[1] Fiske: *Old Virginia and Her Neighbours*, vol. ii, p. 327. *Cf.* Bruce: *Economic History of Virginia*, vol. ii, p. 108.

ginia and Maryland, great as the evils of slavery were in degrading free white labor, there was still room for the white indented servant and the freeman, but in South Carolina that was impossible, and it was a colony not of white men using the labor of slaves, but a colony of slaves with a few white masters. In 1760, of the total population of 150,000 three quarters were said to be slaves, while in the adjoining colony of North Carolina there were only 50,000 slaves in a population of 200,000. In Virginia and Maryland the proprietors lived on their plantations surrounded by their slaves, and the life was both patriarchal and feudal; in South Carolina it was seldom that a rice planter lived on his estate, and he gravitated naturally to Charleston, which occupied the same relation to the colony as London did to the rest of England. In Virginia and Maryland the planter had little fear from his slaves, but in South Carolina that dread was never absent; the planter always went armed (to that we can doubtless trace the demoralizing modern custom of the Southern man carrying a pistol and the freedom with which he uses it on the slightest provocation); and the slave insurrection of South Carolina of 1740 is a part of its early history.

Because most of the landed proprietors of South Carolina lived in Charleston, that city naturally became the centre of the life of the colony and absorbed not only its wealth and fashion, but also its commercial activity. Virginia, as we have seen, was a colony of estates and not of cities or towns; Maryland life at first centred in Annapolis, and Baltimore became the commercial metropolis; but in South Carolina Charleston combined the two. This circumstance made life there more cosmopolitan than in any other city in any of the southern colonies of the day, and as South Carolina had a large seaborne trade there was frequent and close communication with Europe. The isolation of North Carolina, a backwoods settlement, was very marked, and the freedom of intercourse of South Carolina appears all the more striking because of the contrast with its nearest neighbor.

From the point of view of English colonial policy of that time, which regarded a colony as simply a producer of raw material and a consumer of English finished product, which was for the advantage of English merchants and manufacturers, South Carolina was an ideal possession. There were no manufactures, her people were satisfied with the cultivation of the soil, and it brought them wealth and contentment.

CHAPTER XVIII

AN EXPERIMENT THAT FAILED

IN the history of the United States there is no chapter invested with such romantic interest as that of the founding of Georgia, the last of the English Colonies. Neither Massachusetts and its Puritan theocracy; nor Rhode Island, a monument to the liberality of Roger Williams; nor Maryland, where Catholics practiced tolerance and were persecuted; nor Pennsylvania, where Quakers found a home, is comparable to Georgia, established to afford a refuge for unfortunates, with aims so lofty and purposes so ideal that it is a remarkable and unique episode in the march of civilization; and it was typical of that idealistic spirit in the Americans that made them for so many years, and until self-preservation caused more prudent considerations to prevail, to regard America as a haven for the distressed. It failed to accomplish the hopes of its promoters, but the experiment was worth making. Few people remember this early phase of Georgia; the strife of religions, the ambitions of politicians, the folly of rulers, are all too well remembered; but the efforts made in behalf of humanity, on a scale never before or since equaled, have been forgotten.

A lad of good family, James Oglethorpe had been

one of Marlborough's subalterns in his campaigns in the Low Countries; he had fought under Peterborough in Italy and with Prince Eugene against the Turk. Handsome, dashing, with a manner that made him popular with men, and women found captivating; full of courage and high spirits but with excellent control of himself, he was a romantic and fascinating figure. Boswell tells a pretty story showing his spirit and quick wit. When he was only nineteen years old he dined one day with the Prince of Würtemberg, who insolently flipped a few drops of wine in his face. Oglethorpe dare not submit to the insult without protest, for that would have betokened him a coward; and to have hotly resented it might have given him a reputation of turning a pleasantry into a quarrel. Looking the prince squarely in the face, and with the easy manner of a man amused, he said: "That's a good joke, but we do it much better in England," and he flung a full glass of wine in the astonished prince's face. There was consternation for a moment, but an old general who was one of the guests at the table said, "*Il a bien fait, mon prince, vous l'avez commencé*"; and "thus all ended in good humor," Boswell comments in relating the incident.

In 1717 Sir Robert Montgomery attempted to establish a colony in what is now known as Georgia, which lay between the English colony of North Carolina and the Spanish possessions of Florida. Sir Robert was a man of luxuriant imagination.

In his advertisement for settlers he described in glowing terms this wonderful country. "Nature has not blessed the world with any tract which can be preferable to it. Paradise with all her virgin beauties may be modestly supposed, at most, but equal to its native excellencies." But even an earthly paradise could not attract immigrants, and three years later the attempt was abandoned.

Oglethorpe was now in England, a familiar figure at court and at Westminster, where he had been elected to Parliament. He became interested in that barbarous system by which imprisonment for debt was sanctioned, and he was made a member of a parliamentary commission to investigate the debtor prisons. Profoundly moved by the horror of imprisonment for debt and a legal system which made misfortune a crime, he petitioned the privy council for a grant of land lying between the Savannah and Altamaha rivers, on which he proposed to establish a colony for the indigent and insolvent who were willing to make a new start in life.

The scheme was hailed with extraordinary enthusiasm. Oglethorpe was inspired by his love of humanity and his desire to extend a helping hand to his fellowmen who had stumbled; but his associates in the enterprise saw an opportunity to capitalize charity and make it yield handsome dividends. The same spirit that had moved the early Spanish discoverers, that had animated the first English adventurers, was now again to manifest itself, and the copartnership of God and Mammon was once more entered into. The indigent and the insolvent were to be placed on their feet, which was a pious work; but the colonization of Georgia by Englishmen would create a strong military outpost between the English and Spanish possessions, and it was obvious to English statesmen that Spain was a menace to the English colonies in the South and must be kept in check. And in addition, the new colony could be made profitable and swell the commerce of England, which was the ambition of every Englishman. Montgomery's alluring picture of Georgia (so named after George II, who granted the charter) was accepted as truthful by Englishmen, to whom New England was a place of snow and ice and the South a land of perpetual sunshine. Georgia was to be the great storehouse from which England drew her raw supplies. Instead of spending five hundred thousand pounds a year for silk woven in Italy and France, Georgia was to raise raw silk to be woven by English weavers in England, thus giving employment to twenty thousand people in Georgia and forty thousand in England. Wine, oil, dyes, drugs, flax, hemp, and other commodities that England was forced to purchase abroad were to be raised in the English colony of Georgia. Foreign nations were no longer to grow prosperous at the expense of Englishmen, but English money was to remain in England, and

English workmen were not to be reduced to starvation by foreign competition. It was all so simple. The prisons and poorhouses of England were filled with debtors and paupers; it was only necessary to transport them a few thousand miles across the sea and poverty would be replaced by riches and the despondent would become strong men of whom England could feel proud.

The charter was granted in 1732. Money was liberally supplied, the scheme having the powerful patronage of the Church as well as society. To those self-sacrificing clergymen who labored without reward in noisome prisons and among the poor whose condition was so deplorable, this seemed at last a practical way to relieve suffering, and society was dazzled by Oglethorpe's enthusiasm and devotion. He was already distinguished as a soldier, he had mounted the first rounds of a parliamentary career; in every drawing-room there were women whose eyes took on a new light when he approached; life lay before him and offered whatever honors or pleasures he cared to take. And on everything he deliberately turned his back and gave up that which men most covet to suffer the hardships of an emigrant ship of those days and lead his little band of broken-down men to a new life in the wilderness where the Spaniard threatened and the Indian lurked ever alert and treacherous.

The charter granted to Oglethorpe and his associates was unlike that of any other colony. Instead of the government, to which by that time the people had become accustomed, of a governor and council or the representative of the proprietors and a legislature representing the people, a body of twenty-one trustees was created whose corporate existence was limited to twenty-one years, after which the Crown would determine the form of government best suited for the needs of the colony. The trustees were the government of the colony and were given despotic control, but the charter provided that the settlers should enjoy the liberties of free-born British subjects. Slave labor was prohibited, as was also the importation of rum. As Georgia was intended to be a military outpost against the Spaniards, the presence of a large mass of slaves, as in South Carolina, was considered dangerous to the military security of the province.

Early in 1733, Oglethorpe reached Charleston where he was well received, for the South Carolinians were only too glad to have a buffer erected between themselves and the Spaniards. On the site of what is now Savannah the first settlement was laid. The little colony at once went to work, and Oglethorpe took his share of the labor, assisting in putting up the houses and doing his turn at guard duty. Fresh settlers arrived. Parliament made a grant of £10,000; botanists were sent by private subscription to the West Indies and South America to find plants that would grow in the fertile soil of Georgia. If ever there was a petted colony it was this refuge for the unfortunate. Highlanders were brought from Scotland, and they were of better texture and more fitted to cope with the hardships of the wilderness than the spawn of the jails and the poorhouses. There came also Protestants from the archbishopric of Bavaria to escape the persecutions of its primate, who attempted to convert them to the Catholic faith. But in a year or two Oglethorpe and the trustees discovered what since then philanthropists have repeatedly found to their sorrow, that men who have made a failure of life seldom, if ever, reassert qualities of success after they have reached a certain age. There is always a chance for the young man to make a new start under more favorable circumstances, but the man of middle age has lost his power of initiative, his character is no longer plastic, and the pleasing fiction of turning over a new leaf exists in imagination only. The debtors and paupers were not regenerated by their passage across the Atlantic, and they were as worthless in Georgia as they had been in England.

But a danger even greater than the worthlessness of his colonists now threatened Oglethorpe. The relations between England and Spain were daily becoming more strained, and the activity of the Spanish *guardacostas* in enforcing the laws against smuggling, and the contemptuous fashion in which they overhauled and searched British trading vessels, excited so much indignation that it only needed a swashbuckling mariner with an eye to dramatic effect to fan popular fury into a demand for reprisals. Fate is always ready to find its agents, whether for good or evil, and when the valorous Captain Jenkins brought home his carefully preserved dissevered ear and joyfully exhibited it to his countrymen, daily becoming more angry, as proof of Spanish brutality and the indignities to which freeborn Englishmen were subjected, it was enough, and the war of Jenkins's ear resulted.

Georgia was in the track of the storm. The Spaniards were in a position of strong defense at St. Augustine, and from Havana they could easily summon reinforcements and supplies. Oglethorpe acted with his usual decision and perspicacity. As soon as war was declared he called on the neighboring colonies for assistance, to which South Carolina responded with money and North Carolina and Virginia with men and arms, and he attacked and captured the fort at Picolata on the St. John's River and then moved in force to attack St. Augustine, but the place was too heavily fortified and he was obliged to abandon the siege, having suffered considerable loss but having inflicted a still heavier loss upon the enemy. For the next two years military operations on land practically ceased, then the Spaniards attempted to inflict a crushing blow. A great fleet was fitted out at Havana and an assault made on the forts at Frederica, which Oglethorpe repulsed with such heavy loss that the enemy abandoned the attack. The following year the

Spaniards made another attempt, but Oglethorpe forced their hand by taking the offensive, which had no result except to disconcert them. This ended the war, and it left England in secure possession of Georgia and South Carolina.

While Oglethorpe was repelling the Spaniards his colony was not prospering. It has already been said that the trustees prohibited slavery, although Oglethorpe himself owned a plantation worked by enslaved negroes in South Carolina; but the prohibition was based on economic and military reasons, rather than on the ground of humanity. Black labor was considered unsuited for the products that Georgia was to raise, and as one of the main reasons for creating Georgia was to throw up a barrier between South Carolina and the Spanish possessions, the presence of a large slave population easily to be corrupted by Spanish emissaries would doubly have endangered the security of the colony. In less than ten years after the first settlers landed they began to clamor for the right to bring slaves into the colony, and, jealous of the great prosperity of South Carolina and their own seemingly hopeless struggle, they contended that without negroes it would be impossible for the colony to thrive. The trustees attempted to remain true to themselves and firmly resisted the introduction of slavery, but at last they were compelled to give way, and fifteen years after Oglethorpe had led his first band of settlers to Georgia, ships were discharging their cargoes of black chattels, and even before that slaves had been smuggled into the colony from South Carolina.

Although the charter of the trustees was to run for twenty-one years, they surrendered it shortly before it expired by limitation. The great scheme had proved a failure. Once more it had been demonstrated that men are not made by coddling, and that states as well as character are only wrought out by the exercise of individual expression and the struggle that brings out the best of which men are possessed. The silk and the wine and the olives that were to make Georgia prosperous and England rich had not been grown, nor were any attempts made to raise them. The Georgians looked over to South Carolina and saw slaves toiling in the swamp lands and raising indigo and rice, which made their neighbors rich, while they were struggling with poverty; and they wanted slaves so that they might also grow rice and indigo and be surrounded by the same comfort. The alluring vision of a peaceful, happy, contented community was a dream that had never been realized. Of all the English colonies Georgia was the most discontented and the most backward, exceeding even North Carolina in this respect. In Georgia, as in all the Southern colonies afflicted with the curse of slavery, there was the element of "mean whites" (the Georgia "crackers" of to-day can trace their descent through an unbroken line to ancestors who were among

Oglethorpe's first settlers), and slavery there as everywhere else degraded free labor and encouraged thriftlessness and slack habits. There was much crime and lawlessness, there were neither schools nor literature, the people were rude and uncouth, communication was difficult because the roads were mere trails.

When the Crown took over the charter a royal governor was appointed and a form of government established similar to those in the other provinces. Rice and indigo worked by slaves were the principal products of the colony, but lumber and turpentine were also important articles of commerce. Down to the Revolution, when the other colonies were highly developed and had given birth to men of the widest mental attainments, Georgia was still a struggling, backward, illiterate community.

CHAPTER XIX

THE FIRST WRITTEN CONSTITUTION

WHILE a civilization was being developed in the South, the northern colonies, laid on the Pilgrim and Puritan foundation, were growing apace and making progress along their own lines. We have already seen how New England came into being, and it is not necessary for the purpose the writer has in view to trace minutely the growth of Massachusetts during the years immediately following, but some attention must be paid to the origin of the other New England colonies, to complete the historical perspective.

The rigid theocracy established by the Puritan founders of Massachusetts invited to resistance men less inclined to subordinate earthly rule to divine interpretation or who were more liberal in their concept of life; and the foundation of what is now the state of Connecticut has a twofold interest to the student of early American development. Connecticut, or as it first appeared in American history, the settlement of Hartford, was the protest of dissidents against the iron-clad rule of the theocracy, who found that it was easier to abandon Massachusetts and carve out for themselves a new home in the wilderness than to remain and perpetually be at war. Connecticut is further interesting to us because it was the beginning of that great and world-influencing movement, by which the parent colony casts forth a shoot which takes root and flourishes in new soil. Before this time colonies had been formed by conquest or migration from the mother country, but now we are to see the colony sending forth her own pioneers to extend the frontier and increase her strength.

Theocratic tyranny soon bred its discontent. As early as 1633 Thomas Hooker, a clergyman in charge of a congregation at Newton, a man of learning and eloquence, much more tolerant than the majority of the Puritan ministers, with far less pugnacity and hair-splitting narrowness, and a belief in democracy rather than the autocratic rule of the church, to whom the divine right of self-ordained governors was no less repugnant than that of kings, began to agitate resistance to the ecclesiastical oligarchy then in control in Massachusetts; and he found zealous supporters not only in his own congregation, but also in the neighboring towns of Watertown and Dorchester.

The idea of democracy at that time, as a philosophic principle, was very foreign to the ideas of the men whose descendants were to establish it as an enduring form of government; Winthrop had such a poor opinion of power entrusted to the people that to him democracy was "amongst most civil nations accounted the meanest and worst of all forms of government," and he found historical warrant for believing "that it hath always been of least continuance and fullest of trouble"; John Cotton, that "thundering preacher," voiced what was generally believed when he said, "Democracy I do not conceive that God did ordain as a fit government either for church or commonwealth."

The theocracy had a quick and ready means for overcoming resistance to authority and banished those who challenged its rule. It is probable that would have been the fate of Hooker and his associates had they not forestalled action by voluntarily emigrating. Accordingly, the people of the three towns, the able-bodied, the old, and the little children, with their cattle and their household goods, left Massachusetts and turned their faces to the south, where on the banks of the Connecticut River they founded the three towns of Hartford, Windsor, and Wethersfield, Hartford being the most important and occupying in a sense the relation of the seat of the central government to the allied towns. At first these towns, which Massachusetts regarded as one of her outposts, were governed by Massachusetts through a board of commissioners, but that extraordinary craving for self-government, which is written on every page of American history from the landing at Jamestown to the present day, made these Massachusetts emigrants determined to be their own rulers, and the towns elected representatives to a General Court at Hartford, which became the mother town of the new colony and was the beginning of Connecticut as separate and apart from Massachusetts.

On May 31, 1638, Hooker preached a sermon of great eloquence and power, that age has not dimmed nor time robbed of its remarkable conception of the philosophy of democracy; which foreshadowed by 138 years the great basic truths of the Declaration of Independence. "The foundation of authority," Hooker declared, "is laid in the free consent of the people." "Governments are instituted among men deriving their powers from the consent of the governed," the authors of the Declaration of Independence wrote. "The choice of public magistrates belongs unto the people, by God's own allowance," Hooker said, and "they who have power to appoint officers and magistrates, it is in their power, also, to set the bounds and limitations of the power and place unto which they call them." The Declaration of Independence indicted the king for having "obstructed the Administration of Justice, by refusing his Assent to Laws for establishing Judiciary Powers. He has made Judges depend upon his will alone, for the tenure of their offices, and the amount and payment of their salaries."

In the following January a written constitution was adopted, which too many American writers have treated as an incident instead of recognizing that it was an epochal event momentous in the progress of mankind. It was the first civil code reduced to writing adopted on American soil; it was the only written constitution then in existence that organized a form of civil government. Magna Charta was a compact between sovereign and people guaranteeing them certain liberties, but the constitution adopted in that little frame house on the banks of the Connecticut went much further than the compact that the barons wrested from John at Runnymede. Just as Hooker's sermon foreshadowed the Declaration of Independence, so his charter, for he was undoubtedly the moving spirit in its formation and phraseology, was the prototype of the Constitution of the United States.

The Connecticut constitution created, by the federation of the independent towns, an independent republic that contained no reference to any existing sovereign and recognized no government except that which these wanderers from Massachusetts had made for themselves. In that again it served as the model on which in the following century the American constitution was founded, which recognizes neither temporal nor spiritual ruler and acknowledges only the sovereign rule of the people. "It is on the banks of the Connecticut, under the mighty preaching of Thomas Hooker and in the Constitution to which he gave life, if not form, that we draw the first breath of that atmosphere which is now so familiar to us. The birthplace of American democracy is Hartford." [1]

Just as the American Constitution puts in the

[1] Johnston: *Connecticut*, p. 73.

hands of Congress certain enumerated powers and reserves to the states and the people those powers on which silence is maintained, so the Constitution of Connecticut reserved to the towns all power and authority save that vested in the General Court. The President of the American Republic is elected by a majority vote, and the power of the people is lodged in the hands of its representatives on a basis of equality. The Governor of Connecticut, who was to the little republic what the President is to the larger federation, and his council were elected by the people at large, the suffrage being almost universal, but each town had an equality of representation in the Assembly. While Connecticut exercised no such influence on the American people as Massachusetts and Virginia, to it belongs the credit of having brought about at the formation of the Constitution of the United States, the compromise by which the states were given equal representation in the Senate and the composition of the House of Representatives was accepted.

Why the Connecticut Englishmen should have developed an individuality marked and characteristic enough to differentiate them from the Englishmen of Massachusetts and those of the other New England colonies it is not easy to determine, but that distinction was early apparent and has survived. The popular name of Americans among Europeans is "Yankees," and the term is synonymous in the European mind with sharp trading, acquisitiveness, and abnormal curiosity about the affairs of one's neighbors,[1] but among Americans it is only the New Englanders who are regarded as the real Yankees, and their distinguishing qualities are supposed to be typical of the people of Connecticut. As a matter of fact, as every American knows, the Massachusetts man rather resents the appellation of Yankee.

The little federal republic of Connecticut was allowed to develop peacefully and normally; its constitution was not violently wrenched out of shape like that of Massachusetts at the end of the seventeenth century. It silently grew until it became the strongest political structure on the continent.[2]

Side by side with the federal republic of Hartford there grew up another federation under the name of New Haven, which was founded in 1638. As Hooker was the leading spirit at Hartford so

[1] "Rural Yankees, impudent, inquisitive, grasping, sharp, drawling in speech and utterly without manners, — a class which has most fortunately passed away, but which once furnished the stock material for Charles Dickens and other English writers who ridiculed Americans. Occasionally, in remote parts of New England, you may find survivors of this class, and if one fastens himself on you, as they are apt to do, you will never forget him." — Sydney George Fisher: *Men, Women, and Manners in Colonial Times*, vol. ii, p. 140.

"Obadiah or Zephaniah, from Hampshire or Connecticut, who came in without knocking; sat down without invitation; and lighted their pipe without ceremony; then talked of buying land; and, finally, began a discourse on politics, which would have done honor to Praise God Barebones, or any of the members of his parliament." — Mrs. Grant, *Memoirs of an American Lady*, p. 286.

An equally uncomplimentary picture of these inquisitive Yankees may be seen in Washington Irving's *Knickerbocker*.

[2] Fiske: *The Beginnings of New England*, p. 128.

another clergyman, John Davenport, was foremost in the affairs of the younger colony. Davenport had none of Hooker's liberality and tolerance; he was typical of the intense Puritanism of his time, and New Haven was intended to be even more extreme in its theocratic government than Massachusetts. According to Davenport, man found in the Bible a perfect and sufficient rule for the conduct of civil affairs, and membership in the church was a prerequisite of citizenship; it was Massachusetts over again. Just as Hartford had been formed by the federation of the towns, so the New Haven colony came into existence by a union of New Haven, Milford, Guilford, and Stamford. New Haven, similar to Hartford, set up its own establishment without regard to the sovereignty of England or the rights or claims of any other body of Englishmen. The founders of New Haven assumed as an inherent right the right to be independent and, as its corollary, to do as they saw fit. They had not even a shadowy claim to the title of the land which they occupied. They simply planted themselves there and were content to let the future take care of itself.

Connecticut, when these two little republics came into existence, reproduced what had happened in Massachusetts a few years before. The sweetness and mildness of the Plymouth Pilgrims found their counterpart in Hooker and the Hartford colony; the grim intolerance and blind obedience to Biblical law and the passionate zeal to regulate all conduct was the Puritan dower to the New Haven republic. Davenport and his associates read in the Bible that wisdom hath builded her house, she hath hewn out her seven pillars,[1] and in accordance with this injunction each town was governed by seven pillars of the church, who were not only the pillars of the church but also the foundation and capstone of society, as they were the magistrates of the colony, and judges as well as jury. The New Haven fathers would not permit juries because they could find no warrant for the institution in the laws of Moses. In Hartford there was practically universal suffrage; in New Haven only church members were allowed to vote, which resulted in nearly one-half of the settlers being disfranchised and the power of government passing into the hands of the most illiberal element of the community, who used their power with all the perverted zeal that intolerance has always delighted in. It was not sufficient that they regulate the affairs of the little state, but they must needs make men walk according to their own peculiar notions. They were continually prying into what men and women said or thought, and word or thought that departed from the standard bigoted dogmatism set up was swiftly punished.

"Goodman Hunt and his wife, for keeping the councils of the said William Harding, baking him a pasty and plum cakes, and keeping company with him on the Lord's day, and she suffering

[1] Proverbs ix, 9.

Harding to kiss her, were ordered to be sent out of town within one month after the date hereof (March 1, 1643), yea, in a shorter time if any miscarriage be found in them."[1] The way to reform, to subdue the devil and chasten the spirit, lay through the statute-books, for the surest means to make men God-fearing and strengthen them against temptations of the flesh was to enact a law that would provide a punishment for its violation. The laws that New Haven enacted are delicious in their quaintness, and it is these enactments with which that veracious Tory refugee, the Rev. Samuel Peters, tickled the fancy of the world when he published his Blue Laws of Connecticut.[2] There was so little of this spirit in Hartford that its occasional manifestation attracts attention by its rarity. There is mention made of a Hartford man being punished for saying that he looked forward with pleasure to meeting some of the members of his church in hell, and considering the temper of some of those members perhaps the remark was not unwarranted.

They were a godly and proper people, these Connecticut forefathers, to whom virtue was a precious thing and unchastity severely punished, and yet they saw no vice in "bundling," which was carried to greater lengths in Connecticut and Massachusetts than elsewhere, and at last became such a scandal that the church was forced to suppress it. Webster defines the intransitive verb

[1] Johnston: *Connecticut*, p. 99.

[2] See p. 185.

bundle "to sleep on the same bed without undressing; applied to the custom of a man and woman, especially lovers, thus sleeping"; and the last edition of the Century Dictionary gives this definition: "In New England (in early time) and in Wales, to sleep in the same bed without undressing; applied to the custom of men and women, especially sweethearts, thus sleeping." Defenders of the colonists have denied that bundling was a common or generally sanctioned custom, but Stiles, who has written an extremely interesting little book on the subject, which shows careful investigation and judicial impartiality, says:—

"Badinage, ridicule and misrepresentation aside, however, there can be no reasonable doubt that *bundling* did prevail to a very great extent in the New England colonies from a very early day. It is equally evident it was originally confined entirely to the lower classes of the community, or to those whose limited means compelled them to economize strictly in their expenditure of firewood and candlelight. Many, perhaps the majority, of the dwellings of the early settlers, consisted of but one room, in which the whole family lived and slept. Yet their innocence and generous hospitality forbade that the stranger, or the friend whom night overtook on their threshold, should be turned shelterless and couchless away, so long as they could offer him even a half of a bed." [1]

[1] Stiles: *Bundling; its Origin, Progress, and Decline in America*, pp. 66–67.

In Massachusetts the custom was not confined to the lower classes, if contemporary writers are to be believed; and mothers who carefully watched their daughters saw no impropriety in bundling. After the French and Indian wars, the young men returning from camp and army, where they had learned vices and recklessness, deprived bundling of any innocence it possessed. The evil became so apparent that a decided movement was made against it. Jonathan Edwards denounced it from the pulpit, and one by one the ministers who had allowed it to pass unnoticed joined in its suppression.[1]

Stiles says, "We may notice, in this connection, that it is very common, even at the present day, in New England, to speak of one as having 'bundled in with his clothes on,' if he goes to bed without undressing; as for instance, if he came home drunk, or feeling slightly ill, lay down in the daytime, or in a cold night found the blankets too scanty." [2]

Bundling is said by the detractors of America to have originated in America, but like many other American institutions, especially those of which the

[1] Fisher: *Men, Women, and Manners in Colonial Times*, vol. i, p. 287.

[2] Stiles: *op. cit.*, pp. 13–14.

I am told by a woman, who traces her descent back to colonial times and until her marriage lived in Marblehead, that in that quaint old Massachusetts seaport, bundling still survives to a limited extent, but only among the lowest classes.

"It is a certain fact, well authenticated by court records and parish registers, that, wherever the practice of bundling prevailed, there was an amazing number of sturdy brats annually born into the state, without the license of the law or the benefit of clergy." — Irving, *A History of New York*, p. 210.

world no longer approves, it is an exotic. Stiles traces it back to England, Scotland, and Wales, and undoubtedly it was a transplanted custom.

One of the most interesting phases of American development is that marked spirit of justice which made it possible for liberty and bigotry to exist side by side without provoking civil war or conflict. In Massachusetts we have those gentle Pilgrims going their own way without interference from the Puritans made strong by their belief that they were raised up by the Lord for His especial purpose. In Connecticut Hooker preached tolerance and taught men liberality and went about his work unharmed by the zealots of New Haven, whose zeal for conversion was as great as that of the early Spaniards, who knew only one way to convince men of their errors. When Roger Williams revolted against the Massachusetts theocracy he was banished, which was a political necessity, but he was allowed to set up his own government unmolested. This broad spirit of humanity, this recognition of the rights of others, this almost scrupulous regard to obtain nothing by conquest and to abstain from force in dominating weaker colonies — compare this with the prevailing spirit existing in Europe, which was the legacy of history, and see how remarkable, almost inexplicable it appears. The natural temptation of Massachusetts would have been to incorporate Plymouth, peaceably if possible, forcibly if necessary; of Hartford to have regarded with fear and distrust the establishment of New Haven; to have been watchful and suspicious, and to have raised a force to repel invasion or to seek a pretext to use it for aggression. In all the history of the colonies that attempt was never made, and Englishmen who had established settlement or colony had nothing to fear from men of their own blood; nor did they live in constant apprehension of having to yield their independence to satisfy the rapacity of conscienceless adventurers or the ambition of self-constituted rulers.

With the settlement of Connecticut begins the long chapter of Indian warfare that raged throughout the seventeenth century and was closed late in the next only when the red man had been practically exterminated and the superior skill and resources of the white man overmatched the cunning and fanaticism of the savage.

The Indian has been one of the subordinate causes to influence American civilization, not by grafting his own civilization on that of the English, not because the English absorbed him, his customs, language, or religion; not because the Indian in the smallest degree swayed an unyielding and firmly established civilization; but because Indian warfare and the necessity of subduing the Indian to clear the way for the invading white man left its lasting mark on the character of the colonists. Two great barriers challenged the Englishman; the wilderness and the Indians. In New England as well as in the South, later when there was that response to the imperious call of the West, the ground was contested by the aborigines, who resisted the despoiler to the end. Slowly civilization drove back savagery, wresting from it its inheritance, paying in full in blood; and men were made keen and became hardened by the conflict; they were made cruel by contact with a foe whose warfare exacted vengeance to the last drop.

The Indian wars kept alive the military spirit — and while the Americans are not a warlike people, in them the military spirit is highly developed — they made the pioneer and settler live in the fear of surprise and always ready to resist it; it deprived them of that sense of security that might have sunk them in sloth and brought contentment in isolation. Had there been no Indians, the Americans might easily have become a pastoral and agricultural people, physically soft, unsuspicious, fonder of the gentle arts than the ruder struggle of commerce. The Indian hardened the body of the American by making him a soldier, as from youth up he was accustomed to firearms, and at church and in the field his musket was always by his side. It produced that extraordinary military initiative and resource that was the admiration and amazement of European military critics, that made it possible for men in the ranks to rise to command, that made a standing army unnecessary. The readiness with which Americans in their early days took to the field was the result of this training, and the tactics which the Indian had taught them they used against men of their own race. The Indian sharpened the wits of the white man because the cunning of the savage was superior to the slow-moving mind of the Englishman; he taught his own love of cruelty and delight in suffering.

There are to be found American apologists for the American treatment of the Indian; and perhaps these apologies are not without warrant, and we read with horror accounts of massacre, rapine, and torture; the white man no less cruel and merciless than the Indian. But Englishmen were confronting a foe who knew no mercy, and to whom the generosity of the victor in the hour of triumph was interpreted not as the mercy of the strong but the fear of the weak; a foe that understood only the meaning of reprisal; whose respect for their enemy increased the more he imitated their own methods and exacted life for life and tortured and destroyed even as they did. "Often the white men and red fought one another wherever they met, and displayed in their conflict all the cunning and merciless ferocity that made warfare so dreadful. Terrible deeds of prowess were done by the mighty men on either side. It was a war of stealth and cruelty, and ceaseless, sleepless watchfulness. The contestants had sinewy frames and iron wills, keen eyes and steady hands, hearts as bold as they were ruthless."[1] Men on the frontier lived from month to

[1] Roosevelt: *The Winning of the West*, vol. i, p. 191.

month and year to year under the terror which at length taught them to regard their enemies as wild beasts.[1]

A higher civilization was opposed to a lower, a rudimentary race sought to interpose an obstacle to the spread of a race highly developed. It was inevitable that the conflict should come and civilization win the mastery. It was not ethical, perhaps, but it was inexorable.

[1] Doyle: *English Colonies in America*, vol. iii, p. 348.

CHAPTER XX

RELIGIOUS FREEDOM IS BORN

IN the hagiology of each nation, says Emerson, the lawgiver was in each case a man of eloquent tongue, whose sympathy brought him face to face with the extremes of society. In the hagiology of Rhode Island we have the lawgiver of eloquent tongue, a man of such ardent sympathy that he was able to envisage the future, who gathered around him the extremes of society as society manifested itself through its religious views; a man half mystic but yet extremely practical, whose liberality made him far in advance of his time, but who was able to draw the line between liberty and license. The name of Roger Williams is inseparably associated with Rhode Island, and it vividly recalls the narrow formalism of the Puritan, his intense intolerance and the methods he employed to root out any attempt to challenge the supremacy of the theocracy.

There came to Massachusetts in 1631 "the founder of a new state, the exponent of a new philosophy, the intellect that was to harmonize religious differences, and soothe the sectarian asperities of the New World; a man whose clearness of mind enabled him to deduce, from the mass of crude speculations which abounded in the seventeenth-century, a proposition so comprehensive, that it is difficult to say whether its application has produced the most beneficial result upon religion, or morals, or politics."[1] This striking figure was Roger Williams, a Welshman, then about thirty years old, who had taken his degree at Pembroke College, Cambridge, but who had incurred the hostility of Laud for the boldness of his opinions. He was a man of scholarship and ability, with all of a Welshman's fiery love of argument, "conscientiously contentious," as one of his biographers has said; but "most men who contribute materially towards bringing about great changes, religious or moral, are 'conscientiously contentious.' Were they not so they would not accomplish the work they are here to do";[2] pugnacious, turbulent, and at times guilty of "blazing indiscretions," but always overflowing with charity and driven impetuously forward to preach the great doctrine of civil and religious liberty. A very human man this, "lovely in his carriage," whom men of his race trusted and the Indians loved, "a mighty and benignant form, always pleading for some magnanimous idea, some tender charity, the rectification of some wrong, the exercise of some sort of forbearance towards men's bodies and souls."[3] Not the kind of man who would easily fit into "the Puritan starch and uniform,"

[1] Arnold: *History of the State of Rhode Island and Providence Plantations*, vol. i, p. 20.

[2] Adams: *Massachusetts: Its Historians and its History*, p. 25.

[3] Tyler: *History of American Literature*, p. 243.

but one who would rudely shock the narrow formulas of stiff saints cast in the mould of an iron-bound church. He was determined to run counter to the theocratic oligarchy.

Invited soon after his coming to Salem to become assistant to the pastor, he quickly incurred the displeasure of the rulers of Massachusetts by writing a treatise in which he attacked the validity of the Massachusetts patent, holding that the King had no power to grant the land to settlers unless they purchased it from the Indians. Such a doctrine was monstrous, as it struck at the root of all society and would have established the duty of the strong to respect the rights of weak; native races, which, if observed, robbed colonization of its great profit and gave little encouragement to adventurers to risk much for the honor of the nation and their own advantage. Not content with this heinous sin, he must needs still further attempt to disrupt society by boldly announcing that the magistrates had arrogated to themselves too much power, and that the state had no right to control the religious opinion of its subjects. Perhaps it was fortunate for Williams that he gave utterance to these views in Massachusetts and not in England, for there he would probably have been hanged for sedition, at least he would have been branded, and made to stand in the pillory with his ears cropped.

Massachusetts dealt with heresiarchs in another way. The obstinate pastor was brought before the

General Court and offered an opportunity to retract. He stood stubborn in his recusancy. Then began one of those solemn farces which so delighted the Puritans, but which to them was no farce but the great tragedy of Satan fighting to keep his control over a soul brought to damnation through his devilish machinations; to them a ceremony as awful and impressive as the *auto-da-fé*. Hour after hour he was confronted by the accusing dialecticians, but he faced his judges serenely, perhaps secretly glad to be given this great opportunity to spread his doctrines before this high and mighty audience; and a jury, which convicted him before he uttered the first word in his defence, passed sentence of banishment; or in the delightful euphemism of John Cotton, one of his foremost adversaries, he was "enlarged out of Massachusetts." Tempering justice with mercy, he was given six weeks, it then being the depth of winter, to make his preparations for departure, but Williams was no man to sit with hands folded and tongue bridled. Full of energy and defiance, scorning to recant although he had been condemned, he at once began preparations to found a new colony recruited from men who shared his opinions. This contumacy merited extreme measures, and the rulers of Massachusetts made preparations to rid themselves of their danger by putting Williams on a ship about to sail for England, when he received timely warning and plunged into the wilderness. After many adventures he and a few followers laid the foundation of a settlement which is now the city of Providence in the state of Rhode Island. It was land belonging to the Indians on which he set foot, and faithful to his principles he made no attempt to seize it, but bought it from the Indians.

We shall for the moment leave Roger Williams beginning the new life at Providence on amicable terms with the Indians and go back to Massachusetts, because certain events there had a direct bearing on what was to become in the course of time a new state; and we get a very clear insight into the Puritan mind and the state of society in the early days of the Massachusetts colony. Williams arrived in New England in 1631. Three years later there came to Boston William Hutchinson and his wife Anne, who was to play the most conspicuous part in a great religious controversy, but it was something much more vital than a mere theological dispute —"it was the first of many New England quickenings in the direction of social, intellectual, and political development, — New England's earliest protest against formulas."[1] This Mistress Anne Hutchinson was a woman "of haughty and fierce carriage, of a nimble wit and active spirit, and a very voluble tongue, more bold than a man, though in understanding and judgment inferior to many women." This is the portrait drawn by one of her bitter enemies and perhaps exaggerates her

[1] Adams: *Three Episodes of Massachusetts History*, vol. i, p. 367.

most undesirable qualities and ignores those that redeemed her, but in a few vigorous strokes it paints her probably very true to life. Of her "ready wit and bold spirit,"[1] in the moderate words of Winthrop, who had bitter occasion more than once to experience both, there has been given abundant proof. Of her husband little need be said. He is described by contemporaries as "a man of very mild temper and weak parts and wholly guided by his wife."[2] Perhaps it was fortunate. One small frame house would hardly have been large enough to shelter two such turbulent spirits as Mistress Anne. She was at that time about thirty-four years old, a woman whom not even her most devoted eulogist has called beautiful or even pretty, but who possessed that most insidious and greatest of all gifts of her sex, that indefinable and intangible magnetism of sympathy, the possession of which makes a woman become for the moment vividly interested in the man with whom she holds converse and stimulates him and attracts him; which gives more than it takes and leaves the impress of its own individuality. She was not a learned woman, but she had a remarkable native talent for disputation which she clothed in language difficult to confute. That she exercised great power over men and intellectually fascinated them is indisputable.

In her was the spirit of the mystic as well as that

[1] Winthrop: *History of New England*, vol. i, p. 239.

[2] Winthrop: *op. cit.*, vol. i, p. 356.

of the reformer. She drew around her the women of the colony, first, innocently enough, simply repeating to them the sermons she had heard in the meeting-house, but later acting as interpreter and critic. Now we have seen that the Puritans would tolerate no attempt on the part of the people to depart from the Word of God as it was given to them by their ministers, and they, despite all their pious humility and their constant reiteration of unworthiness, were fully conscious of their position of commanding importance in the community, and for the preservation of their own privileged class permitted no rival prophets. Neological tendencies were sternly suppressed. The Puritan ministers at the beginning of Massachusetts were lawgivers as well as teachers, and their authority rested on the blind obedience with which they were obeyed by their congregations. We do not often associate the idea of superstition with the Puritans, and yet, in a sense, the Puritans were no less superstitious than any other religious sect who passively submitted to a narrow and dogmatic creed and disciplined themselves to accept without question the rule of life as expounded to them by their spiritual leaders.

Mrs. Hutchinson not only arrogated to herself, in flat defiance of the clergy, the ability to interpret the Scriptures, but she was possessed of something of which even the most learned and godly among them were deficient. She professed at times to feel the

Spirit of God upon her and to speak from the inward knowledge that had come to her. She disclaimed the gift of prophecy or that she was divinely inspired, although it is not easy to see where she drew the shadowy line, but she asserted that she was apart and different from ordinary women; and this claim to a precious gift was the one thing to condemn her in the eyes of the clergy. Grace came from without, not from within, which was the presumption of sin and not the humility of the regenerate struggling to be made strong. In the eyes of the ministers, Mrs. Hutchinson, by her claim to mantistic qualities, was guilty of blasphemy, and of course there was always the suspicion of the devil's help. Mr. Hales, "a young man very well conceited of himself and censorious of others," after Mrs. Hutchinson's removal to Aquidneck, "was also taken with her heresies, and in great admiration of her, so as these, and other the like before, when she dwelt in Boston, gave cause of suspicion of witchcraft."[1]

It is proof of that immanent sense of personal liberty so deeply rooted in the English character, which has manifested itself in the whole history of the race, that even in that early day of the minister-ridden Puritan colony Mrs. Hutchinson should have been able to gather around her a following who with vigor and courage supported and defended her. Winthrop declared that the whole

[1] Winthrop: *History of New England*, vol. ii, p. 10.

church of Boston, with few exceptions, had become her converts; Welde, who was to become her chief accuser, lamented that persons of quality and gentlemen and scholars were among her adherents. Deep down in the hearts of those gentlemen and scholars, there must have been the quickening thought that Puritan oppression was no less to be feared than the oppression from which they had fled in England; it was a protest against the attempt to stifle individualism. It was the beginning of the great Antinomian controversy that raged with such bitterness in New England until the Puritan theocracy ceased to exist.

Theological controversies, it has been truly observed, are as a rule among the most barren of the many barren fields of historical research; and the literature of which they are so fruitful may, so far as the reader of to-day is concerned, best be described by the single word impossible.[1] It would weary the reader to translate into modern language the curious jumble of words which were the weapons employed by these valiant champions, nor is it necessary in a work of this character. It would be profitless to discuss the merits of the Covenant of Grace as distinguished from the Covenant of Works; and these obscure theological disputes about trifles that mean nothing, which aroused passion and rooted bigotry deeper, and advanced the world not one iota, and contributed nothing to

[1] Adams: *op. cit.*, vol. i, p. 366.

the happiness or the welfare of mankind, seem to us now so childish that we are amazed that men of common sense should so foolishly waste their time and their energies when much better things were waiting to be done.

Mrs. Hutchinson's teachings had now reached that point when they threatened the disruption of the colony, and she was brought to trial before the General Court. It was a trial typical of the time and the Puritan character. The woman, shortly to become a mother, made to stand in the presence of that august tribunal until "her countenance discovered some bodily infirmity," unprovided with counsel, her witnesses browbeaten, the few members of the Court who were well disposed towards her rebuked by their associates, faced her accusers boldly and showed her skill in dispute; she met the subtle arguments of her persecutors with the ingenuity for which she was famous and more than once disconcerted her judges; but nothing moved them. Passionless they would have gazed on the lustrous bosom of Phryne as they looked without emotion on the mock humility of their victim. Pleading, but defiant, when Governor Winthrop pronounced sentence of banishment she asked: "I desire to know wherefore I am banished," to which Winthrop replied: "Say no more. The court knows wherefore, and is satisfied." It was indicative of the farcical proceedings. The Court was satisfied; the reasons it was not necessary to state, for every one understood; the justice of the sentence no one considered. There are Massachusetts historians who regard the trial and banishment of Mrs. Hutchinson as a stain upon the Puritan Commonwealth and wish it could be expunged, but they are oversensitive. The men who banished Mrs. Hutchinson were men of the seventeenth century who were under the influence of their age. To have expected them to show the liberality and tolerance of the twentieth century would have been an anachronism.

The great Antinomian controversy and the banishment of Mistress Anne Hutchinson stamp the character of the Puritan and the peculiar institution which he founded in Massachusetts. It revealed at once his whole theory of government and the relation existing between the church and the state. It is perfectly intelligible and entirely logical when we realize that the Bible was the Puritan Constitution; it is mystifying and confusing when that salient fact has not been grasped. Doyle, with all his learning and painstaking research, seems to have missed the key to the Puritan character, without which it can never be understood. Referring to the church at Salem having appointed, against the remonstrances of the General Court, Roger Williams as its pastor, Doyle says: "For this contumacy, and for its supposed complicity in Williams's seditious courses, Salem was punished by being disfranchised till it made an apology. Such an incident oddly illustrates the manner in which civil and ecclesiastical affairs were blended." [1]

The incident would be more than odd, it would be impossible, had the Puritan been content to render to Cæsar the things that were Cæsar's and been able to accept the modern philosophy that God made man, but man made the State. It was impossible for the Puritan to do this, and in his mind there was never any conflict between human and divine law. He was as convinced of the fallibility of human action when it opposed the provisions of his great code as is an American judge who unhesitatingly declares a statute void because it violates a fundamental inhibition of the American Constitution. The Puritan treatment of Mrs. Hutchinson shows his intense narrowness and how deficient he was in the saving grace of charity. He could argue for days over the meaning of an obscure text in the Bible, but his heart was as iron when he racked the woman shortly to feel the pains of maternity. It was this persecution that, unknown to himself, was to spread colonization and make Massachusetts the mother and maker of states. Again we see the sempiternal revolution of the wheel. Driven forth by religious persecution, the Puritan builds for himself a new state. Driven to persecution by the narrowness of his religion, he in turn becomes the oppressor and furnishes the impetus for the forward march of civilization.

[1] Doyle: *English Colonies in America*, vol. ii, p. 122.

Some of Mrs. Hutchinson's adherents founded towns that afterwards became the state of New Hampshire. Mrs. Hutchinson herself and a considerable following bought from the Indians the island of Aquidneck, and settlements were established at Portsmouth and Newport, which later were incorporated with Williams's colony at Providence and became in time the modern state of Rhode Island.

Just as North Carolina was to Virginia "Rogues' Harbor," where the outcasts of society were made welcome and no one was so inquisitive as to ask the latest arrival why he came or whether he brought his real name with him, — which two centuries later was the etiquette of the western mining-camp, where personal history was always strictly tabooed, — Rhode Island was to the other New England colonies a pit of abomination. It was called in derision and contempt the Isle of Errors and the Religious Sink of New England, for it was the only place where every odd bit of theology could be found and prophets could safely deliver themselves of their inspirations and new sects could be founded without fear of punishment. Cotton Mather, who was not overmuch given to delicate sarcasm, said that if any man lost his religion, he could be sure to find it in Rhode Island. That colony was the seventeenth-century Hyde Park Sunday meetings where every man could call his own audience about him and speak to his heart's content.

One of Mrs. Hutchinson's supporters in Aquidneck was Samuel Gorton, who bred turbulence wherever he lodged. He was "a proud and pestilent seducer," in the vigorous language of that day, which had no reference to his morals but to his irrepressible energy in spreading his horrific doctrines. The modern biographer would term him a crotchety, cantankerous man, decidedly inclined toward anarchy and inconveniently assertive of pretty nearly everything that society disapproves. Doyle describes him as "a singularly puzzle-headed and illiterate man, full of courage and energy, and honest, so far as honesty is compatible with a morbid passion for notoriety which is gained by the upholders of unpopular views."[1] He wrote much, but he had no power of clear expression and it is not easy to follow his argument.

A London clothier, he set up as a preacher without ordination and cherished that same doctrine of divine inspiration which so outraged the Puritans of Massachusetts when proclaimed by Mrs. Hutchinson. Coming to Plymouth, he soon displayed those qualities that made him for many years a thorn in the side of New England. One account has it that the wife of his pastor preferred his teachings to those of her husband, while from another historian we learn that with more zeal than tact he defended his wife's servant who had been severely punished for a trifling infraction of church discipline. He

[1] Doyle: *English Colonies in America*, vol. ii, p. 187.

found it wise to flee Plymouth and seek refuge at Aquidneck, where he celebrated his coming by creating a schism among Mrs. Hutchinson's followers, which led to the founding of Portsmouth. Wherever he tarried trouble was sure to abide, and soon Portsmouth would have no more of him, and for its own peace flogged him and cast him out. We next hear of him at Pawtuxet, which was within the jurisdiction of Providence, where even the broad-minded and tolerant Roger Williams was driven to complaint. Always agitating, his hand ever against the government, "having abused high and low at Aquidneck," Williams plaintively writes, he was now "bewitching and madding poor Providence." It is difficult to understand what power this illiterate and muddle-headed man possessed, but instead of accepting Fiske's conclusion, "probably such success as Gorton had in winning followers was due to the mystical rubbish which abounds in his pages and finds in a modern mind no doorway through which to enter,"[1] it is more probable that in the revolt against theological tyranny and a dim longing for real religious freedom is the explanation to be found. Williams, true to his principles, although disapproving of Gorton, would not silence him, but when he refused to submit to the authority of the magistrates, some of the leading citizens of Providence appealed to Massachusetts for advice and assistance in dealing with this disturber of the

[1] Fiske: *The Beginnings of New England*, p. 167.

peace. It is not necessary to follow in detail future events. Gorton and some of his followers, after a stout resistance, were captured by an armed force and taken to Massachusetts and sentenced to work in irons during the pleasure of the court and strictly forbidden to communicate with any one except the elders and the assistants. But Puritan obstinacy was more than matched by the stubbornness of Gorton who doubtless knew his Epictetus and was strengthened by the philosopher's defiance.

Despite his fetters Gorton continued to propagate his heresies, and he was like to have bewitched Massachusetts as he had poor Providence had not the court amended the sentence to banishment from the colony on pain of death. To Aquidneck, where he had abused high and low, he returned, and because he was a victim of the religious persecution of Massachusetts he was received with sympathy.

I have outlined the adventurous career of this tailor-preacher and mystic because it was the asylum that Rhode Island offered to discordant religious elements that gave it a character unlike those of the other New England colonies and made it possible for the theocracy of New England to be broken down; which was necessary if men were to gain intellectual freedom and escape from the stagnation of the narrow rule of a creed that was a bar to their highest spiritual development. Under the rule of the theocracy the minds of men could only expand along certain lines, but perfect development was impossible. Great and wonderful as was the work wrought by the theocracy and the character which it created, there came a time when instead of making men strong it weakened them by its intolerance and its rigid command of blind obedience; and the power of the theocracy began to crumble when the teachings of Roger Williams and his disciples took root and theological disputes no longer held the first place as the highest expression of intellect.

When, in the progress of society, Buckle says, its theological element begins to decay, the ardor with which religious disputes were once conducted becomes sensibly weakened. That time, in America, had not yet come, but it was foreshadowed; and it was because the narrow theology of Massachusetts broke down before spreading its destructive influence over a wider area and becoming indoctrinated in the race that it was possible for the Americans to be what they are — liberal in religion and thought, with a speculative audacity that has made them ready to embrace every new idea and explore every new realm of mind or deed. They were not clogged by hampering tradition, and of all tradition an intensely formalistic religion is the most impeditive. Buckle adds in the paragraph which has already been quoted — and it concisely reveals the change produced in the Massachusetts character by the displacement of theology as the highest expression of intellectual activity — that "the most advanced intellects are the first to feel the growing indifference, and, therefore, they are also the first to scrutinize real events with that inquisitive eye which their predecessors had reserved for religious speculations. This is a great turning-point in the history of every civilized nation. From this moment theological heresies become less frequent, and literary heresies become more common. From this moment, the spirit of inquiry and of doubt fastens itself upon every department of knowledge, and begins that great career of conquest, in which by every succeeding discovery the power and dignity of man are increased, while at the same time most of his opinions are disturbed, and many of them are destroyed; until, in the march of this vast but noiseless revolution the stream of tradition is, as it were, interrupted, the influence of ancient authority is subverted, and the human mind, waxing in strength, learns to rely upon its own resources, and to throw off incumbrances by which the freedom of its movements had long been impaired." [1]

Gorton, who served a purpose, was an ill-balanced and undisciplined man; Williams, whose light still burns with undiminished brilliance, was of splendid sanity. In that heterogeneous mixture of Antinomians and Gortonites and Quakers and other strange conglomerations of sects there was a serious element of liberal thinkers; men and

[1] Buckle: *History of Civilization in England*, vol. i, p. 554.

women were groping in the dark to free themselves from the slavery and superstition that had for centuries overlaid thought, but which the Reformation had begun to clear away. They were sick, sick unto death, of the mockery of Christ; of the sham and pretence of the church; of religion that was forever preaching damnation but offered never a word of hope; that crucified but bathed no wounds; that to the soul-thirsty gave vinegar and tantalized with a cup of cold water. Long had they been bound only to find themselves free in a wilderness; they were longing to use their freedom, but they did not know how to exert their strength. It was natural, when restraint had been cast off, that they, not having experienced that long discipline which hardens character and brings it under control, should go to extremes and take up with every vagary that promised the intellectual liberty they so ardently craved. Almost each man felt he was privileged to create his own moral code. Some were opposed to all forms of government because it elevated men in authority over their fellows, and they were able to prove to their own satisfaction that Christ taught that all men stood equal before Him. It was sufficient for a man to refuse to obey a law because he was unable to reconcile it with his conscience. Ingenuity could find in the Bible that a man was permitted one wife or many. There was, we are told, either too much marriage or too little. It was a strange, tumultuous, undisciplined, muddle-headed band of extremists, but with the germ of an idea in their not over-logical brains, that the tyranny and precise formalism of Massachusetts drove to seek refuge in Rhode Island.

Out of that ruck rises the majestic figure of Roger Williams, as impressive in its dignity and strength of character and liberality two hundred years in advance of his time as Everest towering over the plains in the mystery of its solitary grandeur. Williams was able to distinguish between liberty and license, to grant freedom to all men, and yet to require the obedience of all to the discipline of law and the will of society. In a letter that has often been quoted he defended himself from the charge that the freedom he contended for led to licentiousness and every kind of disorder, and used the well-known illustration of the captain and the ship. "There goes many a ship to sea," he wrote, "with many hundred souls in one ship, whose weal and woe is common; and is a true picture of a commonwealth, or a human combination, or society. It hath fallen out sometimes, that both Papists and Protestants, Jews and Turks, may be embarked in one ship; upon which supposal I affirm, that all the liberty of conscience that ever I pleaded for, turns upon these two hinges: that none of the Papists, Protestants, Jews, or Turks, be forced to come to the ship's prayers or worship, nor compelled from their own particular prayers or worship, if they practice any." Yet notwithstanding this liberty, he maintains, "the commander of this ship ought to command the ship's course, yea, and also command that justice, peace and sobriety be kept and practised, both among the seamen and all the passengers. If any of the seamen refuse to perform their service, or passengers to pay their freight; if any refuse to help in person or purse, towards the common charges or defence; if any refuse to obey the common laws and orders of the ship, concerning their common peace and preservation; if any shall rise up and mutiny against their commanders and officers; if any shall preach or write, that there ought to be no commanders nor officers, because all are equal in Christ, therefore no masters nor officers, no laws, nor orders, no corrections nor punishments; I say I never denied, but in such cases, whatever is pretended, the commander or commanders may judge, resist, compel, and punish such transgressors, according to their deserts and merits."[1] If Williams had done nothing more than to write this letter, it would have established his perdurable fame.

Massachusetts was the attempt to establish a political community on a basis of religious tyranny, an experiment often before made; Rhode Island, much more wonderful, was to see for the first time a political organization foundationed on religious liberty, which succeeding was powerfully to affect the thought not only of America but of the whole

[1] Arnold: *History of Rhode Island*, vol. i, p. 225; Larned, vol. iv, p. 2713.

world; that was to free men not alone from the thraldom of the church, but was to liberate them from political slavery; that was to spread democratic institutions; for it was only when the power of the autocracy of the church and the oligarchy of an aristocratic political class was broken down that it became possible for democracy to take root. It is a striking contrast this, Massachusetts wedded to its theocracy, and Rhode Island, separated by no impassable natural or artificial barriers, under the very eyes of Massachusetts, peopled by her own people, inspiring liberty. America was wide enough to shelter all; there was room here for the narrow-minded and stern Endicott and the broad and benignant Williams; it was the forerunner of American liberality.

It was an experiment scoffed at, and it was prophesied that a scheme so revolutionary would be of short duration. But it endured. Like every great movement that has influenced the course of civilization, it encountered the contempt and opposition of the adherents of older institutions. Those institutions absorb the highest talent, the greatest ability, all the power that comes from wealth and learning; and the cohesive strength of men leagued to maintain an existing state of society has a disciplinary effect on those who adhere to its conventions and who are contemptuous of the disorganized rabble which the new order at first attracts. There are in every such movement, three successive stages which are common to all social revolutions: first, unrestrained enthusiasm, which is its strength; then more practical considerations prevail, and, finally, if the revolution is to accomplish its work, discipline is enforced and individual enthusiasm subordinates itself to social regulation.

The theocracy of Massachusetts, the aristocratic institutions of Virginia, the alien customs of New York, have disappeared, but the gospel spread by Roger Williams lives.

Rhode Island interests us not at all for any contribution it made to the constitutional struggle or the development of the spirit of constitutional government. It defied no proprietors nor royal governors. It did not threaten the authority of the King. It took no part in upholding the fundamental principle of English political liberty, that in the control of the purse is the real sovereignty of the people. It gave birth to no new social conditions as did Virginia and Maryland and the other southern colonies. It injected no new strain into the English character as did Puritan Massachusetts. But no survey of American psychology is complete without Rhode Island, where was laid the foundation of that liberty of conscience and religious freedom which have had so much to do in making the American character.

CHAPTER XXI

HOW THE DUTCH CAME AND WENT

Of the thirteen original colonies we have thus far dealt with eight, each of which contributed a distinct element to the making of what was later to become the American nation and left its peculiar characteristics upon the psychology of the race, or laid that system of popular and democratic government that logically and irresistibly developed into the political system on which the American Republic rests. The five remaining colonies — New Hampshire, New Jersey, Delaware, New York, and Pennsylvania — demand little attention at our hands at this stage of the inquiry. It is true that of those five colonies two were to become the most important and influential states of the Union and were in the second period of American politico-psychology what Massachusetts and Virginia were in the first; but while Virginia and Massachusetts were the mother who gave birth to a race of giants and suckled them, New York and Pennsylvania were father and tutor to teach them strength and how to walk fearlessly. It will perhaps appear remarkable to him who has read American history and ignored its psychology that this assertion should be made, but if we call the roll of those eight colonies whose establishment has formed the theme of the preceding pages, we shall see how essential they were to the first stage of American development, and how little influence New York and Pennsylvania exercised at that time.

Let us briefly review what each contributed. Massachusetts gave Puritanism and its institutions, the spirit of which still lives; Virginia and Maryland and the other southern colonies, which were their offshoots, the institution of slavery and a social system that produced momentous political consequences which, modified by later economic and political causes, have influenced the American people and make the South to-day different in thought and manner from the North or the rest of the English-speaking world; Connecticut and Rhode Island, the seed of Massachusetts, nurtured more benignantly, were the beginnings of that great liberty of conscience which is the just pride of Americans. Now if we turn to New York, we find that it laid no foundation on which has been erected a diuturnal structure. The civilization of the Dutch succumbed before a more virile race, a race endowed with a peculiar genius to govern and leave its ineffaceable mark. All that the Dutch brought to America—language, customs, political principles—has been overlaid by the speech and institutions and political philosophy of the English, as Herculaneum withered under the scorching ashes of Vesuvius, and became merely a memory on which a newer and more lasting civilization was reared. Search as we may, we can find no trace of the Dutch strain or that the Dutch left any indesinent impress upon the American character or were able to modify a conquering race or impose upon it their own civilization. We have seen that the Indian stimulated certain qualities of the Englishman; the influence exercised by the negro on the character of the white man has been referred to and we shall make more detailed reference to it later; but the Dutch came and went like visitors in a household, whose little peculiarities are the only thing by which they are remembered, but from whom nothing has been learned. The early colonial history of Pennsylvania is no less barren of results, redeemed only by the romantic personality of Penn and the Quaker invasion.

New York as a Dutch colony explains why Holland failed where England succeeded, and it elucidates how it became possible for England to secure the continent while France and Spain labored to no purpose. The English were colonizers as well as traders, the Dutch were traders only; they had no genius for over-sea empire-building. Where the English planted themselves there immediately was instituted a political system that begat a spirit of loyalty to English institutions and at the same time created an intense spirit of independence and pride in the work of their own hands and the colony which they had created. With the Dutch it was different. Neither the States General nor the Dutch West Indian Company had dealt with the New Netherlands to foster any spirit of loyalty, and it was with indifference that its people regarded the political changes that made them at one time owe allegiance to Holland and later to England. "Nothing could show more strongly the lack of any vigorous sense of nationality than the passivity with which the Dutch settlers suffered themselves to be handed backwards and forwards without protest or expression of interest."[1] One cannot picture such a thing in Massachusetts or Virginia; it would be difficult to imagine those stubborn Puritans or those fiery Virginians tamely submitting to be treated as chattels and like fortresses or munitions of war the spoil of the conqueror. There would have been an uprising to tax all the energy of the United Provinces to suppress.

The marked difference in the character of the Dutch and the English and the proof, if additional proof is wanting, that it was the English and not the Dutch who laid the foundation of American psychology, is to be found in the political ties that bound the colonists to England, which led to their independence and their birth as a nation, as contrasted with the slight importance the New Netherland settlers attached to their political relationship to the home government. The Puritan settlers, Goldwin Smith, says, "in common with the other

[1] *Cambridge Modern History*, vol. vii, p. 41.

colonists of the period, retained not only their love of the old land, but their political tie to it. They deemed themselves still liegemen of a sovereign on the other side of the Atlantic. This created a relation false from the beginning. Herein lay the fatal seeds of misunderstanding, of encroachment on the side of the home government, of revolt on that of the growing colony, and ultimately revolution"; and he goes on to say that "the English colony unhappily was a dependency, and when it grew strong enough to spurn dependence there was a bond to be broken which was not likely to be broken without violence and a breach of affection."[1] It is to be regretted that such a clear thinker as Goldwin Smith should have failed to comprehend the exact nature of the relationship that existed between the English colonists and the mother country, the mental attitude of his countrymen both at home and in America, and the causes that produced the discontent of the colonists; and it is only with that knowledge that it becomes possible to understand why the Dutch accomplished nothing.

In previous chapters I have endeavored to correct the widespread but erroneous impression that the Englishman when he emigrated to America, whether as a Puritan colonist or a southern planter or landholder, divested himself of his nationality and ceased to remain an Englishman. But the truth is that in all things, political principles no less

[1] Smith: *The United States*, p. 6.

than in his manners and customs and his religion, he was as much the Englishman in Massachusetts or in Virginia as he had been in Lincolnshire or in Suffolk. These Englishmen did not merely "deem" themselves liegemen of a sovereign; they were. Because they lived in Virginia they were no less Englishmen than those of their kin who were still living in the ancestral halls of Kent; distance neither broke nor weakened the tie. It was because they were Englishmen, it was because they were Englishmen and had not ceased to be Englishmen, that they insisted upon the same rights and privileges, the same liberty, the same safeguards, the same political freedom that were enjoyed by Englishmen elsewhere, that inherently belonged to the Englishman whether he acknowledged allegiance to his sovereign in London or in Jamestown. In the Cambridge synod of 1646 the ministers defined the relations of Massachusetts toward England in these words: "We depend upon the state of England for protection and immunities of Englishmen."[1] "The complaints of the people in the colonies," Straus says, "were at no time because of the form of their government, or that of the mother country, but because of the encroachments upon, and utter disregard of, the natural rights, privileges and immunities to which they deemed themselves entitled, equally with those residing in England."[2]

[1] Adams: *The Emancipation of Massachusetts*, p. 90.

[2] Straus: *The Origin of Republican Form of Government in the United States of America*, p. 3.

We have seen that in the colonies, almost from the very beginning, there were continual uprisings of the people to resist the encroachments of their governors or to assert their prerogatives; they were defiant not only of the local authorities but of the Crown itself when they believed themselves the victims of oppression or tyranny. But it created no false relation; it was, on the contrary, a relation perfectly understood and perfectly satisfactory according to the spirit of the age; and of all things the historian must avoid the error of visualizing the past by the false light of the present — false because modern clearness of thought magnifies and distorts; it is too cruelly keen to make allowances for only a partially developed concept of the philosophy which men once accepted as final. Bacon's rebellion, for example, was no more an effort to "spurn dependence" than the uprising led by Wat Tyler was an attempt to make Kent or Hartfordshire independent principalities; but both were the expression of popular discontent and were the only means then known to correct grievances, to readjust a burdensome and unjust system of taxation, and to secure the reaffirmation of rights which were the immemorial privileges of Englishmen. Just as Tyler rode at the head of his motley rabble three centuries before Bacon aroused the spirit of Virginia, so Cromwell marshaled his hosts nearly a century before Washington created an army. In searching for a precedent the Englishmen of America found the Grand Remonstrance framed by the Puritans of England, and they indicted their sovereign with the Declaration of Independence. But in neither case was it a deliberate attempt to break a bond because it was politically galling. An English sovereign lost his head because he defied the liberties of the people and attempted to set up an autocracy; a later English sovereign lost his colonies because he was deaf to remonstrance and clung to the exploded idea that Englishmen might be taxed without their consent. In the time of Cromwell England was in spirit a republic. The English colonies had long been republican not alone in spirit but in the form of their governments, and in that mood it needed only a choice bit of rhetoric to make them cast out even the semblance of monarchical institutions and openly embrace that form of government for which their training and their natural inclinations had for so long prepared them.

Returning to those Dutch settlers who planted themselves on the Hudson, we see how they differed from the men of English stock who rooted themselves in the North. While English governors and their courts were ruling with a firm and, in many cases, oppressive hand, which made men more determined than ever to resist encroachments and widen their liberty, Dutch stadtholders were engaged in the ridiculous pastime of governing by paper proclamations, which appealed to stolid humor and were to be laughed at over the comforting contentment of pipes. The London Company was invested with political as well as commercial powers; Baltimore's charter, similar to that of every other English proprietor, contained a distinct recognition of the political rights of the settlers; but the company of Dutch merchants which was granted by the States General the exclusive monopoly of trading in the New Netherlands was under no such restrictions, and the Dutch temperament, unlike the English, was too sluggish and too unimaginative to make them passionately demand their political independence. "As a creature of the States General, the West India Company, the declared rival of the French for the Canadian fur trade, managed affairs in the colony with an iron hand. Scant consideration was given the settler. The policy of the company was purely commercial."[1]

It was the English Governor Fletcher who taught these Dutchmen the meaning of political liberty when he said to them: "There are none of you but are big with the privileges of Englishmen and Magna Charta." It has been well said by an American author that the Dutch fought heroically for their independence against the Spaniards, and won the gratitude of the civilized world by driving him out of Northern Europe. But, their independence

[1] *Military Minutes of the Council of Appointment of the State of New York*, vol. i, p. 2.

once attained, they settled down to the substantial enjoyment of it and the commerce of the Indian seas, and have remained in that happy state ever since. They had no passion for conquest, and were not wandering over the earth with empires in their brains, like the English.[1]

In the charter of the Dutch East and West India Companies[2] the right of the colonists—or it would be more proper to call them traders, because they were not colonists in any real sense of the word—to maintain self-government was so completely ignored that no provision was made for popular assemblies or legislatures, nor were the colonists permitted the right to vote, and this effort of the home government to keep their children in a state of perpetual tutelage aroused not even passive resistance. We have only to contrast the rights of the English colonists with the withholding of all rights from the Dutch colonists to see how little foundation there is for the oft-repeated assertion that it is to the Dutch Americans owe the origin of a Republican form of government or the institutions on which American society is founded. The laws under which the English colonists lived were laws framed by themselves, and whether good or bad, at least they had the satisfaction of knowing that they were their own work, that the code they erected for them-

[1] Fisher: *Men, Women, and Manners in Colonial Times*, vol. ii, p. 15.

[2] For the full text of the charter of the West India Company see Van Rennselaer Bowier *Manuscripts*, p. 87 *et seq.*, and the Charter of *Freedoms and Exemptions*, p. 137 *et seq.*

selves was the expression of their own requirements and their own moral nature. If they branded and imprisoned and maimed and hanged, it was because the welfare of the community, as they considered it, demanded drastic discipline. Even their tyranny was intelligent and was not the mere caprice of a William the Testy. It was discipline enforced by a majority of the community and not by governors whose actions they were unable to control; who were as deaf to public opinion as the Spanish governors were to the meek protests of the Indians. The Dutch governors, Irving says in that most delightful of all books, enjoyed that uncontrolled authority vested in all commanders of distant colonies or territories. They were, in manner, absolute despots in their little domains, lording it, if so disposed, over both law and gospel, and accountable to none but to the mother country; which it is well known is astonishingly deaf to all complaints against its governors, provided they discharge the main duties of their station — squeezing out a good revenue.[1] Whatever was wrong could be corrected with a proclamation. If pestiferous New Englanders or trespassing Swedes invaded the territory of the New Netherlands, if sailors were unruly or there was too much private traffic in furs, if Dutch hausvrows were too prone to gossip, the Testy one retired to the solitude of his cabinet and brought forth a proclamation which he issued with

[1] Irving: *A History of New York*, p. 167.

sublime faith in its potency as a cure for all evils. Nothing destroyed his belief in the efficacy of his Edicts. Contrast with that the stern methods of the English both north and south, and the measures they adopted to make men and women walk in the narrow way and respect lawful authority. It was only after Kieft was dismissed that there was some semblance of breaking the autocratic power of the governor by the appointment of a supreme council, and then it began to penetrate the heads of these incompetent colonizers that they could learn from the English. It was recommended that the Dutch should be encouraged to settle in towns and villages "as the English are in the habit of doing," which is still further testimony that in the art of colonization it was from the Dutch the English learned little if anything, while it is to the English the Dutch owe much.

Equally fallacious is the widespread impression that the Dutch were extremely liberal in religious belief, and that the same spirit which made them offer asylum to the Separatists in Holland controlled them in their settlements in the New World. The Dutch of the New Netherlands were no less narrow in the maintenance of one religion than were the Puritans of Massachusetts Bay in their attempts to suppress the "pestilent seducer." The Reformed Church was alone recognized; unlicensed preachers were suppressed and if they persisted, their contumacy was punished by fine and imprisonment; with the exception of Massachusetts, nowhere was such harshness meted out to the Quakers as in New Amsterdam. Perhaps nothing better demonstrates the utter incapacity of the Dutch for colonization and their unfitness to found a colonial empire than their sterility and the slow growth of population. After they had been in possession for more than forty years of the fairest part of America they numbered but ten thousand, while at that time the Puritan colonies, with a much less fertile soil to sustain them and climatic rigors to contend with which sorely tried them, could count their people at not less than fifty thousand. It was impossible for the Dutch to have peopled a continent.

In another way the difference between the Dutch and English character is illustrated. The heart of the Dutch province was Manhattan Island with a far-flung outpost at Albany, and between were scattered farms and straggling settlements. Relatively to that day Albany was as remote from New York as London is from St. Petersburg in ours; in one sense the distance was greater, as there was no telegraph to bridge space and destroy time; there was no constant stream of travelers flowing back and forth to bring half the world in intimate contact. Judging by what happened in New England, seeing what took place in the South, we are warranted in believing that had the English been the first settlers on Manhattan Island and established an outpost up the river at Albany, it would have been only a short time before those Albanian Englishmen would have cut loose from the nominal control of New York and set up a government of their own, in the same way that Connecticut and New Hampshire and Rhode Island came into existence. Englishmen would have felt the imperious necessity of governing themselves and being their own political masters, but the Dutch had no such impulse. They were quite content with their lot; trade they understood, but political science did not vex them; and whether they were ruled by imbeciles in New York or men of intelligence in Holland made little difference so long as they were allowed to drive their bargains and were not disturbed when they smoked their long pipes after their midday meal.

The Dutch brought over with them an aristocratic system of land tenure that was even more harmful than the plantation and manorial systems of Virginia and Maryland. Great estates were in the hands of the patroons, who would not part with an acre but worked them with tenants, which was one of the reasons population increased so slowly and the colony remained in such a backward condition until after the English occupation. Immigrants both from Europe and the English colonies were not content to be the tenants of Dutch masters when in neighboring colonies they could take up land and become its owners. The great estates of the South were made possible by slavery and the shipping of indented white servants, but although the Dutch were keen slave traders and a fairly large number of African slaves were to be found in New York, they were principally used as house servants and seldom employed in field labor. The Dutch had it in their power to attract to their vast territory the best yeomanry of England and the cream of the peasantry of Europe, for as there was little infusion of slave labor the cultivation of the soil by free white men was no degradation; but in this as in so many other things we see Dutch ineptitude. They were unable to grasp their opportunies or to found lasting social institutions. An American biographer of Peter Stuyvesant finds that "in New York City, the high stoop house, and the peculiar observances of New Year's Day which continued until 1870, are two familiar relics of Holland. The valuable custom of registering transfers of real estate has been received from the same source."[1] A pitifully weak foundation on which to attempt to erect a lasting monument to Dutch genius!

Virginian institutions were economically unsound and morally vicious, yet the Virginian was redeemed by his fondness for outdoor sports, his love of adventure, his daring, and the appeal which nature always made to him, and his intellect and creative political genius profoundly excite our admiration. The Dutch overlords were aristocrats of a different calibre. They took their pleasures more reposefully and with that phlegmatic love of ease which was as

[1] Tuckerman: *Peter Stuyvesant*, p. 186.

characteristic of their amusements as it was of their business methods. They gained little because they feared to venture much. It was a natural instinct in the Virginians to gamble; temperamentally they were adventurers, and from being speculators in commerce they became speculative political philosophers, their speculations tempered by a strain of clear thinking and material prudence. The Dutch had no love of speculation; great rashness, which is the audacity of genius, was foreign to their nature as well as their training.

No people who have played a part in affecting the destinies of mankind — and that the Dutch did, no one who is familiar with their history or that of Europe in the sixteenth-century will deny — offer such a curious and puzzling study. They were endowed with many heroic virtues; against the mighty power of Philip II of Spain they successfully offered their puny resistance; no sacrifice was too great for them to make, no torture too great for them to bear; and yet virile, industrious, undegenerate—and those qualities make the mystery all the greater — they have influenced the world so little. On their soil they were the modern Antæus and invincible, but when they wrestled in a new land their sinews were made weak and their strength was gone. Schiller says the pressure of circumstances surprised them and forced a transitory greatness upon them, which "they never could have possessed and perhaps never will possess again"; that necessity created genius and accident made heroes.[1] The crisis produces its genius or hero, who influences not only the thought of his own time but moulds the future. In Holland he did not. The example of the rise of the Dutch Republic could have had little if any influence in bringing about the birth of the American Republic. It is interesting to note that when the United Provinces resolved to renounce their allegiance to the King and to seek foreign assistance, they had no thought of founding a republic, but were ready to submit themselves to a monarch less bigoted and cruel than Philip; [2] and to compare that action with the course of the English colonists when they resolved on independence. Independence did not mean to them simply a change of rulers; they were not willing to free themselves from the connection with the British Crown merely to become the subjects of another King. Circumstances had forced them into revolt, and they staked everything on their own strength. Note again how different were the results of the adoption of the Declaration of Independence in America and the Act of Abjuration, the Declaration of Dutch Independence, in 1581. In America, once independence was resolved upon, the colonists agreed to stand or fall together, and opposition was silenced. The Tories were of course to be reckoned with, but they were able to drive no wedge between the allied colonies. But in Holland "Providence

[1] Schiller: *History of the Revolt of United Netherlands*, Introduction, p. 9.

[2] May: *Democracy in Europe*, vol. ii, p. 48.

did not permit the whole country, so full of wealth, intelligence, healthy political action — so stocked with powerful cities and an energetic population, to be combined into one free prosperous commonwealth."[1] Ambition, venality, religious intolerance, many causes, kept kindred provinces apart which ought to have been united.

Before leaving New York, brief reference must be made to an episode which happened after the English were masters. In itself it means nothing, it had no important consequences, it turned no stream of thought, but it is of interest as showing how the same causes were operating North and South, how the same considerations influenced men throughout the spread of the colonies.

The reader will recall the panic that possessed the Maryland Protestants after the dethronement of James II and the Davis and Pate rebellion. In New York there was a similar panic, there was for the moment equal uncertainty and fear whether the Protestants or Papists would rule; and as authority was broken, the time was opportune for any man of courage or reckless adventure who could play on the fears or passions of the people to seize the government. Such a man was found in Jacob Leisler, but it is difficult to tell whether he is worthy to be placed in the valhalla of history or was merely a historical mountebank, for the estimates of his character and motives are conflicting and there are neither

[1] Motley: *The Rise of the Dutch Republic*, vol. iii, p. 516.

letters nor diaries to reveal the inner nature of the man. His patronymic stamps his nationality. A German merchant, according to some of his biographers a brewer, regarding Papacy with horror, he, if his detractors are to be believed, "seized" New York, while more friendly critics tell us that he was "induced" to become a leader in a great emergency; just as Bradstreet became the head of the provisional government in Massachusetts when a similar movement drove Andros from power. Whether patriot or adventurer, the fact remains that Leisler became the *de facto* governor of New York, and to the sound of trumpets proclaimed William and Mary King and Queen of England and their colonies over the seas. His stormy rule lasted for two years, when he was tried and hanged for high treason. "Calm and impartial judgment, enlightened by truth, now assigns to Jacob Leisler the high position in history of a patriot and martyr," [1] one of his eulogists declares; and another holds it to be "the office of history to bear witness to Jacob Leisler's integrity as a man, his loyalty as a subject, and his purity as a patriot." [2] The founder of the democracy of New York was Jacob Leisler, says still another historian, who adds that "Leisler was truly an honest man, who though a martyr to the cause of liberty, and sacrificed by injustice, aristocracy and party malignity, ought to be consid-

[1] Lossing: *The Empire State*, p. 113.

[2] Frothingham: *The Rise of the Republic*, p. 95.

ered as one in whom New York should take pride — although the ancestors of many of her best men denounced him as a rebel and a traitor."[1]

It was under Leisler's administration that the first Colonial Conference was called to enable the colonies to take concerted measures to repel French aggression and carry the war into Canada. The resultant consequences were neither militarily nor politically important at the time, but it was the germ that was later to bring forth the Great Confederation which was to expand into the Republic.

In the settlement of Pennsylvania as of Maryland one name predominates. There is a certain semblance between Baltimore and William Penn; both were primarily inspired by the same motives; Baltimore, as we have seen, was animated to establish a Catholic colony and at the same time tolerantly to countenance the observance of other forms of religious worship; Penn, even more liberal in his religious views because his creed was broader and less encumbered by ceremonial tradition, found his guidance in the simple doctrine of the equality of man. With him that doctrine was no dogma, but a practical code that governed him in all the relations of life. In the history of the colonies there is no man whose aim was so lofty or whose purposes were so high and who so steadfastly clung to his

[1] Dunlap: *History of the New Netherlands*, vol. i, p. 211.

ideals. A religious enthusiast, a philanthropist in the widest interpretation of the word, a man in whom an exact sense of justice was perhaps the dominating quality, he was still no narrow closet mystic who conceived it unnecessary to take thought of the morrow. The fervid eloquence and zeal of George Fox had made this man turn to Quakerism as the one outlet to satisfy his spiritual nature, the simplicity and charity of all that Fox taught appealed with peculiar force to his impressionable temperament, for Penn's emotions while deep-centred also lay close to the surface, a seeming contradiction but not uncommon in men of great impulses. Baltimore, we have previously had occasion to remark, was no diarist, and we search in vain for any intimate self-revelation of his real character or his innermost feelings; all that we know of him is his record as proprietor and administrator.

About Penn there is no uncertainty. He has left copious letters and essays and pamphlets; he argued openly on the questions of the day; what he thought the world knows. In turning his back on the religion of his fathers, sincerity and conviction alone moved him; he risked disinheritance for the sake of conscience; he was willing to suffer calumny and social ostracism rather than renounce his new-found belief. And yet there was an intensely practical side to Penn's character which made him a great administrator and ranks him foremost among the colony builders; and this spirit of the practical was typical of Puritanism, and Quakerism was merely another expression of the same moral agencies that produced the Puritan.

All that we know as Puritanism, the Puritan in England and America, Calvinism, Quakerism, the forces which they set in motion, forces as old as creation and as eternal as eternity, that produced such men as Wycliffe, Huss, Zwinglius, Calvin, Roger Williams, and William Penn; all the sects and movements now conveniently known as Nonconformism; all the prophets and their disciples, sprung from the same source. It was a spiritual as well as an intellectual revolt; in some respects it was the intellect rather than the spiritual nature of man that made him seek new inspiration; that made him a rebel against superstition and tradition; that made him revolt against injustice and oppression buttressed in a social structure resting on a foundation of moral and intellectual slavery which denied him opportunity. It was a vague but at the same time practical longing for a betterment of conditions; and for so many centuries had men been taught to believe that society and the church were interwoven, that to them it seemed possible to bring about reform only in one way, and that was to escape from the iron hand of the church that stifled their aspirations. No other religio-social movement that has endured, that has been something more than a mere emotional outburst with its appeal to the higher nature of man, has so influenced character and modified society as the great Puritan movement in combining with a singular devotion to a concept of duty and the regulation of life, an intensely practical and commercial spirit; and as I have previously explained, the term "Puritan" is used here in its wider sense and embraces forces that were in existence long before the word Puritan designated exclusively a particular form and observance of religious belief. It was perhaps the strictness of life which it enjoined, the sense of order and thrift which it inculcated, the preciseness with which existence must be regulated, the hatred of all extravagance and waste, whether of emotion or physical vigor; the respect which men were taught to have for their bodies and the inanimate things with which they were surrounded, that made the Puritan so intensely practical, and founded the New England thrift often treated with contempt, but a very vital force in the making of character, which is seen in the difference between the Puritan civilization and the development of the Puritan colonists and the men who settled the South.

The practical side of Penn's character is shown in the settlement of his proprietary grant, his Frame of Government, the treaty he made with the Indians — here the principles that ever controlled him exercised a greater influence than selfish consideration — and his laying out of the city of Philadelphia. Alone among the leaders of the English colonization in the seventeenth century, he can claim to be a city founder. That dignity, the result of symmetry and spaciousness, in which Philadelphia ranks above any city of its own age and kind, is largely due to Penn's wise choice of a site and to his systematic construction.[1] Like Calvert his aim was to found a place of refuge for the people of his faith, but it was only for a short time that Maryland was a Catholic colony and it was never exclusively Catholic, while in Pennsylvania the teachings of George Fox and the influence of Quakerism were the dominating forces; and the political and social life of the colony, and later the state, was influenced by the tenets of the Quaker faith. With Baltimore, as we have seen, toleration must have been more or less a matter of expediency, although in saying that we detract nothing from his liberality and broad statesmanship. With Penn religious equality and personal liberty were a moral conviction without regard to political or other considerations, and he brought to his side men who thought and believed as he did, who were as zealous in maintaining what to them was the right as the Puritans were equally zealous in suppressing every effort to weaken the power of the theocracy.

The Puritanism that was planted on the shores of New England was bound to break down or to be profoundly modified, because it was narrow and dwarfing and was in essence a form of slavery repugnant to men born with the freedom of intellect;

[1] *Cambridge Modern History*, vol. vii, p. 50.

it was the attempt so often made, but which has always been resisted, to substitute for the morality of the intellect blind obedience to a warped creed. The religious and moral code of Penn was broader, and the more narrowly it was followed the more the spiritual nature of its believers expanded. To men seeking to overthrow the trammels of superstition and escape from a system that cast their lives in a contracted mold, the philosophy of the Quaker was more attractive than that of the Puritan; there was a certain flexibility in Quakerism that could adjust itself to changing conditions, while Puritanism was too rigid; it would break under the strain, but it could not bend to the play of forces. Puritanism was as unyielding as a rod of iron; Quakerism was a fine-strung wire vibrating to the music of the soul. The Puritans, all sects, in fact, clung to their dogmas, their doctrines, their sacraments, without which it was impossible to conceive at that time religion could exist. The Quakers had no ceremonies, no liturgy; they were satisfied simply to accept the inspiration of the Scriptures and the divinity of Christ; to cut away all formalism, to bring men to face God rather than to look on their priests, to reject outward observances which mean nothing and obscure those things that Christ taught and all men can believe irrespective of creed or the manner in which it is recited. "The baptism which saves the soul is not dipping in or sprinkling with water, but the answer of a good conscience toward God, by the resurrection of Jesus Christ."

Pennsylvania and New York were the two colonies in which there were from the beginning a conglomerate population and a strong alien element, which made both less strictly English than their neighbors to the north or those more remote of the south. From the time when the Mayflower brought over her first company until we near the end of the first quarter of the eighteenth-century, about 1720, a year that marks the beginning of that great Irish emigration, there was no alien immigration into New England and the population was fed by the arrival of Englishmen and natural increase, the birth rate being higher then than it is now among either the English or Americans of native stock. The people of New England, prior to the tide of European immigration, were a homogeneous race, alike in religion and customs, a fecund people, who became colonizers and "emigrants" in turn, who were filled with the resistless *Wanderlust* that took them to New York and to the South and the West, impelled to seek new homes because population was constantly pressing on the land and exerted a centrifugal force that drove men from the centre to extend their boundaries. In the southern colonies the admixture of foreign blood began earlier, but unlike New York it tinctured rather than colored the English element. Huguenots and the Scotch-Irish, as we have seen, found footing in the South, and about the middle of the eighteenth-century there was a considerable influx of "German Palatines" into Maryland, but this infusion was not great enough to destroy the homogeneity of the southern Englishmen. In New York there were Dutch, English, French, Swedes, Germans, Jews, Walloons, "and a rabble from all parts of the world." New Amsterdam, we are told, had "so many odds and ends of humanity that, twenty years after Hudson had discovered Manhattan, fourteen languages were spoken in its streets";[1] and when the eighteenth-century was rapidly drawing to a close, it was the boast of New York that men speaking the tongue of every civilized people were to be found in the city.[2]

In Pennsylvania there were Swedes, Germans, Welsh, Scotch-Irish, and English. The German element was particularly strong, Penn's liberality offering them that promise of religious freedom which was denied them in their own country. Mennonites, Tunkers and other sects, the German branch of that great movement which produced Puritanism and Quakerism in England, to escape persecution, came in large numbers, and they were followed by Lutherans and members of the German Reformed Church. Soon the allurement of the new world appealed to the Germans, and they came in the eighteenth-century as they continued to come

[1] Avery: *A History of the United States and its People*, vol ii, p. 91.

[2] McMaster: *A History of the People of the United States*, vol. i, p. 55.

in the nineteenth, and are still arriving in the twentieth. Just as at first they fled to escape religious persecution, and at a time nearer to us they left to avoid military service and others came solely because the New World offered a betterment of conditions, so in the early days of Pennsylvania the German immigration soon ceased to be due to religious oppression and was influenced by the same considerations that have always controlled great migratory movements, the hope of better things. All during the colonial period and until the revolution the Germans continued to come in large numbers to Pennsylvania and became such a considerable element in the population that the "Pennsylvania Dutch," as they were commonly called,[1] were in language and manners and customs apart from the English and were little influenced and slowly assimilated by them. Then as now these Germans settlers were distinguished by their industry, sobriety, love of order and thrift; and next to the Puritans the Germans have contributed more to the making of the American character than any other race or strain. Usually the German landed penniless or so near poverty that he had to rely solely upon his own efforts for a living, but he went quickly to work at whatever offered, he was

[1] Until quite recently, Americans commonly spoke of Germans as "Dutchmen," and even now the term "Dutch" is used colloquially or in contempt to describe a German; and the expression "a thick-headed Dutchman,"applied to an obtuse German, or a German immigrant who has recently landed and is unfamiliar with the language or American ways, is frequently heard.

sparing and frugal and looked forward to realizing his ambition, which was to take up a few acres and farm. This was forest land, and before he could put plough to it he must build himself a rude cabin and with axe and torch clear away the trees and the underbrush; but his optimism, his industry, and the help of his neighbors soon put him on his feet, and when his circumstances improved he was able to buy a redemptioner, add more land to his holdings and surround himself with greater comforts. A trait characteristic of the Germans, which from the beginning has always endured, is that they have ever been loyal to their adopted country. There was a strong Tory element in Pennsylvania which exerted a powerful influence against the adoption of the Declaration of Independence, and without Pennsylvania union was impossible; but it was the Germans who beat down Tory opposition and brought the support of Pennsylvania to the other colonies. They were equally loyal to the new-born Republic, and the way in which they responded to Lincoln's call to arms and freely offered their lives to preserve and maintain the Union the muster rolls of the Northern armies eloquently testify; and the prominent part taken by American generals of German birth is a part of the history of that great conflict.

The three remaining colonies, New Jersey, New Hampshire and Delaware, can be dismissed with a few sentences. New Jersey was within the Dutch grant of the New Netherlands, but its existence was of indifferent concern to them and the few who crossed the river and settled there found Swedes from the Delaware, who always trespassed on Dutch soil; and there was of course a scattering of Puritans, for wherever there was vacant land or the promise of founding a successful settlement there the Puritan went.

The genesis of New Hampshire is a counterpart of Connecticut and Rhode Island; they were all three the offshoots of Massachusetts and born in the throes of religious persecution. When Mrs. Hutchinson and her followers were banished from Massachusetts some went to Providence and founded what later became the state of Rhode Island; others settled Exeter, and in the usual fashion of that time soon a new colony arose. Just as Connecticut was founded by the establishment of little towns which were afterwards politically incorporated, so the beginning of New Hampshire came from the four towns of Portsmouth, Dover, Exeter and Hampden, which were founded either by Puritans from England or their coreligionists from Massachusetts. There as elsewhere in New England the church republic was established, the straggling settlement clustering about the rude meeting-house, which was always the heart of the independent state of the Puritans in the New World. The New Hampshire settlements were too weak to stand alone and not strong enough to sink mutual jealousies and find strength in confederation. For twenty years they quarrelled, then they applied to Massachusetts to be taken under her jurisdiction, and forty years later, during which time the towns had made no progress, the English courts decided that Massachusetts had no legal title and New Hampshire became a royal province and was governed from London. There is really no history of New Hampshire apart from Massachusetts in this period, and the influence of Massachusetts was so strong that the younger colony developed no originality and brought no contribution to the thought of the time.

Delaware was originally settled by the Dutch, who claimed it by right of discovery and as embraced in the grant of the New Netherlands although the English also asserted title to it as part of Virginia, which had neither metes nor bounds but extended indefinitely from ocean to ocean. The Dutch established a small settlement in 1631, but their rule was short, as the settlers were massacred to a man by the Indians in revenge for the killing of one of their chiefs. In 1638 Peter Minuit, who had formerly been the agent of the Dutch West India Company and governor of the New Netherlands, but who resented his removal from office, under the patronage of the Queen of Sweden and prominent merchants, led a Swedish colony to Delaware Bay, where a fort was erected and a settlement created at what is now the site of Wilmington. This is the first and only colony founded by Sweden in the New World, but Sweden wrote her brief chapter in American colonization in water. She brought nothing to the common stock; she left not the slightest mark of her nationality or character. Little impression as the Dutch made as colony builders, still less was that made by the Swedes, who bequeathed not even a trace of language, custom or law. At a later stage in the development of the American people we shall have to deal with a great Scandinavian influx, but that has no bearing on the colonial period. The Swedes attach no such sentiment to the spot that was their landing-place in the New World as the English do to Plymouth Rock, but with the Swedes it was merely a passing incident in their life that had no more lasting consequences than the scars of childhood have on a man's nature; with the English it was veritably the rock on which was built a civilization no less than a polity which was to affect all mankind.

The petty quarrels between Dutch and Swedish governors, the transfer of sovereignty to Dutch and English as the results of the fortunes of war, the disputes between proprietors as to boundaries, the inclusion at one time of Delaware in Pennsylvania and its subsequent independence, are of no concern for the purpose we have in view. As a colony Delaware is as nonexistent as New Hampshire or New Jersey; they were members of a family that influenced it neither for good nor evil, they brought to it no added lustre, nor did they bow its head in shame. In a family distinguished for the extraordinary brilliancy and attainments of its sons they, by their commonplace and placid temperament, simply served as a background to make more conspicuous those talents which they were denied.

BIBLIOGRAPHY

ADAMS, BROOKS. The Emancipation of Massachusetts. Boston: Houghton, Mifflin & Co. 1887.

ADAMS, CHARLES FRANCIS. Massachusetts: Its Historians and its History. Boston: Houghton, Mifflin & Co. 1893.

ADAMS, CHARLES FRANCIS. Three Episodes of Massachusetts History. 2 vols. Boston: Houghton, Mifflin & Co. 1892.

American Cyclopædia, The, Edited by George Ripley and Charles A. Dana. 16 vols. New York: D. Appleton & Co. 1883; and Annuals, 1876–1902.

AMES, AZEL. The May-Flower and her Log. Boston: Houghton, Mifflin & Co. 1901.

APGAR, E. A. *See* Sypher, J. R.

Appletons' Cyclopædia of American Biography. 6 vols. New York: D. Appleton & Co. 1889.

ARNOLD, SAMUEL GREENE. History of the State of Rhode Island and Providence Plantations. 2 vols. New York: D. Appleton & Co. 1859.

AVERY, ELROY MCKENDREE. A History of the United States and its People. Cleveland: The Burrows Bros. Co. 1907.

BACON, LEONARD. The Genesis of the New England Churches. New York: Harper & Bros. 1874.

BAGEHOT, WALTER. The English Constitution. New York: D. Appleton & Co. 1877.

BANCROFT, GEORGE. History of the United States of America. 6 vols. New York: D. Appleton & Co. 1888.

BARRY, JOHN STETSON. The History of Massachusetts. 3 vols. Boston: Phillips, Sampson & Co. 1855.

Beard, George M. The Psychology of the Salem Witchcraft Excitement. New York: G. P. Putnam's Sons. 1882.

Beaulieu, Pierre Leroy. The United States in the Twentieth Century. New York: Funk & Wagnalls Co. 1906.

Besse, Joseph. A Collection of the Sufferings of the People called Quakers. 2 vols. London: Luke Hinde. 1753.

Bishop, George. New England Judged by the Spirit of the Lord. London: T. Sowle. 1703.

Bodley, John Edward Courtenay. France. 2 vols. New York: The Macmillan Co. 1898.

Boutmy, Émile. The English People. London: T. Fisher Unwin. 1904.

Bozman, John Leeds. The History of Maryland. 2 vols. Baltimore: James Lucas & E. K. Deaver. 1837.

Bradford, William. History "Of Plimouth Plantation." Boston: Wright & Potter Printing Co., State Printers. 1898.

Brodhead, John Romeyn. History of the State of New York. New York: Harper & Bros. 1853.

Brown, Alexander. The Genesis of the United States. 2 vols. Boston: Houghton, Mifflin & Co. 1890.

Bruce, Philip Alexander. Economic History of Virginia in the Seventeenth Century. 2 vols. New York: The Macmillan Co. 1907.

Bryant, William Cullen, and Sydney Howard Gay. A Popular History of the United States. 4 vols. New York: Charles Scribner's Sons. 1881.

Bryce, James. The American Commonwealth. 2 vols. New York: The Macmillan Co. 1907.

Buckle, Henry Thomas. History of Civilization in England. 2 vols. New York: D. Appleton & Co. 1860.

Byington, Ezra Hoyt. The Puritan in England and New England. Boston: Little, Brown & Co. 1900.

BYRD, Colonel WILLIAM, The Writings of. New York: Doubleday, Page & Co. 1901.

CAIRNES, J. E. The Slave Power. London: Parker, Son & Bourn. 1862.

Cambridge Modern History, The. Vol. VII. New York: The Macmillan Co. 1903.

CAMPBELL, DOUGLAS. The Puritan in Holland, England, and America. 2 vols. New York: Harper & Bros. 1892.

CARLYLE, THOMAS. Heroes and Hero Worship. Boston: Estes & Lauriat.

CARLYLE, THOMAS. Oliver Cromwell's Letters and Speeches. Boston: Estes & Lauriat.

CARROLL, B. R. Historical Collections of South Carolina. 2 vols. New York: Harper & Bros. 1836.

CHANNING, EDWARD. A History of the United States. Vol. II. New York: The Macmillan Co. 1908.

CHANNING, EDWARD. A Student's History of the United States. New York: The Macmillan Co. 1904.

CHANNING, EDWARD, and ALBERT BUSHNELL HART. Guide to the Study of American History. Boston: Ginn & Co.

CLINTON, GEORGE, Public Papers of, with an Introduction by Hugh Hastings, State Historian. 8 vols. Published by the State of New York. 1899.

COMAN, KATHERINE. The Industrial History of the United States. New York: The Macmillan Co. 1905.

DARWIN, CHARLES. The Descent of Man. New York: D. Appleton & Co. 1896.

DARWIN, CHARLES. The Origin of Species. 2 vols. New York: D. Appleton & Co. 1896.

DEXTER, HENRY MARTYN. *See* Mourt's Relation.

DILL, SAMUEL. Roman Society from Nero to Marcus Aurelius. London: Macmillan & Co. 1904.

DOYLE, J. A. English Colonies in America. 3 vols. New York: Henry Holt & Co. 1882.

DUNLAP, WILLIAM. History of the New Netherlands. 2 vols. New York: Carter & Thorp. 1839.

EARLE, ALICE MORSE. Curious Punishments of Bygone Days. Chicago: Herbert S. Stone & Co. 1896.

EARLE, ALICE MORSE. Customs and Fashions in Old New England. New York: Charles Scribner's Sons. 1893.

EARLE, ALICE MORSE. Home Life in Colonial Days. New York: The Macmillan Co. 1898.

EARLE, ALICE MORSE. Two Centuries of Costume in America. 2 vols. New York: The Macmillan Co. 1903.

ELLIOTT, CHARLES W. The New England History. 2 vols. New York: Charles Scribner. 1857.

ELLIS, GEORGE E. The Puritan Age and Rule. Boston: Houghton, Mifflin & Co. 1888.

ELSON, HENRY WILLIAM. History of the United States. New York: The Macmillan Co. 1904.

Encyclopædia Britannica. 9th Ed. (American reprint.) Philadelphia: J. M. Stoddart & Co. 1875.

FERRERO, GUGLIELMO. The Greatness and Decline of Rome. 5 vols. New York: G. P. Putnam's Sons. 1908.

FISHER, GEORGE PARK. History of the Christian Church. New York: Charles Scribner's Sons. 1887.

FISHER, SYDNEY GEORGE. Men, Women, and Manners in Colonial Times. 2 vols. Philadelphia: J. B. Lippincott Co. 1898.

FISKE, JOHN. Old Virginia and her Neighbours. 2 vols. Boston: Houghton, Mifflin & Co.

FISKE, JOHN. The American Revolution. 2 vols. Boston: Houghton, Mifflin & Co. 1891.

FISKE, JOHN. The Beginnings of New England. Boston: Houghton, Mifflin & Co.

FORCE, PETER. Tracts and Other Papers Relating Principally to the Origin, Settlement, and Progress of the Colonies in North America. 4 vols. Washington: Wm Q. Force. 1844.

FROTHINGHAM, RICHARD. The Rise of the Republic of the United States. Boston: Little, Brown & Co. 1902.

FROUDE, JAMES ANTHONY. History of England. New York: Charles Scribner's Sons. 1899.

GRAHAME, JAMES. The History of the United States of America. 4 vols. Philadelphia: Lea & Blanchard. 1845.

GRANT, Mrs. Memoirs of an American Lady. New York: Printed for Samuel Campbell. 1809.

GRAVES, HORACE. The Huguenot in New England. The New England Magazine, vol. XI. 1894.

GREEN, JOHN RICHARD. A History of the English People. 10 vols. New York: Funk & Wagnalls Co.

GREEN, J. R. A Short History of the English People. London: Macmillan & Co. 1875.

GROSVENOR, GILBERT H. The Century Magazine, June, 1905.

GUIZOT, F. The History of Civilization. 3 vols. London: George Bell & Sons. 1885.

HALLAM, HENRY. The Constitutional History of England. 2 vols. New York: A. C. Armstrong & Son. 1897.

HALLOWELL, RICHARD P. The Quaker Invasion of Massachusetts. Boston: Houghton, Mifflin & Co. 1884.

HARRIS, THADDEUS MASON. Biographical Memorials of James Oglethorpe. Boston: Printed for the Author. 1841.

HART, ALBERT BUSHNELL. American History told by Contemporaries. 4 vols. New York: The Macmillan Co. 1908.

HART, ALBERT BUSHNELL. Source Book of American History. New York: The Macmillan Co. 1908.

HASTINGS, HUGH. *See* Clinton, George.

HENING, WILLIAM WALLER. Statutes at Large of all the Laws of Virginia. New York: R. & W. & G. Bartow. 1823.

HERBERT, LEILA. The First American, his Home and his Households. New York: Harper & Bros. 1900.

HILDRETH, RICHARD. The History of the United States of America. 3 vols. New York: Harper & Bros. 1877.

HOAR, GEORGE F. Speech at the Banquet of the New England Society of Charleston, S. C. Washington: The Saxton Printing Co. 1899.

HUME, DAVID. History of England. London: James Dinnis. 1832.

HUTCHINSON, LUCY. Memoirs of the Life of Colonel Hutchinson. London: Henry G. Bohn. 1846.

HUTCHINSON, THOMAS. The History of the Colony of Massachusetts Bay. 3 vols. Boston: Printed by Thomas & John Fleet, 1764.

HUXLEY, THOMAS H. Man's Place in Nature. New York: D. Appleton & Co. 1896.

IRVING, WASHINGTON. A History of New York. New York: G. P. Putnam's Sons.

JAMESON, J. FRANKLIN. Dictionary of United States History. Boston: Puritan Publishing Co.

JEFFERSON, THOMAS. Notes on the State of Virginia. New York: Printed by M. L. & W. A. Davis for Furman & Loudon. 1801.

JOHNSON, EDWARD. Wonder Working Providence of Sions Saviour in New England. London: 1654. Andover: Warren F. Draper. 1867.

JOHNSTON, ALEXANDER. Connecticut. Boston: Houghton, Mifflin & Co. 1903.

JONES, CHARLES C. The History of Georgia. 2 vols. Boston: Houghton, Mifflin & Co. 1883.

KITTREDGE, GEORGE LYMAN. American Antiquarian Society Proceedings. Vol 18. 1907.

KNOWLES, JAMES D. Memoir of Roger Williams. Boston: Lincoln, Edmands & Co. 1834.

LARNED, J. N. History for Ready Reference. 6 vols. Springfield, Mass.: The C. A. Nichols Co. 1901.

LAWSON, JOHN. The History of Carolina. London: Printed for W. Taylor at the Ship. 1714.

LEA, HENRY CHARLES. A History of the Inquisition of Spain. 4 vols. New York: The Macmillan Co. 1906.

LECKY, WILLIAM EDWARD HARTPOLE. A History of England in the Eighteenth Century. 8 vols. New York: D. Appleton & Co. 1882.

LEVERMORE, CHARLES H. The Republic of New Haven. Baltimore: Johns Hopkins University. 1886.

LODGE, HENRY CABOT. A Short History of the English Colonies in America. New York: Harper Brothers. 1881.

LONGFELLOW, HENRY WADSWORTH. Poetical Works of.

LOSSING, BENSON Jr. The Empire State. New York: Funk & Wagnalls. 1887.

LOVE, W. DELOSS, Jr. The Fast and Thanksgiving Days of New England. Boston: Houghton, Mifflin & Co. 1895.

LOW, SIDNEY, Editor. The Dictionary of English History. London: Cassell & Co. 1884.

LOW, SIDNEY. The Governance of England. London: T. Fisher Unwin. 1904.

LOWELL, JAMES RUSSELL. Among My Books. 2 vols. Boston: James R. Osgood & Co. 1876.

MACDONAGH, MICHAEL. The Book of Parliament; London: Isbister & Co. 1897.

MCMASTER, JOHN BACH. A History of the People of the United States. 7 vols. New York: D. Appleton & Co. 1907.

MACAULAY, LORD, Poems of. New York: D. Appleton & Co. 1878.

MACAULAY, LORD. The History of England. 2 vols. London: Longmans, Green, Reader & Dyer. 1873.

MASTERMAN, C. F. G. In Peril of Change. New York: B. W. Huebsch.

MATHER, COTTON. Magnalia Christi Americana. 2 vols. Hartford: Silas Andrus. 1820.

MAY, Sir THOMAS ERSKINE. Democracy in Europe. 2 vols. London: Longmans, Green & Co.

Military Minutes of the Council of Appointment of the State of New York, 1783–1821, compiled and edited by Hugh Hastings, State Historian. 4 vols. Published by the State of New York. 1901.

MOTLEY, JOHN LOTHROP. The Rise of the Dutch Republic. 3 vols. New York: Harper & Bros. 1856.

Mourt's Relation, or Journal of the Plantation at Plymouth, Edited by Henry Martyn Dexter. Boston: John Kimball Wiggin. 1865.

NEAL, DANIEL. The History of the Puritans. 2 vols. London: Printed for J. Buckland. 1754.

O'CALLAGHAN, E. B. History of New Netherland. 2 vols. New York: D. Appleton & Co. 1846.

OLIVER, PETER. The Puritan Commonwealth. Boston: Little, Brown & Co. 1856.

PAINTER, F. V. N. A History of Education. New York: D. Appleton & Co. 1897.

PALFREY, JOHN GORHAM. History of New England. 3 vols. Boston: Little, Brown & Co. 1865.

PARKMAN, FRANCIS. Pioneers of France in the New World. Boston: Little, Brown & Co. 1907.

PETERS, SAMUEL, A General History of Connecticut. London. 1781.

RAMSAY, DAVID. The History of the American Revolution. 2 vols. London: Printed for John Stockdale. 1793.

REICH, EMIL. Success Among Nations. New York: Harper & Bros. 1904.

RIVERS, WILLIAM JAMES. A Sketch of the History of South Carolina. Charleston: McCarter & Co. 1856.

ROOSEVELT, THEODORE. The Winning of the West. 6 vols. New York: The Current Literature Publishing Co. 1905.

SCHARF, J. THOMAS. History of Maryland. 3 vols. Baltimore: John B. Piet. 1879.

SCHILLER, FRIEDRICH VON. History of the Revolt of the United Netherlands. London: The Anthological Society.

SEMPLE, ELLEN CHURCHILL. American History and its Geographic Conditions. Boston: Houghton, Mifflin & Co. 1903.

SEWALL, SAMUEL. Diary of. Massachusetts Historical Society Collections, 5th Series.

SEWALL, WILLIAM. History of the Rise, Increase, and Progress of the Christian People Called Quakers. 2 vols. Philadelphia: Benjamin & Thomas Kite. 1823.

SHALER, N. S. Nature and Man in America. New York: Charles Scribner's Sons. 1891.

SHARPLESS, ISAAC. A Quaker Experiment in Government. Philadelphia: Alfred J. Ferris. 1898.

SMITH, GOLDWIN. The United States. New York: The Macmillan Co. 1907.

SPENCER, HERBERT. First Principles. New York: D. Appleton & Co. 1896.

SPENCER, HERBERT. The Principles of Biology. 2 vols. New York: D. Appleton & Co. 1896.

SPENCER, HERBERT. The Principles of Sociology. 5 vols. New York: D. Appleton & Co. 1896.

SPENCER, HERBERT. The Study of Sociology. New York: D. Appleton & Co. 1896.

Springfield (Mass.) Republican.

STEVENS, WILLIAM BACON. A History of Georgia. 2 vols. New York: D. Appleton & Co. 1847.

STILES, HENRY REED. Bundling; Its Origin, Progress, and Decline in America. Albany: Joel Munsell. 1869.

STRAUS, OSCAR S. Roger Williams, the Pioneer of Religious Liberty. New York: The Century Co. 1894.

STRAUS, OSCAR S. The Origin of Republican Form of Government in the United States. New York: G. P. Putnam's Sons. 1901.

SYPHER, J. R., and E. A. APGAR. History of New Jersey. Philadelphia: J. B. Lippincott & Co. 1870.

TOCQUEVILLE, ALEXIS DE. De la Démocratie en Amérique. 4 vols. Paris: Librairie de Charles Gosselin. 1840.

TOWNSEND, MALCOLM. Handbook of United States Political History. Boston: Lothrop, Lee & Shepard Co.

TRUMBULL, J. HAMMOND, Editor. The True Blue Laws of Connecticut and New Haven. Hartford: American Publishing Co. 1876.

TUCKERMAN, BAYARD. Peter Stuyvesant. New York: Dodd, Mead & Co. 1893.

TYLER, MOSES COIT. A History of American Literature during the Colonial Period. New York: G. P. Putnam's Sons. 1904.

UPHAM, CHARLES W. Salem Witchcraft. 2 vols. Boston: Wiggin & Lunt. 1867.

Van Rensselaer Bowier Manuscripts. Albany: University of the State of New York. 1908.

WALKER, GEORGE LEON. Thomas Hooker. New York: Dodd, Mead & Co.

WALLACE, ALFRED RUSSEL. Natural Selection and Tropical Nature. London: Macmillan & Co. 1891.

WARD, NATHANIEL. The Simple Cobler of Aggawam. London: Printed by J. D. & R. I. for Stephen Bowtell. 1647.

WEEDEN, WILLIAM B. Economic and Social History of New England. 2 vols. Boston: Houghton, Mifflin & Co. 1891.

WENDELL, BARRETT. Liberty, Union, and Democracy. New York: Charles Scribner's Sons. 1906.

WHEELER, JOHN H. Historical Sketches of North Carolina. Philadelphia: Lippincott, Grambo & Co. 1851.

WINSOR, JUSTIN. Narrative and Critical History of America. 8 vols. Boston: Houghton, Mifflin & Co.

WINTHROP, JOHN. The History of New England. 2 vols. Boston: Little, Brown & Co. 1853.

WINTHROP, ROBERT C. Life and Letters of John Winthrop. Boston: Ticknor & Fields. Vol. I, 1864; Vol. II, 1867.

YOUNG, ALEXANDER. Chronicles of the First Planters of the Colony of Massachusetts Bay. Boston: Charles C. Little & James Brown. 1846.

INDEX

The Riverside Press
CAMBRIDGE . MASSACHUSETTS
U . S . A

www.ingramcontent.com/pod-product-compliance
Lightning Source LLC
LaVergne TN
LVHW020553110826
845149LV00002B/248
* 9 7 8 1 4 1 8 1 8 8 4 5 0 *